KAREN BROWN'S

England, Wales & Scotland

Charming Hotels & Itineraries

Karen Brown Titles

Austria: Charming Inns & Itineraries

California: Charming Inns & Itineraries

England: Charming Bed & Breakfasts

England, Wales & Scotland: Charming Hotels & Itineraries

French Country Bed & Breakfasts

France: Charming Inns & Itineraries

Germany: Charming Inns & Itineraries

Ireland: Charming Inns & Itineraries

Italy: Charming Bed & Breakfasts

Italy: Charming Inns & Itineraries

Spain: Charming Inns & Itineraries

Swiss Country Inns & Itineraries

KAREN BROWN'S

England, Wales & Scotland
Charming Hotels & Itineraries

Written by

JUNE BROWN   KAREN BROWN

Illustrations by Barbara Tapp

Cover Painting by Jann Pollard

Travel Press
Karen Brown's Country Inn Series

Editors: Clare Brown, Karen Brown, June Brown, Iris Sandilands
Technical support: William H. Brown III; Aide-de-camp: William H. Brown
Illustrations: Barbara Tapp; Cover painting: Jann Pollard; Cover Design: Tara Brassil
Maps: Susanne Lau Alloway—Greenleaf Design & Graphics
Written in cooperation with Carlson Wagonlit/Town & Country Hillsdale Travel, San Mateo, CA 94401
Distributed USA & Canada: The Globe Pequot Press
Box 833, Old Saybrook, CT 06475, tel: (860) 395-0440, fax: (860) 395-0312
Distributed Europe: Springfield Books Ltd., tel: (01484) 864 955, fax: (01484) 865 443
Norman Road, Denby Dale, Huddersfield HD8 8TH, W. Yorkshire, England
Distributed Australia and New Zealand: Little Hills Press Pty. Ltd.
1st Floor, Regent House, 37-43 Alexander St, Crows Nest NSW 2065, Australia
tel: (02) 437-6995, fax: (02) 438-5762
A catalog record for this book is available from the British Library

Library of Congress Cataloging-in-Publication Data
Brown, June, 1949-
    Karen Brown's England, Wales & Scotland : charming hotels &
    itineraries / written by June Brown and Karen Brown ; sketches by
    Barbara Tapp ; cover painting by Jann Pollard. -- Totally rev. 8th
    ed.
            p. cm. -- (Karen Brown's country inn series)
    Includes index.
    ISBN 0-930328-32-9 (pb)
    1. Hotels--England--Guidebooks. 2. Hotels--Wales--Guidebooks.
    3. Hotels--Scotalnd--Guidebook. 4. England--Guidebooks 5. Wales-
    -Guidebooks. 6. Scotland--Guidebooks. I. Brown, Karen.
    II. Title. III. Series
    TX907.5.G7B76   1996
    647.9441'01--dc20   95-16419
                                                  CIP

To my children
Simon and Clare
in the hope that they will
discover Britain for themselves

Contents

HOTELS

MAPS

USA HOTEL REPRESENTATIVES

INDEX

Introduction

This guide falls into three sections: practical information useful in planning your trip; driving itineraries that take you deep into the countryside through idyllic villages full of thatched-roofed cottages and flower-filled gardens, exploring ancient castles and traversing vast purple moorlands; and lastly, but most importantly, our personal recommendations for outstanding hotels in England, Scotland, and Wales. Every hotel included in this guide is one that we have seen and enjoyed—our personal recommendation written with the sincere belief that where you lay your head each night makes the difference between a good and a great vacation. If you prefer to travel the bed and breakfast way, you may prefer to select places to stay from our companion guide, *England: Charming Bed & Breakfasts*. We encourage you to buy new editions of our guides and throw away old ones—you will be glad you did because we add new listings, update prices, phone, and fax numbers, and delete places that have not maintained standards.

About England, Wales & Scotland

The following pointers are given in alphabetical order, not in order of importance.

CAR RENTAL

If you are coming from overseas it is frequently less expensive to arrange and prepay a car rental before arriving in Britain. Car companies in collaboration with airlines often offer a variety of rental packages. Plan on visiting London either at the beginning or end of your trip. This way you can arrive in London, pick you car up at the airport, tour the countryside, drop the car back at the airport, and take a taxi, bus, or tube from Heathrow, or the train from Gatwick airport into London. If you visit London at the start of your holiday, collect your car from the airport at the conclusion of your stay in London. The trick is to avoid driving in London.

DRIVING

Just about the time overseas visitors board their return flight home they will have adjusted to driving on the "right" side which is the left side in England. You must contend with such things as roundabouts (circular intersections); flyovers (overpasses); ring roads (peripheral roads whose purpose is to bypass city traffic); lorries (trucks); lay-bys (turn-outs); boots (trunks); and bonnets (hoods). Pedestrians are permitted to cross the road anywhere and always have the right of way. Seat belts must be worn at all times.

MOTORWAYS: The letter "M" precedes these convenient ways for covering long distances. With three or more lanes of traffic either side of a central divider, you should stay in the left-hand lane except for passing. Motorway exits are numbered and correspond to numbering on major road maps. Service areas supply petrol (gas), cafeterias, and "bathrooms" (the word "bathroom" is used in the American sense—in

Britain "bathroom" means a room with a shower or bathtub, not a toilet—"loo" is the most commonly used term for an American bathroom).

"A" ROADS: The letter "A" precedes the road number. All major roads fall into this category. They vary from three lanes either side of a dividing barrier to single carriageways with an unbroken white line in the middle indicating that passing is not permitted. These roads have the rather alarming habit of changing from dual to single carriageways at a moment's notice.

"B" ROADS AND COUNTRY ROADS: The letter "B" preceding the road number or the lack of any lettering or numbering indicates that it belongs to the maze of country roads that crisscross Britain. These are the roads for people who have the luxury of time to enjoy the scenery en route and they require your arming yourself with a good map (although getting lost is part of the adventure). Driving these narrow roads is terrifying at first but exhilarating after a while. Meandering down these roads, you can expect to spend time crawling behind a tractor or cows being herded to the farmyard. Some lanes are so narrow that there is room for only one car.

ELECTRICITY

The voltage is 240. Most bathrooms have razor points (American style) for 110 volts. If you are coming from overseas, it is recommended that you take only dual voltage appliances and a kit of electrical plugs. Often your host can loan you a hairdryer and an iron.

Introduction–About England, Wales & Scotland

INFORMATION

The British Tourist Authority is an invaluable source of information. Their major offices are located as follows:

AUSTRALIA–SYDNEY: BTA, 210 Clarence Street, 8th Floor Sydney, NSW 2000, tel: (02) 261 6034, fax: (02) 267 4442

CANADA–TORONTO: BTA, 111 Avenue Road, Suite 450, Toronto, Ontario M5R 3J8, tel: (416) 925-6326, fax: (416) 961-2175

FRANCE–PARIS: BTA, Maison de la Grand Bretagne, 19 rue des Mathurins, 75009 Paris, tel: (1) 4451 5620, fax: (1) 4451 5621

GERMANY–FRANKFURT: BTA, Taunusstrasse 52-60, 60329 Frankfurt, tel: (069) 238 0711, fax: (069) 238 0717

NEW ZEALAND–AUCKLAND: BTA, Suite 305, 3rd Floor, Dilworth Building, corner Queen and Customs Streets, Auckland, tel: (09) 303 1446, fax: (09) 377 6965

USA–CHICAGO: BTA, 625 North Michigan Avenue, Suite 1510, Chicago, IL 60611—walk in only

USA–NEW YORK: BTA, 551 Fifth Avenue, New York, NY 10176, tel: (800) 462-2748 or in NY (212) 986-2200.

If you need additional information while you are in Britain, there are more than 700 official Tourist Information Centres identified by a blue and white letter "i" and "Tourist Information." Many information centers will make reservations for local accommodation and larger ones will "book a bed ahead" in a different locality.

In London at the British Travel Centre at 4-12 Lower Regent Street, London SW1 (near Piccadilly Circus tube station) you can book a room, buy air or train tickets, hire a car or pay for a coach tour or theatre tickets. The Centre also has exhibitions and films. The Centre is open 9 am to 6:30 pm, Monday to Saturday; 10 am to 4 pm on Sunday.

THE NATIONAL TRUST

The National Trust works for the preservation of places of historic interest or national beauty in England, Wales, Northern Ireland, and Scotland. Its care extends to stately homes, barns, historic houses, castles, gardens, Roman antiquities, moors, fells, woods, and even whole villages. During the course of a driving itinerary, whenever a property is under the care of the National Trust we state (NT). You can check times and location with the current edition of *The National Trust Handbook* available from many National Trust shops and overseas from the British Tourist Authority. If you are traveling to Scotland, you will need a copy of *The National Trust for Scotland Guide*. A great many National Trust properties have excellent shops and tea rooms. If you are planning on visiting several sites, consider joining the National Trust as a member, thus obtaining free entry into all properties.

SHOPPING

Overseas visitors can reclaim the VAT (Value Added Tax) that they pay on the goods they purchase. Not all stores participate in the refund scheme and there is often a minimum purchase price. Stores that do participate will ask to see your passport before completing the VAT form. This form must be presented with the goods to the Customs officer at the point of departure from Britain within three months of purchase. The customs officer will certify the form which you return to the store where you bought the goods. The store will then send you a check in sterling for the refund.

WEATHER

Britain has a tendency to be moist at all times of the year. The cold in winter is rarely severe; however, the farther north you go, the greater the possibility of being snowed in. Spring can be wet but it is a lovely time to travel: the summer crowds have not descended, daffodils and bluebells fill the woodlands, and the hedgerows are filled with wildflowers. Summer offers the best chance of sunshine but also the largest crowds. Schools are usually closed the last two weeks of July and all of August—this is the time when most families take their summer holidays. Travel is especially hectic on the weekends in summer—try to avoid major routes and airports at these times. Autumn is also an ideal touring time: the weather tends to be drier than in spring and the woodlands are decked in their golden fall finery.

Introduction–About England, Wales & Scotland

*Overview Map of
Driving Itineraries*

Scotland

Edinburgh

*The Dales and Moors
of North Yorkshire*

The Lake District

York

*Derbyshire
Dales and Villages*

Chester

Chesterfield

Ashbourne

*Cambridge
and East Anglia*

Wales

Coventry

Cambridge

Oxford

*In and Around
the Cotswolds*

Bath

LONDON

Winchester

*Southwest
England*

Exeter

Portsmouth

*Southeast
England*

About Itineraries

Nine driving itineraries map a route through the various regions of England, Wales, and Scotland. At the beginning of each itinerary we suggest our recommended pacing to help you decide the amount of time to allocate to each region. Often all, or a large portion, of an itinerary can be enjoyed using one hotel as a base and staying for several days.

Most sightseeing venues operate a summer and a winter opening schedule, the change-over occurring around late March/early April and late October/early November. If you happen to be visiting at the changeover times, be sure to check whether your chosen spot is open before making plans. We try to give an indication of opening times, but there is every possibility that these dates and times will have changed by the time you take your trip, so before you embark on an excursion, check the dates and hours of opening.

MAPS

At the beginning of each itinerary a map shows the itinerary's routing, places of interest along the way, and towns with recommended hotels. These are an artist's renderings and are not intended to replace commercial maps. Our suggestion is to purchase a large-scale road atlas of England where an inch equals 10 miles. Mark your itinerary route with a highlight pen.

About Hotels

The third section of this guide contains our recommendations for outstanding places to stay in England, Scotland, and Wales. Each listing is very different and occasionally the owners have their eccentricities, which all adds to the allure of these small hotels. We have tried to be candid and honest in our appraisals and tried to convey each hotel's special flavor so that you know what to expect and will not be disappointed. No hotel pays to be included in our guide: they are all places that we have visited, inspected, and stayed—places that we enjoy. Our recommendations cover a wide range: please do not expect the same standard of luxury at, for example, the lovely Wykeman Arms in Winchester as at the luxurious Chewton Glen—there is no comparison—yet each is outstanding in what it offers. We have tried to mention major sightseeing attractions near each countryside listing to encourage you to spend several nights in each location. Few countries have as much to offer as Great Britain—within a few miles of most listings there are places of interest to visit and explore—lofty cathedrals, quaint churches, museums, and grand country houses.

CHILDREN

Places that welcome children state *Children welcome*. The majority of listings in this guide do not "welcome" children but find they become tolerable at different ages over 5 or, more often than not, over 12. In some cases places simply do not accept children. However, these indications of children's acceptability are not cast in stone, so if you have your heart set on staying at a listing that states *Children over 12* and you have an 8-year-old, call them, explain your situation, and they may well accept you. Ideally we would like to see all listings welcoming children and all parents remembering that they are staying in a hotel and doing their bit by making sure that children do not run wild.

CHRISTMAS PROGRAMS

Several listings offer Christmas getaways—if the information section indicates that the listing is open during the Christmas season, there is a very good chance that it offers a festive Christmas package.

CREDIT CARDS

Whether hotels accepts payment by credit card is indicated using the terms AX—American Express, MC—MasterCard, VS—Visa, or simply—all major.

FINDING HOTELS

At the back of the book is a key map of Great Britain plus nine regional maps showing each recommended hotel's location. The pertinent regional map number is given at the right on the top line of each hotel's description. To make it easier for you, we have divided each location map into a grid of four parts, a, b, c, and d as indicated on each map's key. We give concise driving directions to guide you to the listing which is often in a more out-of-the-way place than the town or village in the address. We would be very grateful if you would let us know of cases where our directions have proved inadequate.

RATES

Rates are those quoted to us for the 1996 summer season. We have tried to keep rates uniform by quoting the 1996 rate for a standard double room and for a suite. Not all places conform, so where dinner is included, or the listing only quotes per person rates, we have stated this in the listing. Prices are always quoted to include breakfast (except in London where breakfast is not usually included in the rate), Value Added Tax (VAT), and service (if these are applicable). Please use the figures printed as a guideline and be certain to ask what the rate is at the time of booking. Many listings offer special terms, below their normal prices, for "short breaks" of two or more nights. In many listings suites are available at higher prices.

RESERVATIONS

Reservations can be confining and usually must be guaranteed by a deposit; however, if you have your heart set on a particular place, to avoid disappointment make a reservation. If you prefer to travel as whim and the weather dictate, rooms can often be had in the countryside with just a few days' notice. July and August are the busiest times and if you are traveling to a popular spot such as Bath or York, it is advisable to make reservations. It is always a good idea to have reservations in London.

It is a completely unacceptable practice to make reservations for a particular night at several establishments, choosing at the last minute which one to stay at. Although proprietors do not always strictly adhere to it, it is important to understand that once reservations are confirmed—whether by phone or in writing—you are under contract. This means that the proprietor is legally obligated to provide the accommodation he has promised and that you are bound to pay for that accommodation. If you cannot take up your accommodation, you are liable for a portion of the accommodation charges plus your deposit. If you have to cancel your reservation, do so as soon as possible so that the proprietor can attempt to re-let your room—in which case you are liable only for the re-let fee or the deposit.

There are several options for making hotel reservations:

LETTER: If you write for reservations, state clearly exactly what you want, how many people are in your party, how many rooms you require, the category of room you prefer (standard, superior, deluxe), and your dates of arrival and departure, and enquire about deposit requirements. The hotel usually sends you a map with your confirmation. When you receive a reply, send your deposit.

FAX: If you have access to a fax machine, this is a very quick way to reach a hotel. If the hotel has a fax, we have included the number in the listing.

TELEPHONE: If you are visiting from overseas, our preference for making a reservation is by telephone; the cost is minimal and you have your answer immediately, so if space is not available, you can then decide on an alternative. (If calling from the United States, allow for the time difference [England is five hours ahead of New York] so that you can call during their business day. Dial 011 [the international code], 44 [Britain's code], then the city code [dropping the 0] and the telephone number.) Be specific as to what your needs are, such as a ground-floor room, en-suite bathroom or twin beds. Check the prices which may well have changed from those given in the book (summer 1996). Ask what deposit to send or give your credit card number. Tell them approximately what time you intend to arrive and request dinner if you want it. Ask for a confirmation letter with brochure and map to be sent to you.

USA REPRESENTATIVE: Several of the hotels have United States representatives, often more than one. We have listed the US representatives along with the hotels they book at the end of the guide. This is an extremely convenient way to secure a reservation. However, sometimes representatives make a charge for their services, only reserve the more expensive rooms, or quote a higher price to protect themselves against currency fluctuations.

Introduction–About Hotels

Southeast England

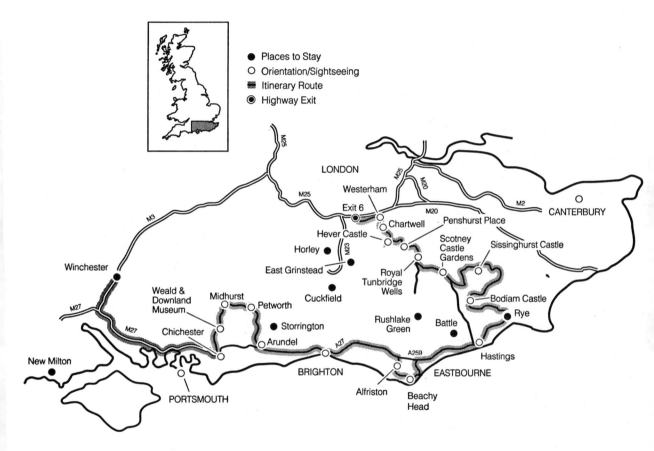

Places to Stay
Orientation/Sightseeing
Itinerary Route
Highway Exit

M25

LONDON

Westerham

Exit 6

Chartwell

Penshurst Place

CANTERBURY

M2

M20

M20

M3

Hever Castle

Horley

East Grinstead

Scotney
Castle
Gardens

Sissinghurst Castle

Winchester

Royal
Tunbridge
Wells

Bodiam Castle

M27

Weald &
Downland
Museum

Midhurst

Petworth

Cuckfield

Rye

M27

Chichester

Storrington

Rushlake
Green

Battle

Hastings

New Milton

Arundel

A27

A259

EASTBOURNE

PORTSMOUTH

BRIGHTON

Alfriston

Beachy
Head

Southeast England

Southeast from London through Kent and Sussex to England's southern coast, the land is fertile and the climate mild. Scores of narrow country lanes twist and turn among the gentle slopes of the pleasant countryside, leading you from Chartwell, Churchill's home, through castles, manors, and some of the most exquisitely beautiful gardens in England to Rye, a town full of history and rich in smugglers' tales. Along the busy, crowded coast you come to Brighton where seaside honky-tonk contrasts with the vivid spectacle of the onion domes of the Royal Pavilion, Arundel with its mighty fortress, and Portsmouth with its historic boats.

Scotney Castle Gardens

Recommended Pacing: Spend two nights in southeast England to enable you to accomplish the first part of this itinerary. Allow a day's drive, with sightseeing, along the coast and into Winchester. Spend two nights in Winchester to give you a complete day for sightseeing.

Chartwell (NT), your first sightseeing destination, is signposted from exit 6 of the M25, through Westerham and onto country lanes. Chartwell was the home of Winston Churchill from 1924 until his death in 1965, when Lady Churchill gave the house and its contents to the nation. To visit this large home and Churchill's studio full of his mementos and paintings is to have a glimpse into the family life of one of Britain's most famous politicians. (*Closed December, closed Mondays and Fridays, tel: 01732-866368.*)

Leaving Chartwell, retrace your steps the short distance to the main road and follow signs for **Hever Castle**, a small 13th-century moated castle that was at one time home to the Boleyn family. Anne Boleyn was Henry VIII's second wife and Elizabeth I's mother. At the turn of the century vast amounts of money were poured into the castle's restoration by William Waldorf Astor, an extremely wealthy American who forsook his native country and became a naturalized British citizen. Because the castle was far too small to provide accommodation for his family and friends, Mr Astor built an adjacent village of snug, Tudor-style cottages and joined it to the castle. While the village is not open to the public, the restored castle, its rooms full of antiques that span the last 800 years, and the park-like grounds are open to the public. (*Open mid-March–November, tel: 01732-865224.*)

Leave the castle heading left in the direction of Tunbridge Wells, turning left down a small country road to **Chiddingstone**, a National Trust village, whose short main street has several 16th- and 17th-century half-timbered houses, a church, and a tea shop. Park by the old houses and follow a footpath behind the cottages to the Chiding Stone, from which the village gets its name: nagging wives were brought here to be chided by the villagers.

Just beyond the village, branch left at the oast house for Penshurst Station and **Penshurst Place**, a 14th-century manor house with an Elizabethan front surrounded by magnificent parkland and gorgeous gardens. Here Sir Philip Sidney—poet, soldier, and statesman—was born and his descendant, Viscount de l'Isle, lives today. The enormous, 14th-century great hall with its stone floor and lofty, ornate, beamed ceiling contrasts by its austerity with the sumptuously furnished state rooms. There is also a fascinating collection of old toys. The gardens are a delight, full of hedges and walls that divide them into flower-filled alleyways and rooms—each garden with a very different character. (*Open April–September, closed Mondays, tel: 01892-870307.*)

Royal Tunbridge Wells lies about 7 miles to the south. In its heyday Royal Tunbridge Wells rivaled Bath as a spa town. The Regency meeting place, The Pantiles, a terraced walk with shops behind a colonnade, is still there as are the elegant Regency parades and houses designed by Decimus Burton. Central parking is well signposted to the rear of the Corn Exchange which contains an exhibit, *Day at the Wells*, which traces the town's growth from the time the spring water became fashionable for its curative powers to its popularity with wealthy Victorians.

Leave Royal Tunbridge Wells on the A267 following signposts for Eastbourne till you are directed to the left through Bells Yew Green to cross the A21 (Hastings road) and enter **Scotney Castle Gardens** (NT), a gorgeous, romantic garden surrounding the moated ruins of a 14th-century castle. (*Open April–mid-November, closed Mondays and Tuesdays, tel: 01892-890651.*)

Leave Scotney Castle Gardens to the left taking the A21 (Hastings road) for a short distance to Flimwell where you turn left on the A268 to Hawkshurst and from here left on the A229 Maidstone road to **Cranbrook**. While it is not necessary to go through Cranbrook to get to Sissinghurst Gardens, it makes a very worthwhile detour because it is a delightful town whose High Street has lots of lovely, white-board houses and shops, a fine medieval church, and a huge, white-board windmill with enormous sails. On the other side of town you come to the A262 where you turn right for the short drive to Sissinghurst Castle Gardens.

Sissinghurst Castle (NT) was a jail for 3,000 French prisoners in the Seven Years' War. Its ruined remains were bought by Vita Sackville-West and her husband, Harold Nicolson, in 1930 and together they created the most gorgeous gardens with areas divided off like rooms and each room a distinctly different, beautiful garden. They also rescued part of the derelict castle where you can climb the tower in which Vita wrote her books. At the entrance to the garden an old barn has been tastefully converted into a tea room and shop. (*Open March–October, closed Mondays, tel: 01580-712850.*)

Continue along the A262 to Biddenden and take the A28 through **Tenterden** with its broad High Street of tiled and weather-boarded houses to the A268 (Hawkshurst road) where you turn right for the short drive to the village of Sandhurst. Here you turn left onto country lanes to **Bodiam Castle** (NT), a small, picturesque, squat fortress with crenelated turrets surrounded by a wide moat and pastoral countryside. Richard II ordered the castle built as a defensive position to secure the upper reaches of the Rother against French raiders who had ravaged nearby towns, but an attack never came. (*Open all year, tel: 01580-830436.*)

Turn left as you leave the castle following a country lane to Staple Cross where you turn left on the B2165 which brings you into **Rye**, a fortified seaport which was often attacked by French raiders. However, the sea has long since retreated, leaving the town marooned 2 miles inland. Find the quaintest street in Rye, **Mermaid Street**, with its weatherboard and tile-hung houses and up one cobblestoned block you find yourself on the doorstep of **The Mermaid Inn**. Opened in 1420, The Mermaid Inn is a fascinating relic of the past. As late as Georgian days, smugglers frequented this strikingly timbered inn and used to sit drinking in the pub with their pistols on the table, unchallenged by the law. Near the Norman Church is the 13th-century **Ypres Tower**—formerly a castle and prison, it is now a museum of local history. **Lamb House** (NT) (on West Street near the church) was the home of American novelist Henry James from 1898 to 1916. To learn more about Rye's fascinating history attend the sound and light show at the **Rye Town Model**. (*Open April–October, tel: 01797-223254.*)

Rye

Leave Rye on the A259 taking this fast road around Hastings and Bexhill to **Eastbourne** where you follow signs for the seafront of this old-fashioned holiday resort and continue on to the B2103 which brings you up and onto the vast chalk promontory, **Beachy Head,** that rises above the town. It is a glorious, windswept place of soaring seagulls and springy turf which ends abruptly as the earth drops away to giant chalk cliffs that plummet into the foaming sea. This is the starting point for the **South Downs Way, a** walking path. Passing the Belle Tout Lighthouse, you come to **Birling Gap,** a beach once popular with smugglers but now favored by bathers. The most dramatic scenery, the **Seven Sisters,** giant, white, windswept cliffs, are an invigorating walk from the tiny village of Friston.

From Friston take the A259 to Westdean where you turn right for **Alfriston,** an adorable village on the South Downs Way which traces its origins back to Saxon times. Behind the main village street in a little cottage garden facing the village green sits the **Clergy House** (NT) with its deep thatch roof, the first building acquired by the National Trust, in 1896.

Either the fast A27 or the slower coastal road (A259) will bring you into **Brighton,** a onetime sleepy fishing village transformed into a fashionable resort at the beginning of the 19th century by the Prince Regent building his fanciful, extravagant **Royal Pavilion** with its onion domes and gaudy paintwork. Follow signs for the town center and park near the pavilion, an extravaganza of a place full of colorful, rather overpowering decor. (*Open all year, tel: 01273-603005.*)

Very near the Royal Pavilion are **The Lanes,** narrow streets of former fishermen's cottages now filled with restaurants and antique and gift shops. The seafront is lined by an almost 3-mile-long promenade with the beach below and gardens and tall terraces above. Many of the once-fashionable townhouses are now boarding houses and small hotels but this does not detract from the old-fashioned seaside atmosphere of the town. Stretching out into the sea, the white, wooden **Palace Pier** harks back to an earlier age.

At the end is a delightful, old-fashioned funfair with a helter-skelter and carousel horses along with other rides.

Leave Brighton along the seafront in the direction of Hove to join the A27 at Shoreham-by-Sea. This section of the A27 passes through suburb after suburb and is the least interesting part of this itinerary. On the outskirts of **Arundel** the massive keep and towers of **Arundel Castle** rise above the town. Built just after the Norman Conquest to protect this area from sea pirates and raiders, the castle contains a collection of armor, tapestries, and other interesting artifacts. (*Open April–October, closed Saturdays, tel: 01903-882173.*)

From Arundel take the A284 inland towards Pulborough and then follow signs through the narrow, winding old streets of **Petworth**, where several of the shops are antique stores, to **Petworth House** (NT), an enormous, 17th-century house in a vast deer park with landscaping by Capability Brown. The house, completed by the 6th Duke of Somerset in 1696, retains the 13th-century chapel of an earlier mansion and houses a proud art collection which includes a series of landscapes by Turner and also paintings by Holbein, Rembrandt, Van Dyck, Gainsborough, Titian, Rubens, and Reynolds. (*Open April–October, closed Mondays and Fridays, tel: 01798-42207.*)

Retrace your route the short distance into Petworth and take the A272 through Midhurst to reach the A286 (Chichester road). **Midhurst** has some fine old houses and attractive inns. Knockhundred Row leads from North Street to Red Lion Street and the old timbered market. Curfew is faithfully rung each evening at 8 pm in the parish church. Legend has it that a rider, lost in darkness, followed the sound of the church bells and found his way to the town. To show his gratitude he purchased a piece of land in Midhurst, now called Curfew Garden, which was presented to the town as a gift and made money available for the nightly ringing of the bells.

Across the South Downs the A286 brings you to the **Weald and Downland Museum**, an assortment of old, humble buildings such as farmhouses and barns brought to and restored on this site after their loss to demolition was inevitable. Inside several of the structures are displays showing the development of buildings through the ages. (*Open March–October, tel: 0124-363348.*)

Leaving the museum, take the A286 around Chichester to the A27 Portsmouth road which leads you onto the M275 to the historic center of **Portsmouth** and your goal, the *H.M.S. Victory* and *Mary Rose*. The ***H.M.S. Victory***, Nelson's flagship at the Battle of Trafalgar in 1805, has been restored and kitted out to show what life was like on board. Nearby, the ***Mary Rose***, Henry VIII's flagship, is housed in a humidified building that preserves its remains which were raised from the sea bed several years ago. The Naval Museum has a display of model ships, figureheads, and a panorama depicting the Battle of Trafalgar. (*Open all year, tel: 01705-812931.*)

Retrace your steps up the M275 and onto the M27 which quickly brings you to the A33/M3 and **Winchester** where a magnificent **cathedral** stands at the center of the city. Park in one of the car parks on the edge of town and walk into the pedestrian heart of the city that was the capital of England in King Alfred's reign during the 9th century and stayed so for 200 years. Construction of the 556-foot-long cathedral began in 1079 and finished in 1404. Treasures include a memorial window to Izaak Walton, a black marble font, seven chancery chapels for special masses, medieval wall paintings, stained glass, and tombs of ancient kings including King Canute. Close by is **Winchester College**, founded in 1382, one of the oldest public schools in England. Leaving Winchester, the M3 will quickly take you back to London.

Southwest England

- ● Places to Stay
- ○ Orientation/Sightseeing
- ▓ Itinerary Route
- ••• Minor Roads

Boscastle
Tintagel
Padstow
A39
A30
A30
A390
A38
Lostwithiel
St Austell
Mevagissey
A390
Truro
Veryan
Portloe
Trelissick Gardens
Portscatho
St Ives
St Just in Roseland
St Mawes
A394
Mawnan Smith
Falmouth
Marazion
Cape Cornwall
St Just
St Michael's Mount
Lands End
Penzance

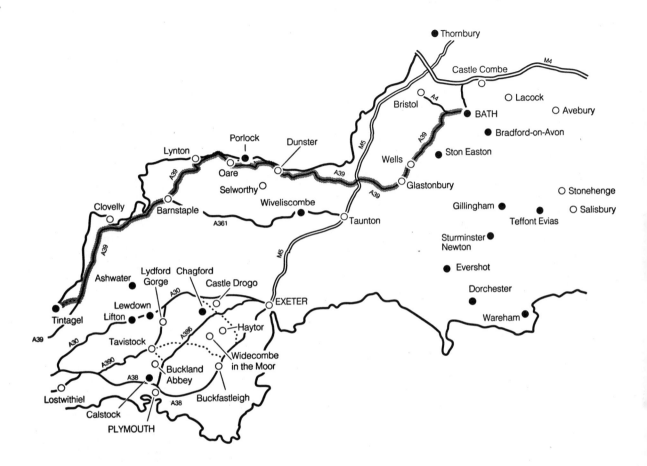

23

Southwest England

Scenery changes noticeably as this itinerary traverses England southwest from Bath through Somerset and along its unspoilt coast, outlining Cornwall, into the heart of Devon. Wild ponies gallop across the expanses of Exmoor. Along the northern coastline, the scenery changes dramatically from wooded inlets dropping to the sea to wild rollers crashing on granite cliffs, giving credence to old tales of wreckers luring ships onto rocky shorelines. Picturesque villages surround sheltered harbors, their quays strewn with nets and lobster pots. Southern ports present a gentler scene: bobbing yachts dot wooded estuaries and gentle waves lap the shoreline. Hedgerow-lined lanes meander inland across Dartmoor's heather-clad moorlands to picturesque towns nestling at her edge. Relax and enjoy your explorations of this westernmost spur of land jutting out into the Atlantic Ocean.

St. Michael's Mount

Recommended Pacing: Spend two full days in Bath to give you time to appreciate the flavor of this lovely city. Use Tintagel as a base for exploring north Devon and Penzance, and Mawnan Smith, Veryan or Talland-by-Looe as a base for exploring Cornwall. Complete the itinerary with a couple of nights in south Devon to enable you to explore the wild beauties of Dartmoor.

The elegant city of **Bath** with its graceful, honey-colored buildings, interesting museums, and delightful shopping area is best explored on foot over a period of several days. Bath, founded by the Romans in the 1st century around the gushing mineral hot springs, reached its peak of popularity in the early 1700s with the arrival of Beau Nash, who opened the first Pump Room where people could take the water and socialize. Architects John Wood, father and son, used the local honey-colored stone to build the elegant streets and crescents in neoclassical Palladian style.

Maps are available from the Tourist Information Centre near the abbey (corner of Cheap and Stall streets). Entry into the **Roman Baths** is via the **Pump Room** which was the place to gather in the 18th and 19th centuries. The Great Bath, a large warm swimming pool built around a natural hot spring, now open to the sky, was once covered. Mosaics, monuments, and many interesting artifacts from the town can be seen in the adjacent museum. (*Open all year, tel: 01225-461111 ext. 2782.*)

Nearby, tucked into a narrow passageway between Abbey Green and North Parade, is **Sally Lunn's House**, a museum and a tea shop. The museum, in the cellar, has the kitchen preserved much as it was in the 1680s when Sally's buns and other baked goods were the favorites of Bath society. Upstairs you can try a freshly baked Sally Lunn bun.

Eighteenth-century society came to be seen at balls and gatherings at the **Assembly Rooms** and authors such as Austen, Smolett, and Fielding captured the social importance of these events. The **Museum of Costume**, in the Assembly Rooms basement, should not be missed. (*Open all year, tel: 01225-46111 ext. 2782.*)

From the Museum of Costume it is an easy walk via **The Circus**, a tight circle lined with splendid houses designed by John Wood I, and Brock Street to the **Royal Crescent**, a great arc of 30 terraced houses that epitomize the Georgian elegance of Bath and are the prime example of John Wood II's architecture. **One Royal Crescent** has been authentically restored to the 18th-century style and contains an interesting kitchen museum and a gift shop. (*Open all year, tel: 01225-428126.*)

Bath has some wonderful restaurants and delightful shops and boutiques: whether you are in the market for antiques or high fashion you will find shopping here a real joy.

While our itinerary takes us south and west from Bath, there are a great many interesting places to the east, listed below, that can easily be visited as day trips from this lovely city.

The village of **Avebury** (NT), made up of a church, several houses, shops, and an old pub, lies within a vast circle of standing stones surrounded by earthworks. The site covers 28 acres. Unlike Stonehenge, where the stones are larger, the site smaller, and the crowds sometimes overwhelming, Avebury is a peaceful spot where, armed with a map, you can wander amongst the stones and wonder why about 4,000 years ago Bronze Age man spent what has been estimated at 1½ million man hours to construct such a temple. (Just off the A4 between Calne and Marlborough.) (*Open all year, tel: 016723-555.*)

Castle Combe is the most photogenic collection of warm, honey-stone cottages snuggled along a stream's edge. (Just south of the M4 motorway between exits 17 and 18.)

Claverton Manor is the American museum in the United Kingdom. Furniture, household equipment, and period rooms show home life in the United States from the 17th to 19th centuries. (3 miles east of Bath.) (*Open April–October, tel: 01225-460503.*)

Lacock (NT) is an exquisite village where no building dates from later than the 18th century, many dating from much earlier. Be sure to visit the Fox Talbot museum of early photographs and Lacock Abbey. The abbey was converted to a manor house in the 16th century but retains its 13th-century cloisters. At The Sign of the Angel is a delightful 15th-century inn, easily distinguished by being the only black and white building in the village. (Between Chippenham and Melksham on the A350.) (*Open March–October, tel: 01249-73459.*)

Salisbury has been a prosperous Hampshire market town since the 13th century. Park your car in one of the large car parks on the edge of town and wander through the bustling town center to **Salisbury Cathedral,** the only ancient English cathedral built to a single design. Completed in 1258, it sits gracefully isolated from the busy town, surrounded by a large green field.

Salisbury Cathedral

Britain's most famous ancient monument is **Stonehenge**. Built over a period of almost 1000 years up to 1250 B.C., this circular arrangement of towering stone slabs was probably meant either to mark the seasons or to be used as a symbol of worship. It is intriguing to ponder what prompted a society thousands of years ago to drag these immense stones many miles and erect them in just such a formation, isolated in the middle of flat Salisbury Plain. Understandably, Stonehenge attracts many visitors. Your visit will be more enjoyable if you are prepared for coachloads of tourists. (On the A303 about 10 miles from Salisbury.) (*Open all year, tel: 01272-734472.*)

When it is time to leave Bath take the A36 following signs for Bristol until you come to the A39 Wells road. **Wells** is England's smallest cathedral city and the cathedral is glorious. Park you car in one of the well signposted car parks on the edge of town and walk through the bustling streets to **Wells Cathedral**. The cathedral's west front is magnificently adorned with 400 statues of saints, angels, and prophets. The interior is lovely and on every hour the Great Clock comes alive as figures of four knights joust and one is unseated. From the cathedral you come to Vicars Close, a cobbled street of tall-chimneyed cottages with little cottage gardens built over 500 years ago as housing for the clerical community. On the other side of the cathedral regal swans swim lazily in the moat beneath the Bishop's Palace where at one time they rang a bell when they wanted to be fed—now visitors' picnics provide easier meals.

Nearby **Glastonbury** is a quiet market town steeped in legends. As the story goes, Joseph of Arimathea traveled here and leaned on his staff which rooted and flowered, a symbol that he should build a church. There may well have been a primitive church here but the ruins of **Glastonbury Abbey** that you see are those of the enormous abbey complex that was begun in the 13th century and closed by Henry VIII just as it was completed. The abbey is in the center of town. Legend also has it that Glastonbury (at that time surrounded by marshes and lakes) was the Arthurian Isle of Avalon. Arthur and Guinevere are reputedly buried here and it is said that Arthur only sleeps and will arise when England needs him. (*Open all year, tel: 01458-32267.*)

Cross the M5 near Bridgwater, detouring around the town, and follow the A39, Minehead road, to **Dunster**, a medieval town dominated by the battlements and towers of **Dunster Castle** (NT). Constructed by a Norman baron, it has been inhabited by the Luttrell family since 1376. While much of the castle was reconstructed in the last century, it has a superb staircase, halls, and dining room. (*Open all year, tel: 01643-821314.*) Park before you enter the town and explore the shops and ancient buildings (including a dormered Yarn Market) of the High Street. On Mill Lane you can tour 18th-century **Dunster Watermill** (NT) which was restored to working order in 1979.

Continue your drive along the A39 watching for a sign directing you to your right to the hamlet of **Selworthy** (NT). Its pretty green, surrounded by elaborate thatched cottages, makes this a very picturesque spot. The National Trust has a small visitors' center and excellent tea shop.

Porlock is a large, quaint, bustling village with narrow streets. As the road bends down to the sea, the hamlet of **Porlock Weir** appears as a few picturesque cottages and the Ship Inn facing a pebble beach and a tiny harbor dotted with boats.

Retrace your steps towards Porlock for a short distance and take the first road to the right, a private toll road that rises steeply out of Porlock Weir. It is a pretty, forested drive along a narrow lane with views of Porlock bay. The toll road returns you to the A39 which you take for a short distance before turning left for the village of **Oare**. R. D. Blackmore who wrote about the people, moods, and landscape of Exmoor used the little church that you see in the valley below for Lorna Doone's marriage to John Ridd. Continue into the village where you can park your car behind the village shop and take a 3-mile walk along the river to Badgworthy Valley, the home of the cutthroat outlaw Doone family.

Continue to Brenden where you turn right, signposted Lynton and Lynmouth, and regain the A39. A short drive through squat, red and green hills brings you to the coast where the road dips steeply and you see the neighboring villages of **Lynton** and **Lynmouth**, with Victorian Lynton standing at the top of the cliff and Lynmouth, a fishing village of old-style houses, nestling at its foot. Park by the harbor and take the funky old cliff railway which connects the two villages.

Leaving Lynmouth, proceed up the hill into Lynton, following signs for the alternative route for light vehicles, Valley of the Rocks. Wend your way through the town and continue straight. Beyond the suburbs the road narrows and you find yourself in a narrow valley with large, rugged rock formations separating you from the sea, then in a more pastoral area with seascapes at every dip and turn.

Deposit your road toll (30p) in the honesty box and follow signs along narrow lanes for **Hunters Inn,** a lovely old pub set in a peaceful valley. From here direct yourself back towards the A39 which bends inland across the western stretches of Exmoor and south through Barnstaple, a market center for the area. Continue along the A39 to Bideford where a bridge sweeps you high above the old harbor.

Just beyond Bucks Cross you see a small signpost for **Hobby Drive**. This narrow coastal road winds through woodlands, provides panoramic views of Clovelly, and brings you out on the road above the village. **Clovelly** is an impossibly beautiful spot, its whitewashed cottages tumbling down cobblestone lanes to boats bobbing in the harbor far below. However, to be able to walk through this picturebook village you have to pay an entrance fee and pass through a very commercial visitors' center, a real tourist trap.

Leave the A39 at the B3263 and detour on narrow country lanes leading to the picturesque little village of **Boscastle**. Braced in a valley 400 feet above a little harbor, the town was named after the Boscastle family who once lived there, rather than an actual castle.

Nearby, **Tintagel castle** clings to a wild headland, exposed to coastal winds, claiming the honor of being King Arthur's legendary birthplace. The sea has cut deeply into the slate cliffs, isolating the castle. Climb the steep steps to the castle and gaze down at the sea far below. Prince Charles, as Duke of Cornwall, owns the castle whose interior is more attractive than the exterior. The town itself, while it is quite touristy, has charm and the most adorable, and certainly most photographed, **Post Office** (NT) in Britain.

Leaving Tintagel, follow signs for the A39, in the direction of Truro, to the A30 which takes you around Redruth, Cambourne, and Hayle to the A3074 to **St. Ives**, about an hour-and-a-half journey if the roads are not too crowded. St. Ives is a former fishing town with cobbled streets and old cottages that has spread to suburban sprawl—it's very crowded in summer. With the decline of fishing came the artists who have done much to preserve its quaint cobbled streets and picturesque old cottages. You may want to avoid it on a crowded summer afternoon.

The most attractive, windswept stretch of Cornwall's coastline lies between St. Ives and Land's End. Stone farm villages hug the bare expanse of land and are cooled by Atlantic Ocean breezes that wash up over the cliff edges. Abandoned old tin mine towers stand in ruins and regularly dot the horizon. On the western outskirts of **St. Just** lies **Cape Cornwall**: rather than visit over-commercialized Land's End, consider visiting here to enjoy a less crowded, more pastoral western view. Pull into **Sennen Cove** with its long curving crescent of golden sand and the powerful Atlantic surf rolling and pounding.

The expression "from John O'Groats to Land's End" signifies the length of Britain from its northeasternmost point in Scotland to England's rocky promontory, **Land's End**, in the southwest. Many visitors to Cornwall visit Land's End, but be prepared to be disappointed—you have to pay to enter a compound of refreshment stands, exhibits, and children's rides to get to the viewpoint.

As the road rounds the peninsula from Land's End it is exposed to the calmer Channel waters, far different from the Atlantic rollers. Mount's Bay is just around the bend from Land's End with the pretty village of **Mousehole** (pronounced "mowzle") tucked into a niche on its shores. With color-washed cottages crowded into a steep valley and multi-colored fishing boats moored at its feet, this adorable village is crowded in summer but worth the aggravation endured in finding a parking spot.

Pirates from France and the Barbary coast used to raid the flourishing port town of **Penzance** until the mid-18th century. Now it is quite a large town, a real mishmash of styles from quaint fishermen's cottages to 60s housing estates, where long, peaceful, sandy beaches contrast with the clamor and activity of dry-dock harbors.

Leave Penzance on the A30 following the graceful sweep of Mount's Bay and turn right onto a minor road that brings you to **St. Michael's Mount** (NT). Its resemblance to the more famous mount in France is not coincidental, for it was founded by monks from Mont St. Michel in 1044. A 19th-century castle and the ruins of the monastery crown the island which is reached at low tide on foot from the town of Marazion. If you cannot coincide your arrival with low tide, do not worry—small boats ferry you the short distance to the island. The steep climb to the top of this fairy-tale mount is well worth the effort. (*Open daily April–October, limited winter opening, tel: 01736-710507.*)

To the east lies **Falmouth**. Overlooking the holiday resort, yachting center, and ancient port are the ruins of **Pendennis Castle**. Built in 1540 to guard the harbor entrance, it was held during the Civil War by the Royalists and withstood six months of siege before being the last castle to surrender to Cromwell's troops in 1646. (*Open all year.*) Falmouth is a bustling town whose narrow, shop-lined streets have a complex one-way system—parking is an additional problem. Unless you have shopping to do, avoid the congestion of the town center and follow signposts for Truro.

The road from Falmouth to St. Mawes winds around the river estuary by way of Truro. A faster and more scenic route is to take the **King Harry Ferry** across the river estuary. If you love wandering around gardens, you will enjoy **Trelissick Gardens** (NT) filled with subtropical plants, located on the Falmouth side of the estuary. (*Open all year, tel: 01872-865808.*)

St. Mawes is a charming, unspoilt fishing harbor at the head of the Roseland Peninsula. Its castle was built by Henry VIII to defend the estuary.

The 20 miles or so of coastline to the east of St. Mawes hide several beautiful villages located down narrow, winding country lanes. **Portscatho** is a lovely fishing village that has not been overrun with tourists. **Veryan** is a quaint village where thatched circular houses were built so that "the devil had nowhere to hide." **Portloe** is a pretty fishing hamlet. The most easterly village is **Mevagissey** whose beauty attracts writers, artists, and throngs of tourists.

Drive north through St. Austell to **Lostwithiel**, the 13th-century capital of Cornwall. Twenty miles to the east, **Liskeard** is crowded in summer, but fortunately much of the traffic has been diverted around the town. Between Liskeard and Tavistock you find **Cotehele** (NT), built between 1485 and 1627, the home of the Edgecumbe family. The house contains original furniture, armor, and needlework. A highlight is the kitchen with all its wonderful old implements. The gardens terrace steeply down to the lovely River Tamar. (*Open April–October, closed Friday, tel: 01579-50434/51222.*)

The A390 crosses the River Tay and brings you into Tavistock. Turn right at the first roundabout in town signposted B3357 Princetown (then the B3212 Mortenhampstead road) which brings you up, over a cattle grid, and into **Dartmoor National Park**. Vast expanses of moorland rise to rocky outcrops (tors and crags) where ponies and sheep graze intently among the bracken and heather, falling to picturesque wooded valleys where villages shelter beneath the moor. From Mortenhampstead it's a half-hour drive to Exeter and the motorway. But, saving the best for last, linger on Dartmoor and enjoy some of the following sights.

The view from atop **Haytor Crags** on the Bovey to Widecombe road is a spectacular one—there is a feel of *The Hound of the Baskervilles* to the place. Softer and prettier is the walk down wooded **Lydford Gorge** (NT) to White Lady Waterfall (between Tavistock and Okehampton). (*Open all year, tel: 0182282-441.*) A cluster of cottages and a tall church steeple make up **Widecombe in the Moor**, the village made famous by the *Uncle Tom Cobbleigh* song: the famous fair is still held on the second Tuesday in

September. The pretty town of **Chagford** at the edge of the moor has attractive houses and hostelries grouped round the market square. **Buckland-in-the-Moor** is full of picturesque thatched cottages. **Buckland Abbey** (NT), a onetime Cistertian abbey and home of Sir Francis Drake, is now a museum with scale model ships from Drake's time to today among its exhibits. At **Buckfastleigh** you can take a steam train for 7 miles alongside the river Dart. Nearby is **Buckfast Abbey**, famous for its tonic wine and colorful stained glass windows. **Castle Drogo** (NT) is a fanciful, castle-like home designed by Edward Lutyens overlooking the moor near Drewsteignton. (*Open all year, tel: 01647-433306.*)

Leaving Dartmoor National Park, A roads quickly bring you to **Exeter,** a city that was much damaged by German bombs in 1942. Happily the cathedral which was begun in 1260 survived. The old town towards the River Exe has many fine old buildings including the Custom House and a maze of little streets with old inns and quaint shops. On Town Quay is a fascinating **Maritime Museum**. (*Open all year, tel: 01392-58075.*) The rebuilt center is a modern shopping complex.

From Exeter the M5 will connect you to all parts of Britain.

In and Around the Cotswolds

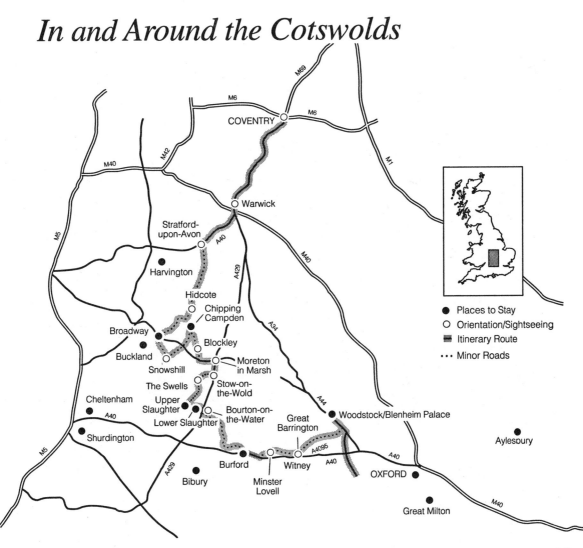

COVENTRY

Warwick

Stratford-upon-Avon

Harvington

Hidcote

Chipping Campden

Broadway

Blockley

Buckland

Snowshill

Moreton in Marsh

The Swells

Stow-on-the-Wold

Cheltenham

Upper Slaughter

Lower Slaughter

Bourton-on-the-Water

Great Barrington

Woodstock/Blenheim Palace

Shurdington

Burford

Witney

OXFORD

Aylesbury

Bibury

Minster Lovell

Great Milton

● Places to Stay
○ Orientation/Sightseeing
▨ Itinerary Route
··· Minor Roads

35

In and Around The Cotswolds

From the gracious university town of Oxford through the quintessentially English Cotswold villages to Shakespearean Stratford and the grand fortress of Warwick Castle, this itinerary covers famous attractions and idyllic countryside nooks and crannies. The Cotswolds is a region of one sleepy village after another clad in the local soft-gray limestone or creamy-golden ironstone, where mellow stone walls, manor houses, and churches cluster along river banks, perch on steep-sided hills, or scatter independently in a pocket of a pretty valley. In Shakespeare's day this was sheep country and the center of England's wool industry. By the mid-1800s the area had fallen into decline, its wool trade usurped by Australia and New Zealand. Thus the area slept, by-passed by the factories and cities of the Industrial Revolution. Now tourists flock to the Cotswolds and yet the region remains remarkably unspoilt: in fact, it appears to thrive on the attention.

Lower Slaughter

Recommended Pacing: Spend a night in Oxford or in nearby Woodstock. Follow this with two nights in a countryside hotel as a base for exploring the beautiful Cotswold villages (consider going into Stratford to see a play one night).

Oxford is a beautiful university town graced by spacious lawns, pretty parks, lacy spires, honey-colored Cotswold stones, romantic pathways, and two picturesque rivers—the Cherwell and the Thames. Follow signs for the city center, park in any of the well signposted, multi-story car parks, and foray on foot to explore. You may want to make your first stop the **Oxford Information Centre** on Gloucester Green, off George Street, to obtain a map. Walking tours of the town start from here. Much of the sightseeing in this the oldest university town centers on its colleges whose open times depend on whether the students are "up" (there) or "down" (not there). Particularly worth visiting are **Christ Church College** with its superb quad and tower designed by Wren to hold the bell Great Tom; **Magdalen College**, the most beautiful college, with its huge gardens making you feel as if you are in the countryside; and **Merton College** whose chapel contains 13th- to 14th-century glass. Apart from the colleges, visit **St. Mary's Church** where you can climb the spire for a marvelous view of the city; the **Ashmolean Museum** with its remarkable collection of paintings, tapestries, and sculptures; the riverside **Botanical Gardens** opposite Magdalen College; **Blackwell's**, the most famous of Oxford's many bookstores; and **The Bear**, on Alfred Street, a marvelous old pub dating from 1242. Punts can be rented on the River Cherwell from beside Magdalen Bridge.

Leaving Oxford, take the A34 (Stratford-upon-Avon) to **Woodstock**, one of England's prettiest country towns. On the outskirts of Woodstock are the famous gates of **Blenheim Palace**, Sir John Vanbrugh's masterpiece, which was built for John Churchill, the 1st Duke of Marlborough. The construction of the house was a gift from Queen Anne to the Duke after his victory over the French and Bavarians at Blenheim in 1704. However, before its completion, Queen Anne's gratitude had waned and the Marlborough family had to pay to have the house finished. The gardens and park-like grounds were landscaped by Capability Brown. Sir Winston Churchill, the grandson of the 7th Duke, was born here on November 30, 1874, and associations with him have accentuated the historical interest of the Palace. (Winston Churchill, his wife, father, Lord Randolph Churchill, and mother, Jenny Jerome, the beautiful daughter of an American newspaper owner, are buried in St. Martin's churchyard in Bladon, 2 miles away.) You drive through the grounds to the house, park on the lawn, and either tour the sumptuous rooms with a group or wander independently. A narrow-gauge railway takes you through the park to the butterfly farm and plant center. (*Open mid-March–October, tel: 01993-811325.*) In contrast to the immense palace and spacious grounds are the compact streets of the little town of Woodstock with its coaching inns, delightful hotel (**The Feathers**), and interesting shops.

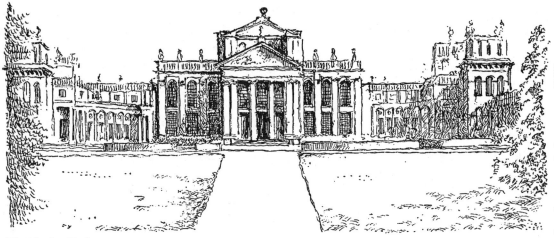

Blenheim Palace

Retrace your steps for a short distance on the A34 in the direction of Oxford and take the A4095 for 7 miles to the mellow-stone town of **Witney** where blankets have been made for over a thousand years and which still preserves its Cotswold market-town atmosphere. The 18th-century **Blanket Hall** was used for weighing blankets and has an unusual one-handed clock.

Minster Lovell is a few miles to the west along the B4047: to reach the old part of the village, follow the brown signs for "**Minster Lovell Hall**." Park at the end of the lane and walk through the churchyard to see the ruined home of the Lovell family in a field by the river's edge. Leave the village by the road to the side of the prettiest building in the village, The Swan, following signs through Astall Leigh and Astall to the A40 which you take in the direction of Cheltenham for a short distance to Burford.

Follow signs for "tourist information" which bring you down the hill into the lovely old-world Cotswold town of **Burford**. The broad High Street sweeps down the hillside, bordered by numerous antique and gift shops, to the bridge spanning the River Windrush. Branching off are delightful, narrow residential streets with flower-filled cottage gardens. In the days when coach and horses was the main form of transport, Burford was a way station. The coaches are long gone but the lovely inns remain: two with the most atmosphere are **The Bay Tree** and the adjacent **Lamb Inn**.

Explore Burford and leave town following the road over the River Windrush. Go left at the mini roundabout, directing yourself down country lanes to **Taynton** with its adorable thatched and golden-stone cottages and on up the valley to Great Barrington and **Little Barrington**, a village of quaint cottages. Turn right along the A40 towards Cheltenham and first right to Windrush where you pick up signs for the drive down country lanes through Sherbourne to Bourton-on-the-Water. (When you come to the A429 turn right and then right into Bourton-on-the-Water.)

Bourton-on-the-Water is a lovely village with a number of riverside greens and low bridges spanning the River Windrush. Go early in the morning, just before sunset, or in the winter to avoid the crowds that overrun this peaceful (albeit somewhat over-commercialized) spot.

Leave Bourton-on-the-Water by going down the main street and turning right for a very short distance on the A429 (in the direction of Cheltenham) to a left-hand turn which directs you down country lanes to the more peaceful side of the Cotswolds as typified by the outstandingly lovely villages of **Lower and Upper Slaughter** with their honey-colored stone cottages beside peaceful streams—just the names on the signpost are enough to lure you down their lanes. From Upper Slaughter follow signs for Stow-on-the-Wold down country lanes through "the Swells," **Lower and Upper Swell**, further picturesque examples of villages with whimsical names.

Stow-on-the-Wold, its market square lined by mellow old gray-stoned buildings, was one of the most prosperous wool towns in England. Most of the 17th-century buildings around the square now house interesting shops. Two of Stow's main thoroughfares—Sheep Street and Shepherds Way—are reminders that selling sheep was once the town's main livelihood. Cromwell converted the 12th-century church into a prison and used it to hold 1000 Royalists captive after a Civil War battle in 1646.

Nearby **Moreton in Marsh's** broad main street, once part of the Roman road known as the Fosse Way, is lined with interesting shops. At the crossroads take the A44 towards Evesham to **Bourton-on-the-Hill**, an appropriately named village whose houses climb a steep hillside. At the top of the hill turn right for Blockley and follow signs for the village center until you pick up signs for Broad Campden and **Chipping Campden**, with its High Street lined with gabled cottages and shops topped by steep tile roofs. **Woolstaplers Hall** is now a museum of photographic and medical equipment and home of the tourist information center.

Cross the A44 and a country lane brings you to **Snowshill** and **Snowshill Manor** (NT), a Tudor manor packed with collections of musical instruments, clocks, toys, and bicycles. (*Open May–September, closed Mondays and Tuesdays, tel: 01386-852410.*)

Just down the lane, flowers dress the lovely weathered-stone houses of **Broadway**, a town that is often described as the perfection of Cotswold beauty. The **Lygon Arms** is as famous as the town, a magnificent 14th- to 16th-century hotel whose public rooms are exquisitely furnished with antiques. In summer the town is thronged with tourists so it is best to visit early or late in the day.

Turn right up the main street and first left on the B4632 (signposted Stratford), through peaceful **Willersey** where ducks sail serenely on the village mere and Weston-sub-Edge, to the outskirts of Mickleton where you turn right for **Hidcote Manor Gardens** (NT), one of the most delightful gardens in England. Created early this century by Major Lawrence Johnston, it is a series of individual gardens each bounded by sculpted hedges and linked paths and terraces. Each "mini-garden" focuses on a specific theme or flower. There are stunning displays of old roses and in summer the perennials are a blaze of color. (*Open March–October, closed Tuesdays and Fridays, tel: 01386-438333.*) Next door, another outstanding garden, **Kiftsgate Court**, has exquisite displays of roses. (*Open April–September, Wednesday, Thursday, and Sunday.*)

Leaving Hidcote, return to Mickleton and turn right onto the B4632 into **Stratford-upon-Avon**, the birthplace of the greatest poet in the English language, William Shakespeare. Stratford-upon-Avon is always impossibly crowded with visitors—if crowds are not to your liking, give it a miss. William Shakespeare was born in 1564 in a half-timbered house on Henley Street, educated at the King's New Grammar School and, in 1597, six years before his death, he retired to **New Place**, one of the finest and largest houses in Stratford. Simply engraved stones in front of the altar of the **Holy Trinity Church** mark the burial spot of Shakespeare and some other members of his family. It is a fairly large town, with beautifully renovated timbered buildings and lovely shops. The town's glory, however, is brought expertly to the stage at the **Royal Shakespeare Theatre** and at its associate theatre, **The Other Place**. (*Open April–December.*)

Warwick Castle

Anne Hathaway married William Shakespeare in 1582, but until then she lived in a darling thatched cottage at **Shottery**, a small village just a stone's throw from Stratford-upon-Avon. You will see paintings and photographs of this picture-book cottage all over the world. (*Open all year.*)

When you leave Shottery head back towards the center of Stratford and take the A46 to Warwick. **Warwick Castle** is a magnificent, 14th-century fortress of formidable towers and turrets. The fortress dominates a choice spot on the river bank and its striking structure is beautifully preserved. Climb the towers, explore the armory and torture chamber below, then visit the Manor House. As you walk through the house you see what it was like to attend a house party given by the Earl and Countess of Warwick in 1898. The house has retained its period furniture and Madame Tussaud's has populated the rooms with wax figures from the past. Here a servant pours bathwater into a bath for a guest while downstairs guests listen to a recital being given by Dame Clara Butt. The gardens are decorated by arrogant, strutting peacocks. (*Open all year, tel: 01926-492797.*)

Wander into **Warwick** with its mixture of Georgian and old timber-framed houses. At the town's west gate stands the **Leycester Hospital**, for 400 years an almshouse for crippled soldiers. (*Closed Sundays, tel: 01926-492797.*) In Beauchamp Chapel lies the tomb of Elizabeth I's favorite, the Earl of Leicester.

The large industrial city of **Coventry** lies just to the north—it is worth a visit to see **Coventry Cathedral,** one of Europe's finest examples of modern architecture. On a night in 1940 Hitler's bombers destroyed 40 acres of the city center, including the cathedral. A new city center and a new cathedral were built after the war. The blackened ruins of the old cathedral form the approach to the new, with a cross made of two charred roof timbers on the old altar, inscribed "Father Forgive." In the new cathedral magnificent stained-glass windows by modern artists all lead the eye to a massive stone altar with its abstract cross and crucifix. Behind it is a 75-foot tapestry of the "Redeeming Savior of the World." From Coventry fast motorways will connect you to all parts of Britain.

Cycling through Suffolk

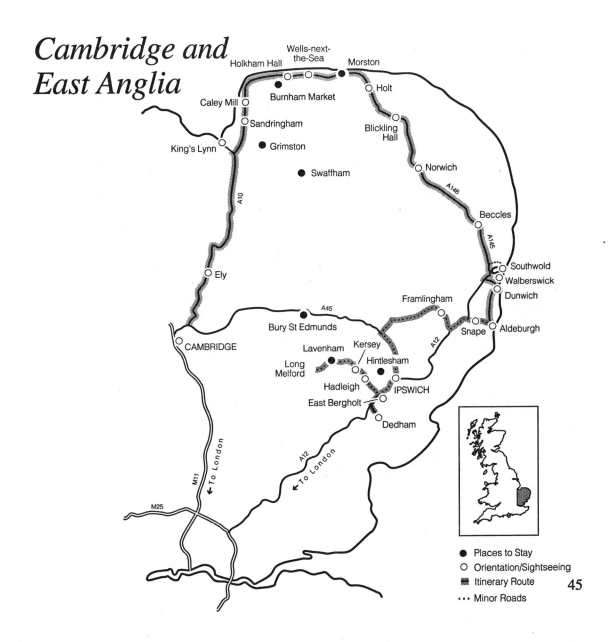

Cambridge and East Anglia

Holkham Hall
Wells-next-the-Sea
Morston
Caley Mill
Burnham Market
Holt
Sandringham
Blickling Hall
King's Lynn
Grimston
Swaffham
Norwich
A146
A10
Beccles
A145
Ely
Southwold
Walberswick
Dunwich
Framlingham
A45
Aldeburgh
Snape
CAMBRIDGE
Bury St Edmunds
A12
Lavenham
Kersey
Long Melford
Hintlesham
Hadleigh
IPSWICH
East Bergholt
Dedham
M11
To London
A12
To London
M25

● Places to Stay
○ Orientation/Sightseeing
▓ Itinerary Route
••• Minor Roads

45

Cambridge and East Anglia

Many visit the famous university town of Cambridge, but few travelers venture beyond to explore the bulge of England's eastern coastline with its sky-wide landscapes, stunning sunsets, lofty windmills, and unspoilt villages. This itinerary takes you from the vast fenlands, drained by the Dutch in the 17th century, along the pancake-flat Norfolk coastline with the sea often just out of sight beyond fields and marshes, into Norwich with its ancient streets and vast cathedral, through sleepy Suffolk villages full of quaint cottages to "Constable Country" where John Constable painted so many of his famous paintings. Be sure to visit Cambridge, but expand your trip to explore this quiet corner of Britain.

Kersey

Recommended Pacing: Spend one night in Norfolk, two if you have the luxury of time, and two in Suffolk, which gives you ample time to explore its quaint villages.

Leaving London, navigate yourself onto the M11 for the fast, two-hour drive to **Cambridge**, a city which contains much new building, but at whose heart is a fascinating university complex whose history spans over 700 years. Park your car in one of the well marked car parks near the town center, buy a guidebook, and set out to explore, for this is a city for strolling and browsing.

At most times visitors can go into college courtyards, chapels, dining halls, and certain gardens. **King's College Chapel** is one of the finest buildings in England, with Rubens' masterpiece, the *Adoration of the Magi*, framing the altar. Be sure not to miss **Clare College, Trinity College**, and **St. John's College**, which backs onto the enclosed stone "Bridge of Sighs." Explore the various alleys and streets on foot, row, or punt, drifting under the willow trees that line the River Cam. Boats are for hire at Silver Street Bridge and Quayside.

Leaving Cambridge on the A10 towards **Ely**, you soon come to open countryside offering sky-wide horizons of flat farmland that are soon punctuated by the soaring mass of **Ely Cathedral**, a building so large that it seems to dwarf the little market town that surrounds it. Until the surrounding fens were drained, Ely was an island, surrounded by water, and the cathedral must have appeared even more magnificent than it does today. This awesome structure was built in 1083, awesome not only for its sheer size but because it is an amazing piece of engineering, its huge tower held up by eight massive oak timbers each more than 60 feet in length.

Leaving Ely, regain the A10 following it around Downham Market to **King's Lynn**, a large, bustling town with a well marked historic core. A market is held every Saturday and Tuesday and the port has many fine old buildings: the **Guildhall** (1421), the **Customs House** (1683), and **St. Margaret's Church**. The father of George Vancouver, who explored the northwestern coast of North America and after whom the Canadian city and island are named, was a customs officer hereabouts.

Leaving King's Lynn, follow signs for the A149 in the direction of Hunstanton. After several miles turn right for **Sandringham**, one of the Royal Family's homes, and almost immediately first left to take you on a scenic drive through the woodlands that surround it. This huge Victorian house was bought in 1861 by Edward VII, at that time Prince of Wales, because he did not like Osborne House on the Isle of Wight. From mid-April to the end of September from 11 am (all week except Fridays and Saturdays) the grounds and several rooms in the house are open to the public—provided that the Royal Family is not in residence. (*Tel: 01553-772675.*)

Leave the car park to your left, passing the main gates (the Norwich gates, a wedding gift to Edward from the city of Norwich), and go left through Dersingham to regain the A149. In summer the air is heavy with the scent of lavender and the fields surrounding **Caley Mill** are a brilliant purple for this is one of the country's centers for the cultivation of lavender. There is a gift shop selling every imaginable lavender product.

After bypassing Hunstanton, the A149 becomes narrower, pottering along through attractive villages of pebble-and-red-brick cottages (Thornham, Titchwell, Brancaster, Staithe, and Overy Staithe) as it traces the flat Norfolk coast with the sea often just out of sight beyond fields and marshes. This is not a coastline of dramatic cliffs and headlands—the land merely ends and the sea begins.

On the outskirts of **Holkham** you follow the wall surrounding **Holkham Hall** to its driveway. This magnificent, 18th-century Palladian mansion, the seat of the "modern" Earls of Leicester, contains paintings by Rubens, Van Dyck, Poussin, and Gainsborough; 17th- and 18th-century tapestry and furniture; thousands of items of bygone days, such as steam engines, kitchen equipment, smithy tools, ploughs, and fire engines; and Greek and Roman statuary. (*Open June–September, closed Fridays and Saturdays, tel: 01328-710227.*) Detour into **Wells-next-the-Sea**, one of the few villages along this coast to have a waterfront. Leave the coast behind and turn inland following the B1156 through Holt in the direction of Norwich to **Blickling Hall** (NT), a grand, 17th-century red-brick house set in acres of parkland. The house if full of fine pictures, tapestries, and gracious furniture. (*Open April–October, closed Mondays and Thursdays, tel: 01263-733084.*)

Following signs for Norwich, join the A140 which takes you to the heart of this sprawling city. **Norwich** is rich in historic treasures including a beautiful Norman cathedral, topped by a 15th-century spire, with a huge close running down to the River Wensum. The castle, built by one of William the Conqueror's supporters, is now the **Castle Museum**. (*Open all year, closed Sundays, tel: 01603-223624.*) **Strangers Hall**, a 14th-century home, has its rooms furnished in the styles of different periods. **Elm Hill** is a cobbled street with shops and houses from the 14th to the 18th centuries. **Colman's Mustard Shop** in Bridewell Alley is a major tourist attraction. Norwich has an interesting market (*closed Sundays*) and some very nice shops and restaurants.

From the ring road surrounding Norwich take the A146 in the direction of Lowestoft. Turn on the A145 through Beccles to the A12 where you turn left and first right on the A1095 into **Southwold**, a quiet, sedate Victorian/Edwardian seaside resort, with its most attractive houses lining the seafront and its narrow rows of shops forming the town center. Across the river estuary lies **Walberswick**, a pretty little fishing/holiday village of cottages and a pub, reached by a little ferry that plies back and forth (or the longer road route that traces the estuary).

Regaining the A12, turn left, towards Ipswich, for a short distance to the village of **Blythburgh** to visit its church which is so imposing in size that hereabouts it is referred to as **Blythburgh Cathedral**. The size of the church is indicative of the community's importance in years gone by when it was a thriving port, with its own mint, on the estuary of the River Blyth. Its prosperity declined and the church was neglected until it was restored this century. Carvings of the Seven Deadly Sins decorate the pew-ends and the rare, wooden Jack-o'-the-Clock.

A short distance farther along the A12 brings you to the left-hand turn for **Dunwich**—cross the heathlands and go through the village to the car park in front of the **Flora Tea Rooms** which serves excellent fish and chips, tea, and, coffee beneath the pebbly bank which separates it from the sea. The fish comes fresh from the fishermen who draw their boats up on the beach. Along the headlands lie the few remains of the medieval port of Dunwich which was almost completely swept out to sea in 1326 by a great storm. What was left has continued to be eroded by the sea. Local legend has it that before a storm the bells of Dunwich's 15 submerged churches can be heard ringing.

A short drive brings you to **Minsmere Nature Reserve**, a celebrated place for birdwatching, and through Westleton to **Aldeburgh**, a charming town whose streets are lined with Georgian houses and whose High Street has antique and other interesting shops. The local council still meets in the half-timbered **Moot Hall** (1512). Benjamin Britten, who directed the Aldeburgh music festival for 30 years until his death in 1976, based his opera *Peter Grimes* on a poem by local poet George Crabbe.

Head inland on the A1094 turning left onto the B1069 into **Snape** to arrive at **Snape Maltings**, a collection of red-brick granaries and old malthouses which has been converted into a riverside center with interesting garden and craft shops, art galleries, tea rooms, and a concert hall, home of the Aldeburgh music festival every June. From here you can take a boat trip on the River Alde which meanders through the marshes to the sea.

Continue inland and map a quiet country route through sleepy Suffolk villages and rolling farmland to **Framlingham**, a quiet market town where Mary Tudor was proclaimed queen of England in 1553. The town is dominated by 12th-century **Framlingham Castle** with tall, gray-stone walls linking its towers. (*Open Easter–September, tel: 01728-723330.*)

Two miles away at **Saxtead Green** a 200-year-old **Post Mill**, one of Suffolk's few remaining windmills, stands guard over the green. (*Open April–September, closed Sundays.*)

From Saxtead Green follow the A1120 towards Ipswich and the A45 as it skirts Ipswich and joins the A12 (direction Colchester) at a large roundabout (it is busy dual carriageways like these that keep the small roads quiet and peaceful). Leave the A12 at the third exit, following signs to your left for **Dedham**, a pretty village settled along the banks of the lazy River Stour made famous by John Constable who painted its mill and church spire on several occasions. (Even though it is just a river bend away from East Bergholt, Constable's birthplace, today you have to go between the two villages by way of the busy A12.) Sir Alfred Munnings, the painter of horses, lived in **Castle House** which is now a museum containing examples of his work.

Retrace your steps to the A12 and return in the direction of Ipswich following signs for **Flatford** and **East Bergholt** where John Constable was born in 1776, the son of the miller of Flatford Mill. The little hamlet of Flatford, now a National Trust property, is signposted in East Bergholt. A one-way lane directs you to the car park above the hamlet (it is not well signposted and you may have to stop and ask the way). The collection of cottages has been restored to the way it was in Constable's time and a tea room serves scrumptious afternoon teas and sandwiches. If the weather is fine, you can take a picnic, hire a rowing boat, and while away an afternoon on the river. The National Trust shop sells a packet which includes a map identifying where Constable painted some of his most famous pictures and postcards of the paintings so you can wander along the riverbank and pinpoint the very spot where he painted his father's mill, Willy Lott's cottage, or the boatbuilders at work. The scene has changed little since those times— apart from the tourists. Constable said of the area, "Those scenes made me a painter." (*Open April–October, tel: 01206-298260.*)

Leaving the Constable complex, the road returns you to East Bergholt where you turn right to go through the village and take the B1070 to **Hadleigh**, a large market town whose High Street has some lovely old houses. On the edge of the town cross the A1071 and then take the first left and first right to bring you onto the main street of **Kersey**, the most picture-book perfect of all Suffolk villages, whose narrow main street is lined with ancient weavers' cottages, grand merchants' houses, and old pubs, all jostling one another for roadside space and each colorwashed a different color. In the middle of the village a stream runs across the road and drivers must take care to avoid the village ducks.

Regain the A1141 and a short drive brings you through **Monks Eleigh** with its thatched cottages and large craft shop selling traditional corn dollies to **Lavenham** which in Tudor times was one of England's wealthiest towns. Now it is a sleepy village where leaning timbered houses line its quiet street and continue into the market square with its 16th-century cross and **Lavenham Guildhall** (NT) which houses displays of local history and the medieval wool industry. (*Open April–October, tel: 01787-247646.*) If you are captivated by the serenity of Lavenham, morning coffee or afternoon tea at the lovely **Swan Hotel** serve as a pleasurable excuse to linger.

Country lanes take you across country the 5 miles to **Long Melford** whose long, broad, tree-lined main street houses many antique shops and leads to the village green which is overshadowed by the magnificent, 15th-century Holy Trinity Church. A short walk away, the red-brick, turreted **Melford Hall** (NT) contains a wealth of porcelain, paintings, and antiques and a display of Beatrix Potter's paintings—she was a frequent visitor here. (*Open May–October, closed Mondays, Tuesdays, and Fridays, tel: 01787-880286.*)

Leaving Long Melford, you can go south to the A12 or east to the M11 which quickly return you to London.

Derbyshire Dales and Villages

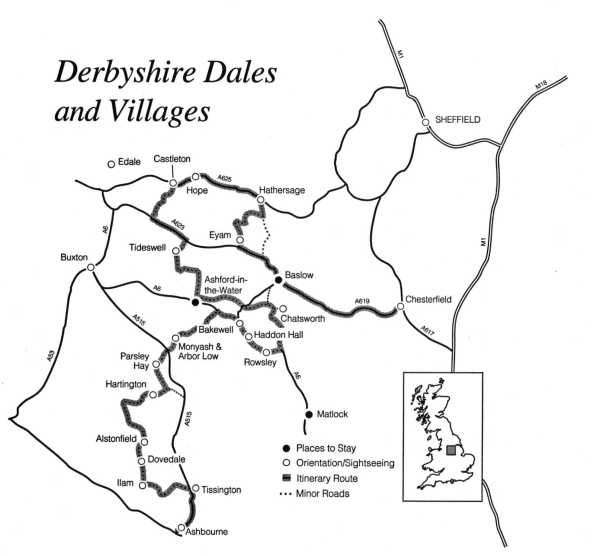

Derbyshire Dales and Villages

Every structure in this itinerary—manor houses, churches, cottages, farmhouses, shops—even the walls that trim the fields making a patchwork of the landscape—is built of gray stone. This is the Peak District, a National Park, where you can enjoy the beauty of a wild landscape of rolling rocky pastures, sheltered valleys, and windswept moors laced by swift rivers tumbling through deep dales—Monks Dale, Monsal Dale, Miller Dale, and, the most beautiful of all, Dovedale where the River Dove flows through a rocky, wooded ravine and is crossed by stepping stones. While this is a driving itinerary, to really appreciate the wild beauty of this area you have to forsake your car and proceed on foot—on the many miles of well marked footpaths—or rent a bike and pedal the cycle routes that travel disused railway lines and quiet country lanes.

Chatsworth House

Derbyshire Dales and Villages

Recommended Pacing: Select a base for this itinerary. To cover all our sightseeing suggestions will take two full days.

This itinerary begins in **Ashbourne**, a small market town just south of the Peak District National Park where on Thursdays and Saturdays market stalls crowd the town square. Close by, on St. John Street, visit the **Gingerbread Shop** which sells aromatic Ashbourne gingerbread and baked goods from a restored 15th-century timber-framed shop that gives you a glimpse of how beautiful Ashbourne must have been during its heyday. (*Cycle hire for the Tissington Trail is Ashbourne Cycle Hire, Mapleton Lane, Ashbourne, Derbyshire, tel: 01335-43156.*)

Leave Ashbourne on the A515, Buxton road, and watch for a discreetly signposted right-hand turn which brings you through a broad avenue of trees to **Tissington** with its Jacobean manor house, Norman church, limestone cottages, and ducks swimming on the village pond. Tissington is reputedly the birthplace of the Derbyshire village tradition of well dressing, giving thanks for the unfailing supply of fresh water that the village wells provided by creating intricate, large mosaic pictures from flower petals and placing them beside the village wells. These spectacular displays are very interesting to visit, so in the course of this itinerary, the dates that villages dress their wells is mentioned in parentheses, for example, "Tissington (*wells dressed for Ascension day*)." If you carry on through the village and across open farmland you come to a ford where the road splashes through a brook.

Retrace your steps to the A515 and cross it, heading through **Thorpe** village and down into **Dovedale**. Dr. Johnston gave it a glowing testimonial: "He who has seen Dovedale has no need to visit the Highlands." Cars can go no farther than the car park whence you walk into the dale, crossing the River Dove on stepping stones and entering a rocky ravine. The farther you walk into the dale the more you are tempted to continue as round each river bend beautiful scenery unfolds—fantastic rock formations, steeply wooded hillsides, and the noisy, tumbling water. The length of the dale is a delightful 4-mile walk. Walkers can be dropped at the car park and picked up in Milldale by Viators Bridge.

At a bend in the road sits **Ilam** (pronounced I lamb), a picture-postcard estate village, built to house the workers on what was once a shipping magnate's vast holdings. On to **Alstonfield** (pronounced Alstonfeld) and the **Post Office Tea Shop** which serves scrumptious scones and cream. (Turn right here if you are picking walkers up in nearby Milldale.)

Well Dressing

Drive into **Hartington** (*wells dressed on second Saturday in September*) with its white limestone cottages, shops, and pubs. Admire the mallards waddling by the village pond and visit the **cheese shop**, an outlet for the last of Derbyshire's cheese factories producing Hartington Stilton and Buxton Blue.

Leave Hartington on the B5054, Ashbourne road, and take the first left, signposted Crowdicote, following the narrow dale. As the dale widens, turn right to **Parsley Hay**. (*Parsley Hay Cycle Hire, Parsley Hay near Buxton, Derbyshire, tel: 01298-84493.*) From here you can cycle the **Tissington Trail** towards Ashbourne or the **High Peak Trail** to Cromford. At the main road turn left (towards Buxton) and immediately right towards Monyash then right again following discreet signposts for **Arbor Low**, Derbyshire's answer to Stonehenge, except that the huge monoliths have all fallen to the ground and you will probably be the only visitors. The stones are set atop a bare hill, swept by cold winds, and reached by tramping across fields from a lonely farm. Pause and wonder why man built here 4,000 years ago.

Retrace your path to the Monyash road, turning right in the village onto the B5055 which leads you into **Bakewell** (*wells dressed on last Saturday in June*), a lovely market town ringed by wooded hills where a picturesque, 700-year-old arched and buttressed bridge spans the swiftly flowing River Wye. The Tourist Information Centre in the splendid, 17th-century **market hall** has displays on the Peak District and information pamphlets. Behind it are set the market stalls where every Monday a farmers' market is held—offering everything from lengths of dress fabric to underwear and pigs. You can buy the original Bakewell tarts (known as puddings in Bakewell) from **Ye Olde Original Pudding Shop** and the splendid **Bakewell Pudding Factory** on Granby Arcade. The town has some excellent shops (china, antique, clothing, and hardware). Up the hill, just behind the church, is The **Old House Museum**, a folk museum, displaying kitchen and farm equipment. (*Open April–October, tel: 01629-81347.*)

Three miles along the A6 in the direction of Matlock lies **Haddon Hall**, a 14th-century manor, home of the Duke of Rutland. This house is more interesting to tour than the opulent Chatsworth House (which is your next stop) because it lacks the vastness and grandeur of Chatsworth and you can really imagine that people actually lived in these aged rooms hung with threadbare tapestries and decorated with magnificent woodcarvings. Parts of the chapel walls are covered with barely discernible frescos that date back to the 11th century. In summer the gardens are a fragrant haven with a profusion of climbing roses and clematis decorating the house and the stone walls of the terraces. (*Open April–September, tel: 01629-812855.*)

Continue along the A6 to **Rowsley** where you can tour **Caudwell's Mill**, a water-powered flour mill, and visit the craft shops. Leaving Rowsley, take the first left (B6012). Pass the edge of Beeley, cross the River Derwent on a narrow humpbacked bridge, and enter the vast Chatsworth estate. (Immediately on your left is the **Chatsworth Garden Centre** which, in addition to a vast array of all things garden, has a gift and coffee shop.) The road leads you through rolling green parkland to **Chatsworth House**, the enormous (the roof alone covers 1.3 acres) home of the Duke and Duchess of Devonshire. While the Duke and Duchess occupy a portion of the house, you can walk through the opulent halls admiring priceless paintings, furnishings, silver plate, and china. Best of all, though, are the acres and acres of landscaped gardens with the great fountain playing and the lawns above the house, laid down in 1760 and groomed ever since (except in wartime). The tea shop is a must. If you are traveling with children, they will enjoy a visit to the farm and the adventure playground. (*Open April–October, tel: 01246-582204.*)

The picturesque village of **Edensor** (pronounced Ensor), mentioned in the Doomsday Book of 1086, was much rebuilt and moved here in the 19th century by a duke who did not want to see it from his park. Kathleen Kennedy, JFK's sister, lies buried near the handsome old church.

Leave the estate in the direction of Baslow and take the first left, B6048, to **Pilsey** where the farm shop sells an interesting variety of nifty gifts and produce from the Chatsworth estate. As the B6048 merges with the main road take the first right on the A6020

(Ashford) following it to **Ashford-in-the-Water** and cross the river into this picturesque village strung along the River Wye. "Sheepwash" is the oldest and quaintest of the village's bridges. Built for packhorses and now closed to traffic, it gets its name from the adjacent stone enclosure in which sheep used to be washed.

Follow the narrow lanes upwards to **Monsal Head** where the ground seemingly falls away and opens up to a magnificent vista of the River Wye running through **Monsal Dale**. Go straight across, beside the Monsal Head car park, and follow the road as it winds down into and along the dale to **Cressbrook mill**, where the road climbs steeply past the terraces of mill cottages clinging precariously to the hillsides. The first terrace is where pauper apprentices lived and higher up are the more opulent foremen's houses. Emerging from the dale, the narrow road skirts stone-walled fields to **Litton** (*wells dressed in June*), a delightful stone village round a green where you turn left for Tideswell.

The magnificent, spacious, 14th-century church at **Tideswell** (*wells dressed on Saturday nearest John the Baptist day, June 24th*) is so impressive that it is often described as "the cathedral of the Peak." It was built between 1300 and 1370 when Tideswell was an affluent place and it is fortunate that Tideswell fell upon hard times so that parishioners could not afford to update their church as ecclesiastical fashions changed.

Leaving Tideswell, you come to the A623 and turn left in the direction of Chapel en le Frith to Sparrowpit where you turn right at the Wanted Inn. Passing an enormous quarry, you see that half the mountain is missing—gone to build all the lovely stone houses and cottages. When you come to a brown-and-white country sign stating "Castleton Caverns, Peveril Castle, light traffic only," turn right into Winnats Pass which drops you down a steep ravine between high limestone cliffs.

As the ravine opens up to the valley, **Speedwell Cavern** presents itself. This is one of several famous caverns (mixtures of natural cavities and lead-mine workings resplendent with stalagmites and stalactites) found around Castleton. Speedwell differs from the other caverns in that it is reached by a 105-step descent to a motor-boat which takes you along an underground canal to a cavern which was the working face of the former Speedwell Mine where Blue John (a corruption of the French *bleue-jaune,* blue-yellow), a translucent blue variety of fluorspar found only in this area, was mined. (*Open all year, tel: 01433-20512.*)

Castleton

Before you head off to explore other nearby caves (Blue John, Treak Cliff, and Peak), head into **Castleton,** a village huddled far below the brooding ruins of **Peveril Castle** where Henry II accepted the submission of Malcolm of Scotland in 1157. Henry had the keep built in 1176, while other parts were added in later years. (*Open all year.*)

Below the castle is the huge mouth of **Peak Cavern**, an enormous cave that once sheltered ropemakers' cottages. The soot from the chimneys of this subterranean village can be seen on the cave's roof. Regrettably, the entrance to the cave has been marred by the erection of a high wooden barrier giving access to the cave only to those willing to pay an entrance fee. In the narrow village's streets you will find cafés, pubs, and several shops selling the polished Blue John set into bracelets, rings, and the like.

This is walking country and you might consider walking up **Mam Tor** (the big bulky mountain beside Winnats Pass) known hereabouts as "Shivering Mountain" because its layers of soft shale set between harder beds of rock are constantly crumbling. Those in search of a longer walk may wish to go to nearby **Edale** where the **Pennine Way** starts its 250-mile path north.

Leave Castleton on the A625 traveling along the broad Hope valley through **Hope** (*wells dressed last Saturday in June*) and Bamford to **Hathersage**, a thriving, non-traditional Derbyshire village strung out along the main road. Its tourist attractions center on its 14th-century church, St. Michael and All Angels, built by a knight named Robert Eyre. Memorial brasses to the Eyre family are in the church and Charlotte Brontë used the village as "Morton" in *Jane Eyre*. In the graveyard is the reputed grave of Little John, the friend and lieutenant of Robin Hood.

Leaving the churchyard, backtrack on the A625 for a short distance, taking the first left (B6001), signposted Bakewell, beyond the village where you turn right, opposite The Plough, up a narrow country lane signposted "Gliding Club." This country lane takes you through the hamlet of **Abney** past the gliding club and the historic **Barrel Inn** (offering views of the valley, good pub food, and refreshing ale) and brings you into **Eyam** (pronounced Eem) (*wells dressed last Saturday in August*).

This large mining and quarrying village was made famous by its self-imposed quarantine when plague hit the village in 1665. It was thought that the virus arrived in a box of cloth from London brought by a visiting tailor. The rector persuaded the community to quarantine themselves to prevent the plague spreading to outlying villages and for over a year the village was supplied by neighboring villagers who left food and supplies at outlying points. Tragically 259 people from 76 families perished. Little plaques on Eyam's cottages give the names of the victims who lived there; the church has a plague register and just inside the door is the letter written by the young rector when his wife succumbed (Katherine Mompesson is buried near the Saxon cross in the churchyard). The most poignant reminder of these grim days lies in a field about ½ mile from the village where within a solitary little enclosure, known as the **Riley Graves**, are the memorials to a father and his six children, all of whom died within eight days of each other.

Leave Eyam in the direction of Bakewell, traveling down a steeply wooded gorge which brings you to the A623. Following signs for Chesterfield, you drive down narrow **Middleton Dale** whose limestone cliffs are so sheer they almost block the sunlight from the road to **Stoney Middleton**, an appropriately named village huddling beneath the cliffs. It does not look at all inviting from the main road but its quiet side streets and pretty church are full of character.

Driving a few miles farther along the A623 brings you to the winding lanes of **Baslow** where the River Derwent flows past tidy houses on the northern edge of the Chatsworth estate. From here fast roads will bring you to **Chesterfield** (visit the leaning spire and if it is a Monday, Friday, or Saturday, you will enjoy the interesting open-air market) where you can join the M1 at junction 29.

The Dales and Moors of North Yorkshire

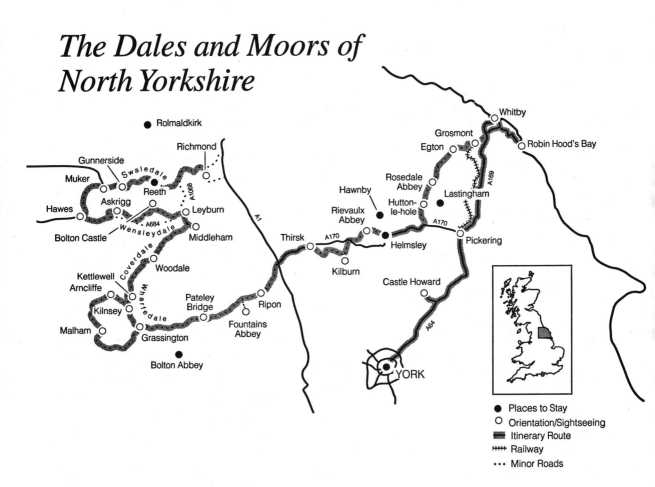

Rolmaldkirk

Richmond

Gunnerside

Muker

Swaledale

Reeth

Askrigg

Hawes

A1068

Leyburn

Bolton Castle

A684

Wensleydale

Middleham

Coverdale

Woodale

Kettlewell

Arncliffe

Wharfedale

Kilnsey

Pateley Bridge

Ripon

Malham

Grassington

Fountains Abbey

Bolton Abbey

A1

Thirsk

A170

Kilburn

Castle Howard

Hawnby

Rievaulx Abbey

Rosedale Abbey

Hutton-le-hole

Helmsley

A170

Grosmont

Egton

Lastingham

A169

Pickering

A64

YORK

Whitby

Robin Hood's Bay

● Places to Stay
○ Orientation/Sightseeing
▓ Itinerary Route
╫ Railway
••• Minor Roads

63

The Dales and Moors of North Yorkshire

After exploring historic York, this itinerary samples the wild and beautiful countryside of two National Parks: the North York Moors and the Yorkshire Dales. This is an area of rugged, untamed, harsh beauty in its landscape and its stout stone villages. With seemingly endless miles of heather-covered moorlands, few roads, and even fewer sturdy villages sheltering in green valleys, the North York Moors appear vast and untamed, dipping to the sea to embrace the villages and towns of the east coast. Across the flat expanse of the Vale of York lie the Yorkshire Dales, characterized by sleepy rivers weaving through peaceful valleys and by gray-stone walls bounding the fields and tracing patterns on the countryside to the moorlands above. Here every valley has a name and a very different character—Swaledale, Littondale, Coverdale, and Wharfedale. Scattered throughout Yorkshire are small gray-stoned villages with a cluster of stone houses, a hump-backed bridge, a friendly pub, and an ancient church.

Recommended Pacing: Spend two nights in York to appreciate the flavor of this historic city. Follow this with the minimum of one night on or near the North York Moors (Hawnby, Helmsley, or Lastingham) and two nights in the Yorkshire Dales.

If you delight in historic towns, you will love **York,** a compact city brimful of history encircled by 700-year-old walls with great imposing gates known as "bars." There has been a settlement here since Roman times and by the time of the Norman Conquest it was, after London, the principal city of England.

Your first stop in York should be the Tourist Information Centre on St. Leonards, near Bootham Bar. Avail yourself of a detailed city map and ask about walking tours that will, in the space of several hours, orient you to this historic city.

Walk the narrow, cobblestoned streets with such appealing names as The Shambles, Stonegate, and Goodramgate past timbered buildings whose upper stories lean out, almost forming a bridge over the streets. While interesting shops abound, the **National Trust Shop** on Goodramgate and **Betty's Bakery and Tearooms** on St. Helen's Square are ones to target.

York's magnificent cathedral is known simply as **The Minster**, a huge structure that towers above the skyline and dwarfs everything else around it. It was begun in 1220 and you can quickly appreciate why it took over 250 years to complete. Entering through the Great West Door you see the vast nave stretching out in front of you and fluted pillars rising to flying buttresses reaching high above. There are more than 100 stained-glass windows and the huge east window is almost the size of a tennis court. Guided tours leave at regular intervals. Nearby the **Treasurer's House** (NT), a 17th-/18th-century townhouse on the site of the former residence of the Treasurers of York Minster, has a fine collection of furniture and an exhibition showing the development of the house from Roman times. (*Open April–October, tel: 01904-624247.*)

The **Jorvik Viking Centre**, Coppergate, is set below ground amidst the most complete Viking dig in England. Electric cars take you on a Disneyland ride backwards through history to a re-created Viking village—complete with sounds and smells of Viking Jorvik. Then they move you forward to the dig itself and a display of the artifacts which have been recovered. Because there is often a long line it is best to be there first thing in the morning for opening at 9 am. (*Open all year, tel: 01904-643211.*)

Enjoy another trip back in time at York's outstanding **Castle Museum.** One section of the museum is a reconstructed Victorian cobbled street, with houses, shops, jail, and a hansom cab in recognition of inventor Joseph Hansom who was born in Mickelgate. (*Open all year, tel: 01904-653611.*) Opposite the museum you can climb to the ramparts of **Clifford's Tower,** a stubby, 13th-century keep set high on a mound. From its ramparts you have a panoramic view of York. (*Tel: 01904-646940.*)

Located beyond York's walls, just a short walk from the magnificent Victorian railway station, is the **National Railway Museum,** Leeman Road, crammed with famous steam locomotives including the world's fastest (202 mph), Mallard, and a wealth of railway items. (*Open all year, tel: 01904-621261.*)

Depart York on the A64 Scarborough road for the fast drive to **Castle Howard** which is well signposted to your left just 4 miles from Malton. Designed by Sir John Vanbrugh for the 3rd Earl of Carlisle, a member of the Howard family, Castle Howard was built between 1699 and 1726—one glimpse of this majestic building and you understand why it took 27 years to complete. Its immense façade reflects in a broad lake and it is surrounded by a vast parkland and approached down a long, tree-lined avenue. It isn't really a castle at all but one of England's grandest homes, as impressive inside as out, full of fine furniture and paintings. This grand setting is better known to many visitors as "Brideshead" from the television dramatization of Evelyn Waugh's *Brideshead Revisited*. It is still owned by the Howard family. (*Open March–October, tel: 0165384-333.*)

From nearby Malton take the A169 through Pickering and across the vast expanse of the North York moors to **Robin Hood's Bay,** the most picturesque of villages situated beneath a cliff top, a maze of huddled houses clinging to the precipitous cliff. Park in the large car park above the village and follow the long, steep street down to the shoreline, peeping into little alleyways and following narrow byways until you emerge at the slipway. Pieces of Robin Hood's Bay have been washed away, and in an attempt to minimize further damage to this little fishing village, much of the cliff has been reinforced by a large sea wall.

The ruins of **Whitby Abbey** face the cold North Sea and the old seaside town of **Whitby**, built on either side of the River Esk. It's a lovely sight: majestic ruins high on a bleak, windy headland, rows of cottages climbing up the hillsides, and, gazing over the scene, a statue of the town's most famous mariner, Captain Cook. Cook circled the world twice, explored the coasts of Australia and New Zealand, and charted Newfoundland and the North American Pacific coast before being killed by natives in Hawaii. His home on Grape Lane is a small museum. Near Cook's statue is a whalebone arch commemorating this photogenic old town's importance as a whaling port. The whaling ships are a thing of the distant past: now just a few fishing boats bob in this large, sheltered harbor. Explore the area of the town that lies below the abbey, for this is the quaintest, most historic portion of Whitby. During the summer the town is filled with holidaymakers.

Leave Whitby on the A169, Pickering road, and follow signs to the right for the **North York Railway**, a road that winds you to **Grosmont**, the terminus of a glorious, 18-mile steam railway that runs to and from Pickering. The railway opened in 1863 with horse-drawn carriages—steam engines came 11 years later. The line was closed by British Rail in 1965 and reopened by train enthusiasts. The railway shed is full of steam locomotives of all colors and you can see engines being prepared for their daily shift and watch restoration from the viewing gallery. (*Tel: 01751-72508, fax: 01751-76970.*)

From nearby Egton a narrow road leads you up from a lush valley and onto acres of gently rolling moorland, with a mass of purple heather stretching into the distance, a dramatically empty, isolated spot, then drops you into another green valley where stone walls separate a patchwork of fields around the tiny village of Rosedale Abbey. Go straight across the crossroads, up the steep bank, and across another stretch of vast moorland, keep to your right at the fork in the road, and you arrive in the most picturesque village on the North York Moors, **Hutton-le-Hole**. A tumbling stream cuts through the village and children play on close-cropped grassy banks between the sturdy stone houses. At the heart of the village lies **Ryedale Folk Museum** where paths lead from a museum of domestic bygones through a collection of ancient Yorkshire buildings (from simple cottages to an elaborate cruck-framed house) rescued from demise and restored on this site. (*Open March–October, tel: 017515-367.*)

The Dales and Moors of North Yorkshire

Farther on from Hutton-le-Hole you join the A170 which brings you to **Helmsley**, a pretty market town beneath the southern rim of the moors. Around the market square (*market day Friday*) are interesting shops and the lovely **Black Swan Hotel**. At the edge of town sits a ruined castle enclosed by Norman earthworks.

About 4 miles beyond Helmsley (take the B1257 signed Stokesley) lie the ruins of **Rievaulx Abbey** (pronounced ree-voh), the delicate and beautiful ruins of York's first Cistercian abbey, standing quietly beside a picturesque group of thatched cottages. The abbey fell into debt and declined until it was dissolved by Henry VIII. Today it is a graceful, ghostly ruin, often shrouded in mist. Follow the narrow lane beside the cottages, turn right over the little humpbacked bridge, proceed through Scrawton, and turn right on the A170 (Thirsk road) for a short distance to a left-hand turn which zig-zags you down **Sutton Bank** (on a clear day park in the car park at the top and enjoy the skywide view of the Vale of York) then drops you down the Hambleton Hills escarpment.

A delightful side trip can by taken by turning left at the bottom of the escarpment and following the narrow lane which brings you to **Kilburn**, a village known for its fine oak furniture. Quality oaken furniture found all over the world can easily be traced back here to the workshop of Robert Thompson. He died in 1955, but craftsmen he trained still use his carved signature, a small church mouse, signifying "poor as a church mouse" to identify their work. It is fun to tour the workshops and watch skilled craftsmen quietly hand-carving beautiful oaken objects with a wavy, adzed surface.

Returning to the main road, you soon come to **Thirsk**, its very pleasant cobbled market square overlooked by shops (*market day Monday*). From Thirsk the A61 traverses rich farmland, crosses the A1 and meanders you through **Ripon** to the market square (*market day Thursday*) where you follow well marked signs for Fountains Abbey.

Cistercian monks arrived in sheltered **Fountains Abbey** (NT) in 1132, at about the same time they came to Rievaulx, but, unlike Rievaulx, this abbey prospered, so that by the end of the 13th century it had acquired vast estates and the abbey was home to over 500 monks. However, its prosperity did not save it from the axe of Henry VIII who sold the monastery, leaving the abbey to fall into majestic ruin. Considering that for hundreds of years it was used as a quarry for precut stone, the complex is remarkably intact. Wander over the closely cropped grass to the soaring walls of the church. Examine the few remaining floor tiles, gaze at the flying buttresses soaring high above, wander through the cloisters, and wonder at the glory that was Fountains Abbey so many years ago. Walking paths abound: a particularly pretty path leads you across grassy meadows to the adjacent National Trust property of **Studley Royal**, an 18th-century deer park and water garden. (*Open all year, tel: 01765-86333.*)

Turn west (B6265) through Pateley Bridge and climb higher and higher onto bleak moorlands through Greenhow and down the fellside through fields trimmed with white stone walls to Hebden and into **Grassington**, a neat village of narrow streets and cobbled squares full of shops and cafés. It's this itinerary's introduction to the Dales National Park and very crowded in summer, so you may want to park at the National Park Information Centre (useful for maps and information) and walk into town.

To experience some magnificent scenery take a breathtaking circular drive from Grassington and back again through Littondale, over the fells to Malham Cove, and back to the B6160 on the outskirts of town. Leave Grassington on the B6265, cross the River Wharfe, and turn right onto the B6160 which leads you up **Wharfedale** towards Kettlewell. Just after passing the huge crags that hang above Kilnsey, turn left up a narrow lane for Arncliffe. The road meanders deep into **Littondale**, a narrow, steep-sided, very pretty dale. At the cluster of cottages that make up Arncliffe turn left for Malham and follow the narrow road as it zigzags you up the side of the dale. As the road reaches the top there is a spectacular view back into Littondale. The high, bleak moorland suddenly ends and to your left lie immense curving cliffs that drop 240 feet into a green valley. This is **Malham Cove**, one of Yorkshire's most celebrated natural features. Huddled in the valley below lies the village of **Malham**. Country lanes direct you through Kirby Malham, Airton, Winterburn, Hetton, and Threshfield to rejoin the B6160 that takes you back into Wharfedale.

Retrace your steps and head north to **Kettlewell**, a pretty village at the foot of Great Whernside. In the 8th century this was an Anglican settlement, then after the Norman Conquest formed part of the estates of the powerful Percy family. A small road leads you to the right over Great Whernside and into quiet **Coverdale** through **Woodale**, **Horsehouse,** and **Carlton**, little villages that shelter in this pretty valley with the moors looming above. Horses are a feature of **Middleham** for there are many famous racing stables in this attractive town of gray-stone houses beneath the ruins of Middleham Castle.

Cross the River Ure and follow the A6108 into Leyburn then turn left on the A648 and right on country lanes through Redmire to the crumbling ruins of **Bolton Castle** which stands grim and square, dwarfing the adjacent village, overlooking distant Wensleydale. You can tour several restored rooms. The castle's most famous visitor was Mary, Queen of Scots, who was held prisoner here for six months in 1568.

Minor roads take you up Wharfedale through Carperby (detour into **Aysgarth** if you would like to walk to **Aysgarth Falls**, a series of spectacular waterfalls where the River Ure cascades down a rocky gorge) and Woodhall to the picturesque Dales village of Askrigg. Cross the river to Bainbridge and take the A684 into **Hawes**, a bustling village whose narrow streets abound with interesting shops, good pubs, and cafés. After exploring, leave town in the direction of Muker. As the road climbs from the valley go right, following signs for Muker via **Buttertubs**. This is one of the highest mountain passes in England (1,682 feet), rising steeply from Wensleydale, crossing dramatic high moorlands, and depositing you in narrower, wilder **Swaledale**. The road gets its name "Buttertubs" from the deep, menacing, limestone pits some distance from the road near the summit.

At the T-junction follow the road to the right and cross the little bridge into **Muker,** the most charming of Swaledale's little villages—just the place to stop for a refreshing cuppa.

As you travel down Swaledale there's a feeling of remoteness: sturdy, gray-stone barns dot the stone-walled fields that checker the valley floor and rise to the green fells. **Gunnerside**, Norse for Gunner's pasture, where a Viking chieftain herded his cattle long ago, is now an appealing village.

Through Low Row, Feetham, and Healaugh the enchantment of being in a narrow, secluded valley continues till at **Reeth** the landscape opens up and the feeling of being in a wild and lonely place is gone. On the village green you will find the **Burgoyne Hotel,** a delightful place to stay. You continue on to Richmond through pretty countryside.

Richmond sits at the foot of Swaledale, a network of cobbled alleys and streets stretching from its cobbled square. At its center sits an ancient church with shops set into its walls. Overhanging the River Swale, **Richmond Castle** was built by Norman lords within 20 years of the Norman Conquest. Over the years only a few Scottish raiders tested the defenses of this guardian of North Yorkshire. Sweeping views across dales down to the Vale of York can be enjoyed from the top of its 11th-century ruins.

The nearby A1 will quickly guide you north into Scotland or return you south towards York.

The Lake District

CARLISLE ○

Bassenthwaite
Lake

Cockermouth ○

Bassenthwaite
Lake ●

A66

Keswick ○

Newlands ●

Derwent
Water

A591

A591

Crummock
Water

Buttermere

Rosthwaite ○

Thirlmere

Ullswater ●

Ullswater

Grasmere ●

Ambleside ●

Little Langdale ○

Coniston ○

A593

Far
Sawrey ○

Windermere ●

Hawkshead

Coniston
Water

Windermere

Sizergh
Castle ○

A5074

Levens
Hall ○

A590

M6

M6

● Places to Stay
○ Orientation/Sightseeing
▓ Itinerary Route
••• Minor Roads

The Lake District

For generations the beauty of the Lake District has inspired poets, authors, and artists. It is a land of tranquil lakes of all shapes and sizes, quiet wooded valleys, and awesome bleak mountains, a land where much of the natural beauty is protected by the National Trust who work hard to keep this a working community of sheep farmers and to keep man in harmony with nature. One of the most determined preservers of the Lake District was Beatrix Potter who used much of her royalties from her famous children's books to purchase vast tracts of land and donate them to the nation. It is a region to be explored not only during the summer when the roads are more heavily traveled and the towns crowded, but also in the early spring when the famous daffodils brighten the landscape and well into the autumn when the leaves turn to gold and dark storm clouds shadow the lakes.

Recommended Pacing: Base yourself at one of the hotels we recommend in the Lake District. If you cover all of our sightseeing recommendations you will need four nights, though three would probably suffice.

From junction 36 on the M6 motorway take the A590 in the direction of Barrow and a few minutes' drive brings you into the grounds of **Sizergh Castle** (NT), not a mighty fortress but a lovely, mostly Tudor house, the home of the Strickland family for over 700 years. The house is fully furnished—just as though the family has gone out for the day and you are a visitor to their home. There is an excellent tea shop in the old cellar and a portion of the grounds presents an impressive rock garden. (*Open March–October, closed Fridays and Saturdays, tel: 01593-60070.*)

Return to the A590 and in just a minute you are at another fine Tudor manor house, **Levens Hall**. The property is most famous for its topiary gardens which have remarkably remained unchanged since 1690, when they were landscaped by a Frenchman, Guillaume Beaumont. (*Open Easter–September, tel: 015395-60321.*)

Join the A5074 Windermere road and on the outskirts of the town follow signs to the ferry which takes you across the broad expanse of **Windermere** for the short drive to the tiny villages of **Near Sawrey** and **Far Sawrey**, discovered by Beatrix Potter on childhood holidays. She was so charmed by the villages that out of the royalties from *Peter Rabbit* she bought **Hill Top Farm** (NT) in Near Sawrey. It was here in a vine-covered, stone cottage set among trees and a garden of flowers that she dreamed up childhood playmates such as Jemima Puddleduck, Mrs Tiggy Winkle, the Flopsy Bunnies, Cousin Ribby, and Benjamin Bunny. Because of its popularity the house is open on a very limited basis, but the National Trust shop by the roadside is open more often and you can walk through the garden to the front door. (*Open March–October, closed Thursdays and Fridays, tel: 015394-36269.*)

In nearby **Hawkshead**, a pretty village with a pedestrian center, there is a delightful **Beatrix Potter Gallery** (NT) containing an exhibition of her original drawings and illustrations of her children's books, together with a display of her life as author, farmer, and preserver of her beloved Lake District. (*Tel: 015394-33883.*) A short drive brings you to **Coniston**, a delightful village of gray-stone buildings at the head of **Coniston Water**. John Ruskin, the eloquent 19th-century scholar, lived on the east side of the lake at **Brantwood**. His home contains many mementos and pictures. (*Open mid-March–mid-November, tel: 015394-41396.*) You will find a small **Ruskin Museum** with drawings and manuscripts in the village. (*Open Easter–October.*)

Travel a short distance along the A595 Ambleside road and turn left to wind along a country lane up into a quiet, less touristy part of the Lake District. Stop for refreshment in **Little Langdale** at the **Three Shires**, a delightful walkers' pub that also offers accommodation. Leaving the village, you enter a wild, bleak, and beautiful area. The lane brings you to Blea Tarn and just as you think you are in the absolute midst of nowhere and contemplate turning around, you come to a cattle grid and a fork in the road—take the right-hand fork signposted Great Langdale and follow the narrow road through wild and lonely countryside, down a steep pass, and through a lush valley into **Great Langdale**, another off-the-beaten-path village popular with walkers. Leaving the village, the road winds you up onto the moor and drops you back onto the A595 where a left-hand turn quickly brings you into Ambleside.

Ambleside is a bustling, busy town at the head of Lake Windermere with lots of shops selling walking equipment and outdoor wear, and gray Victorian row houses huddling along its streets. Leave town in the direction of Keswick (A591), watching for a right-hand turn to **Rydal Mount**, the home of William Wordsworth, the poet, from 1813 to his death in 1850. The house is furnished and contains many family portraits and possessions. A keen gardener, Wordsworth laid out the 4½ acres of informal gardens. (*Open March–November, closed Tuesdays, tel: 015394-33002.*)

Wordsworth fans will also want to stop at **Dove Cottage** where Wordsworth lived from 1799 to 1808 and the adjacent **Wordsworth Museum**. (*Open March–December, tel:*

015394-36544.) Park by the tea room on the main road and walk up to the museum to buy your ticket. Try to visit early in the day as they restrict a tour to the number of people who can comfortably fit into Wordsworth's tiny living room. The docent who led our tour was a true Wordsworthian, mixing together lots of "juicy" information on Wordsworth, his family, and friends with many insights into his poetry. As you tour the few meager rooms it is hard to believe that this was home to one of the leading poets of the era, housing six adults and three children. Poet laureates write poems on royal events, but

Dove Cottage, Grasmere

not Wordsworth: he was the only poet laureate to write not a word on such occasions— but he relished the royal stipend. Just off the busy main road, the adjacent village of **Grasmere** is full of charming shops and galleries

Regaining the A591, it is a delightful drive into Keswick through in turn wild, rugged, and pastoral scenery. Take small roads to the west of **Thirlmere** as the views from the west of the lake are much better than from the A591. The lively market town of **Keswick**, cozily placed at the northern end of **Derwent Water**, is full of bakeries, sweet shops (selling fudge and Kendal mint cake), pubs, restaurants, and outdoor equipment suppliers. There are plenty of car parks near the town center, though on a busy summer afternoon you may have to drive around for a while before you secure a spot. The **Moot** (meeting) **Hall** at the center of the square is now the National Park Information Centre—full of maps, books, and good advice.

Returning to your car, head towards Derwent Water, taking the B5298 to Borrowdale for a spectacular drive between Keswick and Cockermouth, a journey not to be undertaken in bad weather. Follow Derwent Water to **Grange** where inviting woodlands beckon you to tarry awhile and walk, but desist because the most spectacular walking country lies ahead. Passing through the village of Rosthwaite, the narrow road begins to climb, curving you upwards alongside a tumbling stream to the high, treeless fells before suddenly tipping you over the crest of the mountain and snaking you down into the valley to **Buttermere** and **Crummock Water** whose placid surfaces mirror the jagged peaks that surround this wooded, green valley. The mountains here are over 500 million years old, among the oldest in the world. Walking paths beckon in every direction—though these are not paths to be trod without equipment and maps, for the fickle weather can turn from sun to storm in just a short while. Leaving this lovely spot, the narrow road quickly brings you into the center of bustling **Cockermouth** where Wordsworthians have the opportunity to visit **Wordsworth House** (NT), his birthplace on Main Street. (*Open April–October, closed Thursdays, tel: 01900-82405.*)

From Cockermouth follow signs for the A66 and Keswick along a country road that parallels the A66 to the head of **Bassenthwaite Lake**. At the junction cross the busy A66 onto a quiet country side road to visit the **Pheasant Inn**, a superb example of the very best of traditional pubs. From here the A66 quickly speeds you alongside Bassenthwaite Lake, around Keswick, and to the M6 motorway. However, if you have time for one more idyllic lake, take the A5019 through Troutbeck to **Ullswater** where you turn left to trace the lake to **Aira Force** (NT), a landscaped Victorian park with dramatic waterfalls, arboretum, and rock gardens (there is also a café). After a walk along the shores of Ullswater Wordsworth wrote his poem *Daffodils*. The dramatic scenery is still very much as it was in his day. Leaving Ullswater, return to the A66 and join the M6 at junction 40, with convenient connections to all parts of Britain.

The Lake District

Scotland

Achiltibuie
Inverewe Gardens
Ullapool
A835
Loch Torridon
A832
Shieldaig
Nairn
A96
Muir of Ord
Kyle of Lochalsh
Inverness
Rothes
A855
Dunvegan Castle
Cawdor Castle
Dufftown
A4
Kildrummy Castle
Castle Fraser
Portree
A850
A82
A941
A97
ABERDEEN
Sleat
A851
Grantown-on-Spey
Craigievar Castle
A87
Whitebridge
Loch Ness
Mallaig
Fort Augustus
Braemar
Ballater
A93
Banchory
Genfinnan
A9
A830
A82
Balmoral Castle
Fort William
A93
Glencoe
A924
Pitlochry
A82
Aberfeldy
A9
Dunkeld
Port Appin
Killin
A984
Kinclaven
A85
Perth
A93
Callander
Auchterarder
A84
Dunblane
M90
Stirling
GLASGOW
M74
EDINBURGH

● Places to Stay
○ Orientation/Sightseeing
▨ Itinerary Route
⋯ Minor Roads

79

Scotland

This itinerary begins in Scotland's capital, Edinburgh, journeys to Inverness via Pitlochry, samples magnificent castles and portions of "The Whisky Trail," traces the shore of Scotland's most famous lake, Loch Ness, wends through the glens, and travels over the sea to Skye. It then takes you up into the beauties of Wester Ross where Inverewe Gardens blossoms in a harsh landscape, on to Fort William, Callander, and Glasgow with the magnificent Burrell Collection. At every turn there are echoes of history and romance—Nessie the legendary monster of Loch Ness, homes that sheltered Bonnie Prince Charlie and Flora Macdonald, and the lands where Rob Roy Macgregor roamed. The roads are few and often narrow and the long distances between villages and small towns add to the feeling of isolation. The fickle Scottish weather offers no guarantee that the dramatic scenery will be revealed, but what you can be assured of is a warm, friendly welcome from the hospitable Scots.

Eilean Donan Castle

Recommended Pacing: Spend a full day (two if possible) sightseeing in Edinburgh. With an early-morning start you will find yourself at Kildrummy Castle by nightfall (skip Perth sightseeing). If you prefer a more leisurely pace, also include an overnight in Pitlochry. Overnight around Inverness because it's an all-day drive from Inverness to the Isle of Skye, then spend two nights on Skye—more if you prefer a more leisurely pace. If you are venturing up the Wester Ross, plan on spending two nights there. A day-long drive from Skye will find you in Edinburgh by nightfall. If you are not a cities person, skip Glasgow and stay instead in or around Callander.

Edinburgh is Scotland's beautiful capital, dominated by Edinburgh Castle sitting high ·above the city. Before the castle lies the long green band of gardens that separates Edinburgh's Old Town, with its narrow streets crowded with ancient buildings, and New Town where Edinburgh's shopping street, Princes Street, is backed by wide roads of elegant Georgian houses. The city's principal sights are easily explored on foot, but as an introduction to Edinburgh take one of the double-decker sightseeing buses from Waverley Bridge opposite the Tourist Information Office (*tel: 0131-5571700*) and railway station. The tours run every 15 minutes and wind a circular route through the city with an audio-taped and live-from-the-driver commentary on the significance of the buildings along the route. Your ticket is valid for the whole day and the bus makes several stops so that you can take the entire tour for an overview of what there is to see and then later use it as transportation between the sights.

The most popular time to visit Scotland's capital is during the **Edinburgh Festival**. The city glows for the last three weeks of August: pipers dance down the streets and kilts are worn almost as a uniform. The hum of bagpipes sets the stage, and parades, flags, presentations, floodlights, and color appear everywhere. The Military Tattoo provides tradition, The Fringe offers everything from the avant-garde to the eccentric along with jugglers, mimes, and buskers, making this the most comprehensive international arts festival in the world. (*Program bookings and tickets: The Festival 0131-2264001, The Tattoo 0131-2251188, The Fringe 0131-2200464.*)

Some of Edinburgh's major sights are:

Princes Street, the elegant main thoroughfare, its north side lined by shops and its south side bordered by gardens.

The Georgian House (NT), at 7 Charlotte Square, is typical of the elegant Georgian homes found in New Town. From the kitchen, through the drawing room to the bedrooms, the house is furnished and decorated much as it would have been when it was first occupied in 1796 and gives you an insight into the way the family and servants of the house lived. (*Open April–October, tel: 0131-2265922.*)

Majestically perched on the edge of the city is **Edinburgh Castle,** looming against the skyline. There has been a castle here throughout the city's history with today's comprising a collection of buildings from the little 11th-century St. Margaret's chapel, through medieval apartments containing the Scottish crown jewels to more modern army barracks. From the castle ramparts the view over Edinburgh is spectacular. (*Open all year, tel: 0131-2259846.*)

From the castle gates you enter a famous sequence of ancient streets, referred to as The Royal Mile, where you find **Gladstone's Land** (NT), a building which typifies the more pleasant side of what life must have been like in the crowded tenements of Old Town Edinburgh. The house is arranged as a 17th-century merchant's house with the ground floor set up as a cloth merchant's booth and the upstairs as a home. (*Open April– October, tel: 0131-2265922.*)

On the High Street is the great **St. Giles Cathedral,** whose role has been so important in the history of the Presbyterian Church. John Knox preached from its pulpit from 1561 until his death in 1572, hurling attacks at the "idolatry" of the Catholic Church.

John Knox's home is just a little farther down the High Street. (*Open all year, tel: 0131-5569579.*)

Edinburgh Castle from the Princes Street Gardens

At the end of The Royal Mile lies **Holyrood House**, the historic home of the Stuarts, to which Mary, Queen of Scots came from France at the age of 18. The six years of her reign and stay at Holyrood made a tragic impact on her life. Shortly after marriage to a meek Lord Darnley, the happiness of the couple dissolved and their quarrels became bitter. Lord Darnley was jealous of Mary's secretary and constant companion, David Rizzio, and conspired to have him stabbed at Holyrood in the presence of the queen. Just a year later, Lord Darnley himself was mysteriously murdered and gossip blamed the Earl of Bothwell. Mary, however, married the Earl promptly after Lord Darnley's death and rumors still question the queen's personal involvement in the murder. Conspiracies continued and Scotland's young queen fled to the safety of the English court. However, considering her a threat to the English Crown, Queen Elizabeth I welcomed her with imprisonment and had her beheaded 19 years later. Bonnie Prince Charlie was the last Stuart king to hold court at Holyrood in 1745. Today Holyrood, whose apartments are lavishly furnished with French and Flemish tapestries, is used by the British monarch as an official residence in Scotland. (*Closed Sundays in winter and when Royal Family in residence, tel: 0131-5567371.*)

Leaving Edinburgh, follow signs for the **Firth of Forth Bridge** and Perth. After crossing the Firth of Forth, the M90 takes you through hilly farmland to the outskirts of Perth where you take the A93 following signs for Scone Palace.

Before reaching the palace you can detour off the main road to visit the city of **Perth,** known as the "Fair City," which straddles the banks of the Tay. A lovely city, it was the capital of Scotland until 1437 and the murder of James I. Following his death, his widow and young son, James II, moved the court to Edinburgh. One of Perth's most important historic buildings is **St. John's Kirk,** a fine medieval church that has been attended by many members of English and Scottish royalty. Also of interest are the **Perth Museum and Art Gallery** (*open all year*) and the **Museum of the Black Watch,** which is housed in **Ballhousie Castle.** (*Open Easter–October, closed Sundays, tel: 01738-71781.*)

Scone Palace is a 19th-century mansion that stands on the site of the Abbey of Scone, the coronation palace of all Scottish kings up to James I. By tradition the kings were crowned on a stone that was taken from the abbey in 1297 and placed under the Coronation Chair in Westminster Abbey. This token of conquest did nothing to improve relations between Scotland and England. The present mansion is the home of the Earl of Mansfield and houses a collection of china and ivory statuettes. (*Open April–September, tel: 01738-52300.*)

Continuing along the A93, shortly after leaving the abbey you pass through **Old Scone.** This was once a thriving village but was removed in 1805 by the Earl of Mansfield to improve the landscape and only the village cross and graveyard remain to mark the site.

Continue through Guildstown to **Stobhall,** a picturesque group of buildings (*not open*) grouped round a courtyard. Once the home of the Drummond family, much of the structure dates back to the 15th century.

Cross the River Isla and continue alongside the enormous beech hedge that was planted in 1746 as the boundary of the Meikelour estate. At the end of the hedge turn left to the village of **Meikelour**. The focal point of the village is the 1698 mercat cross, opposite which is an old place of punishment known as the Jougs Stone. Driving through the village you join the A984 Dunkeld road.

Continue through Caputh to **Dunkeld**. Telford spanned the Tay with a fine bridge in 1809, but this picturesque town is best known for the lovely ruins of its ancient cathedral. Founded in the 9th century, it was desecrated in 1560 and further damaged in the 17th-century Battle of Dunkeld. The choir has been restored. Stroll to **Dunkeld Cathedral** by way of Cathedral Street where the little 17th- and 18th-century houses have been restored by the National Trust.

Leaving the town, cross Telford's bridge and take the A9 for the 11-mile drive to **Pitlochry** where the Highlands meet the Lowlands of Scotland. The town owes its ornate Victorian appearance to its popularity in the 19th century as a Highland health resort. Now it is better known for its **Festival Theatre** whose season lasts from May to October and attracts some 70,000 theatergoers each year.

In the 1940s the local electricity company built a hydroelectric station and dam across the salmon-rich River Tummel on the outskirts of town. It is hard to imagine a power station being an asset to the town but this is certainly the case here. From the observation room at the dam you can see fish on the run as they climb the 1,000 foot **fish ladder** around the dam and fight their way upstream to spawn in the upper reaches of the river. A special exhibition is devoted to their life cycle and the efforts being made to conserve them. (*Open April–October, tel: 01796-3152.*)

The drive from Pitlochry to Braemar is spectacular. The A924 winds up from Pitlochry to the moorlands behind the town. Alternating lush green fields and heather-clad hills give way to heather-carpeted mountains as you approach the glorious Highland scenery of **Glen Shee** (A93). At the edge of the village of **Spittal of Glenshee** large orange gates are swung across the road when it is closed by winter storms. The road begins its steep climb across the heather up the Devil's Elbow to the ski resort at the summit and drops down to the green lush valley of the River Dee and **Braemar**.

Here in this picturesque valley the clans gather for Scotland's most famous Highland games, the **Braemar Gathering**. A brilliant spectacle of pipe bands, traditional Scottish sports, and Highland dancing, the event is usually attended by the Queen and her family. Also in the village of Braemar is the cottage in which Robert Louis Stevenson lived the year he wrote *Treasure Island*.

Following the River Dee, a short drive brings you to **Braemar Castle**, a doll-sized castle on a little knoll surrounded by conifers—a hint of the magnificent castles that wait you. Following the rushing River Dee, a turn in the road offers a splendid view of **Balmoral Castle**, the Royal summer residence. It's a very overrated Victorian pile of a building built in 1853 in the Scottish baronial style at the request of Queen Victoria and Prince Albert. When the Royal Family are not in residence you can visit the gardens and view the exhibition in the castle ballroom. (*Grounds open May, June, and July whenever the Royal Family is not in residence, tel: 013397-42334.*)

Coming into the tiny hamlet of **Craithe**, park in the riverside car park and stroll up to **Craithe Church** whose foundation stone was laid by Queen Victoria in 1895. The Royal Family attend services here when in residence at Balmoral just across the river.

Continue into **Ballater**, an attractive, small town internationally famous for its Highland games held in August. These include many old Scottish sports and the arduous hill race to the summit of Craig Cailleach. Continue along the A93, watching for the signpost that directs you left for a drive of several miles to **Craigievar Castle** (NT). This single-turret, pink-washed fortress surrounded by farmland is the most appealing of fairy-tale castles. Up the narrow spiral staircase the rooms are small and familial and furnished as though the laird and his family are still in residence. Willie Forbes, better known as Danzig Willie because he made his money trading with Danzig, bought an incomplete

Craigievar Castle

castle here in 1610. He wanted the best that money could buy and gave the master mason free reign with the castle's beautiful design. The best plasterers were busy, so Danzig Willie waited many years for the magnificent molded plasterwork ceilings that were completed the year before his death in 1627. (*Open 2–6 pm, May–September, tel: 0133-983635.*)

Twenty miles away lies **Castle Fraser** (NT), a grander, more elaborate version of Craigievar set in park-like grounds with a formal walled garden. Begun in 1575, the castle stayed in Fraser hands until the early part of this century. It contains a splendid Great Hall and what remains of an alleged eavesdropping device known as the "Laird's Lug." (*Open 2–6 pm, May–September, tel: 0133-03463.*)

Regain the A944 which takes you through Alford and on towards Rhynie. Detour from the main road to visit the romantic ruins of **Kildrummy Castle** (A97). Overlooking the ruins and surrounded by acres and acres of beautiful gardens is **Kildrummy Castle Hotel**, one of our favorite Scottish country house hotels.

The road from Kildrummy to **Dufftown** via the little Highland villages of Lumsden, Rhynie (where you leave A97 and turn left on A941), and Cabrach takes you across broad expanses of moorland. Dufftown was laid out in the form of a right-angled cross by James Duff, the 4th Earl of Fife, in 1817. Turn right at the Tolbooth tower in the center of the square and you come to the **Glenfiddich Distillery**, the only distillery in the Highlands where you can see the complete whisky-making process from barley to bottling. (*Closed last two weeks December, tel: 01340-20373.*)

Malt whisky is to Scotland what wine is to France. The rules for production are strict: it must be made from Highland barley dried over peat fires using water from streams that have run through peat and over granite and it must be distilled in onion-shaped copper stills and stored in oak vats. A map is available from the tourist office in Dufftown that gives details of which distilleries are open and when.

Once a Highland fortress but now sadly in ruins, **Ballathie Castle** stands on the hill overlooking the distillery.

Four miles down the A941 you come to **Craigellachie** village and distillery (the home of White Horse Whisky). Turn left on the A95 for Grantown-on-Spey and follow the Spey valley through pleasant countryside to **Ballindalloch Castle**, the beautiful home of the Macpherson-Grants. An interesting selection of tastefully furnished rooms and a tea shop are open to the public. This elegant home with its lovely gardens shows the transition from the tower house of Craigievar to the country mansion so idealized by the Victorians in the Highlands. (*Open Easter–September, tel: 0180-72206, fax: 0180-72210.*)

A short distance brings you to the **Glenlivet Distillery**. (*Open mid-March–October, tel: 018073-427.*)

Cross the River Spey at Advie and continue into Grantown-on-Spey on the narrow road that follows the north bank of the river. From Grantown-on-Spey the A 939 leads towards the holiday resort of Nairn. After about 15 miles take a small road to the left signposted for **Cawdor Castle**. This was the castle Shakespeare had in mind when he set the scene of Duncan's death in *Macbeth*. The present-day Thane of Cawdor shares his family home and gardens with the public. Portraits, tapestries, lovely furniture, and, of course, tales of romance and mystery blend to make this an interesting tour. (*Open May–September, tel: 016677-615.*)

An 8-mile drive brings you to the cairn that marks the site of the battle of **Culloden** (NT) where on a rainy day in 1746 Bonnie Prince Charlie marched his tired, rain-soaked Highlanders into hopeless battle with the English: 1,200 Highlanders were killed. This was the last battle fought on British soil and Charles's defeat led to the decline of the Highlands and the destruction of the clan system. After the battle the British hunted Charles for five months before he escaped to France. A museum documents this sad incident and on the surrounding moorland red flags outline the Scots battle plan while yellow flags denote the English. (*Open all year, tel: 01463-790607.*)

Nearby **Inverness** is known as the "Capital of the Highlands." Straddling the River Ness, the town takes its name from the river and the Gaelic word "inver" meaning river mouth. Leave the town on the A82 (Fort William road) and after a mile you come to the Caledonian Canal which links the lochs of the Great Glen together to provide passage between the Irish and the North Seas—the canal splits Scotland in two and without it boats would have to risk the dangerous passage around the northernmost stretches of Scotland.

Leave Inverness on the A82 (Fort William road) following the northern shore of Scotland's deepest (700 feet), longest (24 miles), and most famous lake, **Loch Ness**. This is the legendary home of the Loch Ness Monster or "Nessie," as she is affectionately known. So, keep an eye on the muddy gray waters of the lake and you may see more than the wind ruffling its surface. If she doesn't happen to surface for you, visit the **Loch Ness Monster Exhibition** at **Drumnadrochit**, which documents sightings that go back to the 7th century. Photographs of eel-like loops and black heads swimming give credence to the legends. (*Open all year*.)

Monster-spotting is a favorite pastime around Loch Ness and visitors gaze from the ramparts of **Urquhart Castle** because some of the best sightings have been made from here. The ruined castle dates from the 14th century and has a long and violent history. (*Open all year*.)

Following the shores of Loch Ness, a 19-mile drive brings you to **Fort Augustus**, a village that stands at the southwestern end of the loch. Park your car by the **Caledonian Canal** and wander along its banks to see the pleasure craft being lowered and raised through the locks. Thomas Telford, the famous engineer, spent from 1803 to 1847 building the sections of this canal that connects the North Sea and the Atlantic without boats having to navigate around the treacherous Cape Wrath.

A few miles to the southwest, the little village of **Invergarry** is framed by spectacular mountain scenery. The village was burnt to the ground after the battle of Culloden because it had sheltered Bonnie Prince Charlie before and after the battle. Turn west in the village and follow the A87, through breathtaking Highland scenery, for 50 miles to Kyle of Lochalsh. The wild, rugged scenery changes with every bend in the road as you drive high above the lochs across empty moorlands then descend into glens to follow the shores of lochs whose crystal-clear, icy waters reflect the rugged mountain peaks. Habitations are few and far between yet, until the Highland chiefs decided, in the 18th century, that sheep were more profitable than tenants, the hillsides held crofts, schools, and chapels.

As you trace the shore of **Loch Duich**, on the last lap of the journey to Skye, **Eilean Donan Castle** appears, linked to the rocky shore by a bridge. The castle is named for a saint who lived here in the 7th century. It is a massive, walled keep that during subsequent centuries defended the coast against Danish and Norse invaders. More recently it has been restored and it is fascinating to go into rooms with 14-foot-thick walls and to climb to the battlements to see the loch spread out before you. (*Open Easter–September, tel: 0159985-202.*)

From the busy fishing port of **Kyle of Lochalsh** the road bridge takes you "over the sea to Skye" (toll £6.20). There is an exhilarating feel to the often mist-shrouded shores of the **Isle of Skye** where mystery and legends intermingle with dramatic scenery. Islanders still make a living crofting and fishing, though tourism is becoming ever more important. This is the home of the Scottish heroine Flora Macdonald who disguised Bonnie Prince Charlie as her maid and brought him safely to Skye after his defeat by the English at the battle of Culloden.

Set out to explore Skye's coastline where magnificent mountains rise from the rocky shore and sea lochs provide scenic sheltered harbors. Skye has very good roads, although often quite narrow, making it easy to tour portions of the island in a day. (A trip from Portree around the northern end of Skye, west to Dunvegan, and back to Portree by the hill road from Struan is all that you could expect to do comfortably in one day.) If the weather is inclement and mist veils the island, content yourself with a good book by the fireside, for what appears stunningly beautiful on a fine day can appear dreary when sheathed in fog.

Follow the A850 (signposted Portree) through the scattered village of Broadford set along a broad, sheltered bay. Skirting the shoreline, you pass the island of Scalpay before tracing the southern shoreline of Loch Ainort. The surrounding humped peaks of the Cullin Hills are spectacular as you follow the road through Sconser and Sligachan to Portree.

Portree, the capital of Skye, is its most attractive town. Pastel-painted houses step down to the water's edge, fishing boats bob in the harbor, and small boats arrive and depart from its pier. Climbing away from the harbor, the town's streets are lined with attractive shops. If you have not booked your ferry passage from Armadale to Mallaig you can do so at the Caledonian MacBrayne ferry office behind the bus station *(tel: 01478-612075)*. The town derives its name from Port an Righ meaning King's Haven, following the visit in 1540 of James V who made a vain attempt to reconcile the feuding Macleod and Macdonald clans. If you base yourself in Portree, there is no better place to stay than at the home of Hugh and Linda Macdonald, **Viewfield House**.

Leaving the town, turn right onto the A855, a narrow, single-lane road with passing places, which takes you north. As you approach the shores of Lochs Fada and Leathan the jagged, craggy peaks of **The Storr** (mountains) come into view. Standing amongst them is the **Old Man of Storr,** one of the most challenging pinnacles for mountain climbers.

Around the island's northernmost headland the crumbling ruins of the Macdonalds' **Duntulm Castle** stand on a clifftop promontory overlooking the rocky shores of Duntulm Bay. A short drive brings you to the **Skye Croft Museum** where four traditional Highland crofts have been restored and appropriately furnished to show a family home, a smithy, a weaver's house, and a small museum. These little cottages with their thick stone walls topped by a thick straw thatch were the traditional island dwellings—very few good examples remain, though, as you travel around the island, if you look very carefully, you can see several traditional cottages in various states of ruin. Flora Macdonald is buried in a nearby graveyard. *(Open Easter–October, closed Sundays, tel: 0147-052279.)*

Returning to the main coastal route (A855), a short drive takes you through Kilmuir and down a steep hill into the scattered hamlet of **Uig** whose pier is used by ferries to the Outer Hebrides. It is here that Bonnie Prince Charlie and Flora Macdonald landed after fleeing the Outer Hebrides. Continue to Kensaleyre and half a mile beyond the village turn right onto the B8036. When this road meets a T-junction turn right onto the A850 for the 22-mile drive to the village of **Dunvegan.**

Just to the north of the village is **Dunvegan Castle**, the oldest inhabited castle in Scotland and the home of the Macleod family for over 700 years. It stands amidst hills and moorlands guarding the entrance to a sheltered bay. After parking your car walk through rhododendron-filled gardens to the fortress. The castle's 15th-century section is known as the Fairy Tower after the threadbare Fairy Flag that hangs in one of the chambers. Legend has it that this yellow silk flag with crimson spots is the consecrated banner of the Knights Templar, taken as a battle prize from the Saracens. It is said to have the magical properties to produce victory in battle, the birth of sons, and plentiful harvests. Other relics include items relating to Bonnie Prince Charlie. During the summer you can take boat excursions to view the nearby seal colonies. (*Open April–October, tel: 0147-8022206.*)

The A863 winds you down the western side of Skye. If you wish to visit the island's only distillery, take the B8009 to **Talisker** where the **Talisker Distillery** offers guided tours and a tasting. (*Open weekdays April–October, tel: 0147-842203.*)

Follow the narrow, single-track A851 across open moorland to **Sleat** (pronounced Slate) which refers to the complete southern peninsula of Skye where most of the land is divided into two estates: Clan Donald lands to the south and those of Sir Iain Noble to the north. Sir Iain is a great promoter of Gaelic which is undergoing a revival in the western Highlands. On a rocky spit of land almost surrounded by water, the whitewashed **Eilean Iarmain** hotel, a shop, and a huddle of cottages face **Isle Ornsay**—a postage-stamp-sized island whose lighthouse was built by Robert Louis Stephenson's grandfather. (The lighthouse cottage's most famous occupant was Gavin Maxwell.) Across the sound mountains tumble directly into the sea adding a wild, end-of-the-earth feel to this hamlet.

A few more miles of narrow roads bring you to the **Clan Donald Centre** where the stable block serves as a tea room and gift shop whence you walk through the wooded **Armadale Castle** grounds to an exhibition on the Lords of the Isles and Gaelic culture. (*Open Easter–October, tel: 0147-14305.*)

SKYE TO FORT WILLIAM VIA MALLAIG

If time or weather prevent you from following this itinerary north into Wester Ross, you can board the ferry for **Mallaig** in nearby **Armadale**. The ferry sails five to six times a day during the summer months and reservations should be made before sailing—it is suggested that you purchase your tickets from either the Caledonian MacBrayne ferry offices in Kyleakin (*tel: 01599-4482*) or Portree (*tel: 01478-612075*). The ferry company requires that cars arrive half an hour before sailing time. It takes 1½ hours to drive from Portree to the ferry, so unless you are an insomniac do not book the 9 am ferry. Leaving Mallaig, you cannot get lost for there is only one narrow road, "The Road to the Isles," that leads you out of town (A830).

If the weather is fine, you may want to pause at the spectacular white beaches that fringe the rocky little bays near **Morar**. The narrow road twists and turns and passing places allow cars going in opposite directions to pass one another. The village of **Arisaig** shelters on the shores of **Loch Nan Ceal** with views, and ferries, to the little islands of **Rhum** and **Eigg**.

From Arisaig your route turns eastwards following the picturesque shores of **Loch Nan Uamh,** best known for its associations with Bonnie Prince Charlie and the Jacobite Rising of 1745. The clan leaders met in a house nearby and after his defeat the prince hid near here before being taken to the Outer Hebrides—a cairn marks the spot where he left Scotland.

More than 1,000 clansmen gathered at **Glenfinnan** at the head of **Loch Shiel** to begin the 1745 Jacobite Rising. The place where they are said to have hoisted the Stuart standard is marked by a tall castellated tower. You climb the tower stairs to the statue of a Highlander overlooking the icy waters of the mountain-ringed loch. At the adjacent visitors' center the prince's exploits are portrayed.

Leaving the monument to Bonnie Prince Charlie's lost cause, follow the A830 for the 15-mile drive through Kinlocheil and Corpach to **Fort William.** As you approach the town the rounded summit of Britain's highest mountain, **Ben Nevis,** appears before you.

Plockton on Loch Carron

SKYE TO FORT WILLIAM OR INVERNESS VIA WESTER ROSS

If you love Skye with her magnificent seascapes and mountains, then you will adore the Wester Ross coastline that stretches from Kyle of Lochalsh to Ullapool and beyond. It is a long day's drive from Kyle to Ullapool and the scenery is so magnificent that you may want to break the journey and spend several days in the area. Traditionally, **Wester Ross** has most sunshine in May and June, it rains more in July and August, then brightens up in September. Scottish weather is very fickle in May: we went from seven days of glorious sunshine to seemingly endless days of lashing rain. A great deal of the drive from Kyle of Lochalsh to Ullapool is on single-track road—one lane of tarmac just a few inches wider than your car (with passing places).

From **Kyle of Lochalsh** turn left to **Plockton** to see the hardy yucca palms that bravely grow in the harborside gardens in this pretty village that hugs a sheltered spot of the wooded bay. Leaving Plockton, the road traces Loch Carron and after passing the Stratcarron Hotel, at the head of the loch, turn left on the A896 for Tornapress and on to Shieldaig.

If the weather is sunny, rather than continuing along the A896 from Tornapress to Shieldaig, take the coastal road around the headland following signposts for Applecross. You will be rewarded by a most challenging drive and spectacular scenery. The narrow road twists and turns as it climbs ever higher up the **Bealach-nam-Bo** pass with the mountains rising closer and taller at every turn. Crest the summit, cross a boulder-strewn moorland dotted with tarns (tiny lakes), and drop down into **Applecross**, a few whitewashed houses set in a lush green valley with salmon-pink sandy beaches. Grazing sheep fill the coastal fields and the occasional whitewashed croft faces across the water to the Isle of Raasay and, beyond that, the misty mountains of Skye. Rounding the peninsula you come to **Ardehslaig**, a few white cottages set round a rocky inlet with boats bobbing in the tiny sheltered harbor. Turn into **Shieldaig** where little cottages line the waterfront facing a nearby island densely forested with Scotch pines. It's an idyllic, peaceful spot and **Tigh an Eilean** (House by the Island) with its shop, pretty hotel, and pub makes an excellent place to break your journey.

A deceptive few yards of two-lane road quickly turn to single track as you travel along the south shore of **Loch Torridon** where the **Loch Torridon Hotel** sits on its bank and through Glen Torridon to turn left on the A832, an arrow-straight, two-lane highway. After half a mile you find a whitewashed visitors' center on the left. The road traces Loch Maree with tempting glimpses of the glassy loch between groves of birch trees.

The soft lushness and straight road give way to wild moorland and a single-track road to **Gairloch** with its wide bay of pink sand, scattered houses, cemetery, and golf course.

Heading inland to cross the peninsula you come to **Inverewe Gardens** (NT). Osgood Mackensie bought this little peninsula in 1862, a barren site exposed to Atlantic gales but with frosts prevented by the warmth of the Gulf Stream. He planted belts of trees for shelter, brought in soil, and began his garden, a lifetime project that was continued by his daughter who handed over Inverewe to the National Trust in 1952. The lushness of the gardens is a striking contrast to the miles of grandiose, barren scenery that surround it. The surprise is not so much what the garden contains as the fact that it exists at all on a latitude similar to that of Leningrad. The gardens, shop, and tea room are a venue that will occupy several hours. The National Trust brochure outlines a suggested route along the garden's pathways, but you can wander at will down the twisting paths through the azaleas, rhododendrons, and woodlands. Colorful displays are to be found in most seasons: in mid-April to May, rhododendrons; May, azaleas; June, rock garden, flower borders, and roses; September, heather; and November, maples. (*Open all year, tel: 0144-586229.*)

Leaving Inverewe, another 35 miles finds you at the head of **Loch Broom** at an impressive vantage point that offers magnificent views down the valley across lush farmland to the distant loch. Travel down the hill and turn left into the green valley for the 12-mile drive to Ullapool.

Ullapool has a beautiful setting: cottages line the quay and overlook a jumble of slipways, quays, vessels from huge international trawlers to small wooden fishing boats, fishing gear, and nets. On the distant shore heather-clad hills rise steeply from the waters of Loch Broom. The port is a bustle of freighters and foreign fishing boats and is the terminal for the car ferry to Stornoway on the Isle of Lewis. Summer visitors add to the throng. You can always find good food and a reviving cup of coffee (and accommodation) at **The Ceilidh Place**. The most outstanding place to stay, the **Altnaharrie Inn**, lies across the loch.

North of Ullapool there's a lot of heart-stopping scenery but beyond the Summer Isles there are no good places to stay. Journey to the **Summer Isles** by boat to see the seals and seabirds. Travel to **Lochinver** with its breathtaking views of beautiful coastline and visit the **Inchnadamph Caves** and the ruin of **Ardvreck Castle**.

Leaving Ullapool, a 60-mile drive (A835) will return you to Inverness from where it's a 3-hour drive down the A9 to Edinburgh. Or retrace your steps down the northern shore of Loch Ness and continue into Fort William (A82).

Bordering the shores of **Loch Linnhe, Fort William** is the largest town in the Western Highlands. While the town itself cannot be described as attractive, it is the economic hub of the area and it is always crowded with tourists during the busy summer months.

From Fort William the A82 takes you southwest along the southern shore of Loch Linnhe, then turns you inland over the pass of **Glen Coe**, notorious for the massacre of the Macdonalds by the Campbells in 1692. After accepting their hospitality, the Campbells issued an order—written on the nine of diamonds playing card—to kill their hosts, the Macdonalds. The pass of Glen Coe is barren and rocky and the road south travels across this seemingly empty land. A short detour to **Killin** with its craft shops and impressive waterfalls provides an enjoyable break on a long drive.

The area of low mountains and serene lakes around **Callander** (a most attractive town) is known as **The Trossachs**. This is the country of Sir Walter Scott's novel *Rob Roy* and his poem *Lady of the Lake*. Robert MacGregor, "Rob Roy," existed as a romanticized 17th-century Robin Hood, who stole from the rich and gave to the poor. However, some regarded him more realistically as a thief and rustler! Scott's "lady" was Ellen Douglas, and her "lake" was **Loch Katrine**. (*Loch Katrine boat trips May–September, tel: 0141336-5333.*) There are a number of lovely lakes to view in this area, such as **Loch Achray** and **Loch Venachar**.

A few miles distant lies **Stirling**, dominated by its imposing Renaissance castle. **Stirling Castle**, once the home of Scottish kings, is perched high on a sheer cliff overlooking the battleground of **Bannockburn** where the Scots turned the English back in their attempt to subdue the Highland clans. (*Open all year, tel: 01786-62517.*)

From Stirling the M80 will quickly bring you to **Glasgow**, Scotland's most populous city. Its established tradition as a port and industrial center has in recent years been surpassed by its reputation as the home of **The Burrell Collection**, Scotland's most outstanding museum. Take the M8 towards the airport to the M77: the museum is housed in the grounds of **Pollock House**. It is important to remember that this modern museum building houses the collection of one man, Sir William Burrell (1861–1958). William joined his family's shipping company and by the age of 40 had made his fortune, so he was able to spend the rest of his life amassing his vast art collection. He recorded his purchases in 28 notebooks and housed his collection in his home, Hutton Castle. At 82 he bequeathed his vast collection to his native city with the strict condition that they house it in a rural setting no farther than 16 miles from the Royal Exchange. It was not until 1983 that the collection opened to the public. At Burrell's request, **Hutton Castle**'s hall, drawing room, and dining room with their fine paneling, precious antiques, and lovely tapestries have been incorporated into the museum. The collection of European paintings, tapestries, bronzes, Chinese ceramics, and ancient artifacts is so vast that only parts of it can be displayed at any one time. (*Open all year, tel: 0141-6497151.*)

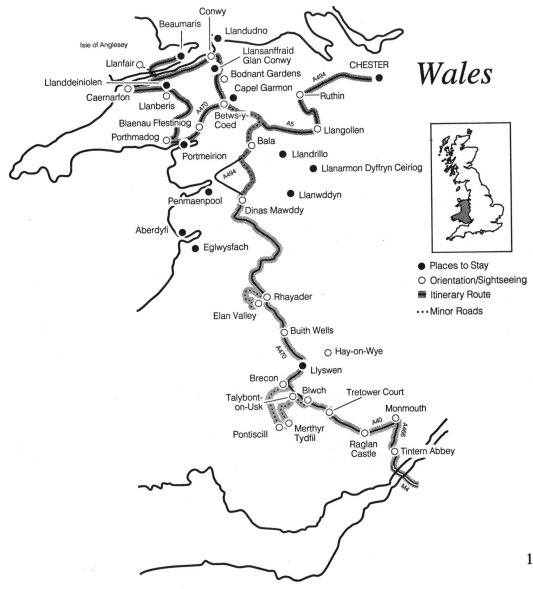

Conwy

Beaumaris

Llandudno

Isle of Anglesey

Llanfair

Llansanffraid
Glan Conwy

Llanddeiniolen

Bodnant Gardens

CHESTER

Wales

Caernarfon

Capel Garmon

Llanberis

Ruthin

Blaenau Ffestiniog

Betws-y-
Coed

Llangollen

Porthmadog

Bala

Portmeirion

Llandrillo

Llanarmon Dyffryn Ceiriog

Penmaenpool

Llanwddyn

Dinas Mawddy

Aberdyfi

Eglwysfach

● Places to Stay

○ Orientation/Sightseeing

Itinerary Route

• • • Minor Roads

Rhayader

Elan Valley

Buith Wells

Hay-on-Wye

Brecon

Llyswen

Talybont-
on-Usk

Blwch

Tretower Court

Monmouth

Pontiscill

Merthyr
Tydfil

Raglan
Castle

Tintern Abbey

Wales

Wales has myriad towns and villages with seemingly unpronounceable names, its own language, an ancient form of Celtic, its own prince, Charles, narrow-gauge steam railways that puff contentedly through glorious scenery, and more castles per square mile than anywhere else in Europe. The Welsh have always been fiercely independent. Consequently, they built fortifications to defend themselves while a series of mighty fortresses was commissioned by Edward I from which the English could sally forth to subdue the fiery Welsh. Today these mighty fortresses are some of Wales's greatest treasures. Another popular attraction is the "Great Little Trains," narrow-gauge steam railway lines, with hard-working "toy" trains that once hauled slate and still steam through gorgeous countryside. And at journey's end there is bound to be a steaming cuppa to be enjoyed with bara brith, a scrumptious currant bread. As the signs say, *Croeso i Cymru*—Welcome to Wales.

Conwy Castle

Wales

Recommended Pacing: One night in southern Wales is all you need to accomplish the sightseeing outlined in this itinerary as, in our opinion, Wales's most magnificent scenery and stunning castles lie to the north in and around Snowdonia National Park. Allow at least two nights in northern Wales.

Leave England on the M4 crossing the Severn toll bridge. The first indication that you are in another country is that all road signs appear in two languages, Welsh first, English second. As you leave the bridge take the first left turnoff signed A466 Monmouth and the Wye Valley. The road winds a course up the steep-sided, wooded valley to **Tintern Abbey**, a romantic ruin adored by the sentimental Victorians. Drive alongside the ruin to the car park at the rear by the tourist office. Stretch your legs with a quick walk round the ruin or, if you would like to visit the prettiest spot on the 168-mile length of **Offa's Dyke**, the tourist office will provide you with a detailed instruction sheet called *Offa's Dyke and the Devil's Pulpit Viewpoint*. Offa's Dyke was a great earthwork built over 1200 years ago at the direction of King Offa to divide England and Wales. (*Open April–October, tel: 012918-251.*)

Follow the river as it winds into Monmouth and turn left on the A40 towards Abergavenny. Traveling this dual carriageway quickly brings into view the substantial ruins of **Raglan Castle** in a field to your right. Because it is on the opposite side of a divided highway you need to do an about-face at the first roundabout. Raglan Castle is the last of the medieval castles, dating from the more settled later Middle Ages when its builders could afford to indulge in decorative touches. It was begun in 1431 and its Great Tower was rendered the ruin you see today by Oliver Cromwell's demolition engineers. A huge fireplace and the windows are all that remain of the Grand Hall but with imagination and the aid of a map you can picture what a splendid place this must have been. You can climb the battlements and picnic in the grassy grounds. (*Open April–October.*)

Stay on the ring road around Abergavenny and 2 miles after passing through **Crickhowell**, a one-time stagecoach stop for coach travelers on the way to Brecon, turn right on the A479 to **Tretower Court and Castle**. The castle, a sturdy keep, was usurped as a habitation in the 14th century by nearby Tretower Court, a grand mansion that was the home of the Vaughan family for three centuries. As you walk through the home's empty medieval hall and along its stone passageways you can imagine how splendid a home it was. Leaving Tretower, continue down the lane, beside the house, and turn right on the A40. (*Open all year, tel: 01874-730279.*)

If the weather is fine, you can enjoy an almost circular driving tour through the **Brecon Beacons** by turning left towards Llangynidr and, after crossing the river, taking a right turn to Cwm Cronon and Talybont-on-Usk where you turn left and follow a beautiful wooded valley alongside lakes and over the hills to Pontiscill. On a fine day it is a spectacular drive along a narrow paved road, but this is not a trip to be appreciated when the clouds hang low over the mountains and visibility is not good. From Pontiscill the road weaves down to the outskirts of Merthyr Tydfil where you turn right on the A470 along another lovely valley and climb the stark, bare escarpment over the pass to Brecon.

If you do not deviate through the Brecon Beacons, remain on the A40 where views of the Usk Valley and the mountains present themselves as the road climbs to the village of Blwch. Bypass the market town of Brecon and take the A470 (Buith Wells) to **Llyswen** where you can enjoy refreshment or an overnight stay at either **The Griffin Inn** or **Llangoed Hall**. (From Llyswen an 18-mile round-trip detour will afford you the chance to explore the many bookstores and antique shops of **Hay-On-Wye**.)

It's a lovely drive to Buith Wells as the road follows the River Wye through soft, pretty countryside. Crossing the river, head to **Rhayader** where an opportunity to enjoy a beautiful (in fair weather) drive through wild, rugged moorlands rising from vast reservoirs is afforded by turning left in the village for the **Elan Valley**. Your first stop lies beneath the looming dam at the information center where a small display outlines the importance and history of clean drinking water and gives details on the vast reservoirs that provide 76 million gallons of drinking water a day. Returning to the road, follow it as it traces the reservoir through fern-covered mountains. A right-hand turn returns you to the center of Rhayader and the A470.

From Rhayader the A470 takes you quickly north. After the junction with the A458 be on the lookout for a small sign that directs you into the pretty roadside village of Dinas Mawddy and along a narrow lane that climbs and climbs above the green fields into stark mountains, crests the pass, and winds down and around the lake to the outskirts of Bala. Here you make a right-hand turn then go immediately left on the A4212 (Trawsfyndd road) for a short distance to the B4501 which quickly brings you to Cerrigydrudion. There you turn left on the A5 to **Betws-y-Coed**, set in a narrow, densely wooded valley at the confluence of three rivers. Crowds of visitors come to admire this town that was popularized by the Victorian painter David Cox.

From Betws-y-Coed take the A470, following the eastern bank of the River Conwy north as it winds its way to the sea. After passing through the village of **Tal-y-Cafn**, look for **Bodnant Gardens** (NT) on your right. Garden lovers will enjoy almost a hundred acres of camellias, rhododendrons, magnolias, and laburnum which provide incredible displays of spring color. Above are terraces, lawns, and formal rose and flower beds; below, in a wooded valley, a stream runs through the secluded, wild garden. (*Open mid-March–October, tel: 01492-650460.*)

The swell of **Conwy Bay** is flanked by high cliffs and the town of Conwy is unforgettable for its picturesque castle set on a promontory at the confluence of two rivers and for the town's wall—over ¾ mile in length with 22 towers and 3 original gateways. **Conwy Castle** was begun in the 13th century for Edward I and suffered the scars of the turbulent years of the Middle Ages and the Civil War. The defensive complex includes an exhibit on Edward I and his castles in Wales. On the top floor of the

Chapel Tower is a scale model of how the castle and the town might have appeared in 1312. (*Open April–October, tel: 01492-592398.*)

Leaving the castle, cross the road to the quay to visit a tiny home which claims to be the smallest house in Britain, then turn onto the High Street and visit the oldest house in Wales, **Abercony House** (NT). (*Open April–October.*)

Leave Conwy and follow the A55 as it hugs the coast in the direction of Caernarfon. Rather than going directly to Caernarfon, follow signs for Bangor (A5122) and call in at **Penrhyn Castle** (NT), a fabulous sham castle built as a grand home by a local slate magnate in the 19th century. This impressive house of intricate masonry and woodwork is filled with stupendous furniture. (*Open April–October, tel: 01248-353084.*)

Cross over the Menai Straight to the **Isle of Anglesey** on the Menai suspension bridge, the first of its kind, built by that famous engineer, Thomas Telford, then follow the road that hugs the coast to **Beaumaris** with its closely huddled houses painted in pastel shades strung along the road. **Beaumaris Castle**, the last of the castles built by Edward I in his attempt to control Wales, is a squat, moated fortress with grassy grounds inside thick walls facing a harbor full of sailboats. (*Open all year, tel: 01248-810361.*)

Return to the Menai bridge and, if you are inclined to have your picture taken by the sign of the town with the longest name in the world, follow directions to **Llanfair**, the abbreviation (that fits on signposts) for Llanfairpwllgwyngyllgogerychwyndrobwyllllan-tysiliogogogoch which means "St. Mary's Church by the white aspens over the whirlpool and St. Tysilio's Church by the red cave." The drab little town has little to recommend it but commercial opportunists have cleverly situated a large shopping complex directly next to the station.

The A5 (Bangor road) quickly returns you to the mainland via the Britannia road bridge where you pick up signs for **Caernarfon**. Edward I laid the foundations of **Caernarfon Castle** in 1283 after his armies had defeated the princes of North Wales. Many revolts against English rule took place in this imposing fortress and during the Civil War it was

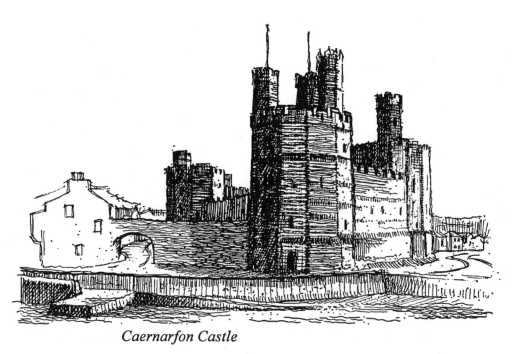

Caernarfon Castle

one of Cromwell's strongholds. The first English Prince of Wales was born here in 1284. The investitures of the Duke of Windsor in 1911 and of Prince Charles in 1969 as Prince of Wales both took place in this majestic setting. This is the most massive and best preserved of the fortifications in this itinerary. It takes several hours to clamber up the towers, peep through arrow slits in the massive walls, and visit the exhibitions on the Princes of Wales, Castles of Edward I, and the Museum of the Royal Welsh Fusiliers. (*Open April–October, tel: 01286-77617.*)

Leave the coast at Caernarfon with the beauty of Snowdonia ahead of you, following the A4086 Llanberis road. The **Snowdonia National Park** is a region of wild mountains which, while they cannot be compared in size to the Alps or the Rockies (Snowdon rises to 3,560 feet), are nevertheless dramatically beautiful with ravines and sheer cliffs whose sides plummet into glacier-cut valleys sparkling with wood-fringed lakes and cascading waterfalls.

The village of **Llanberis** is the starting point for the ascent of the highest mountain in Wales, **Mount Snowdon**. Easier than the rugged walking ascent is the two-hour round-trip journey on the **Snowdon Mountain Railway**, an adorable "toy" steam train that pushes its carriages up the mountainside on a rack-and-pinion railway. The little train winds you along the edges of precipices and up steep gradients to the mountain's summit. If the weather is fine (the train runs only in clear weather) and especially if it is July, August, or the weekend, arrive early to secure a pass that entitles you to return at an appointed time for your adventure. On the day we visited a 10:30 am arrival assured us of a place on the 4:30 pm train. Remember to take warm clothing with you as it is always cold on the summit. (*Open April–October, tel: 01286-870223.*)

When you return from your mountain adventure make your way to the other side of the lake to ride the **Llanberis Lake Railway** (rarely do you have to book in advance). The adorable little train that once served the slate quarries now puffs along 2 miles of track by the edge of the lake beneath the towering mountains. On fine days you have lovely views of Snowdon.

When you leave Llanberis the road climbs the pass and the scenery becomes ever more rocky and rugged: small wonder that Hillary and Hunt trained for the 1953 Everest ascent in this area. At the Pen-y-Gwryd hotel turn right on the A498 for Beddgelert. The landscape softens as you pass Lake Gwynant and, with the River Glaslyn as its guide, the road passes through a valley that is softer and more pastoral than those of Snowdonia's other lakes.

Crowding the river bank where three valleys meet is the little village of **Beddgelert**, nestled in the foothills of Mount Snowdon. From Beddgelert, the road follows the tumbling River Glaslyn which settles into a lazy glide as it approaches **Porthmadog**, the terminus of the hard-working little **Ffestiniog Narrow-Gauge Railway** which runs to and from nearby Ffestiniog. The train provides riders with a mobile viewpoint from which to enjoy the most spectacular scenery as it follows the coast and chugs up into rugged Snowdonia, at one point traveling almost in a circle to gain altitude, to terminate its journey at Blaenau Ffestiniog. Here, in summer, you can connect with a bus that takes you for a visit to the nearby slate caverns before taking you back to the station for your return journey to Porthmadog. This rugged little train for many years carried slate from the mines to the port of Porthmadog. (*Open April–October, tel: 01766-512340, 2½ hours return journey*.)

A short drive on the A487 brings you to Minffordd where you turn right to the extravagant fantasy village of **Portmeirion** which looks like a little piece of Italy transported to Wales. It has a piazza, a camponile, and an eclectic mixture of cottages and buildings squeezed into a small space and surrounded by gardens full of subtropical plants and ornate pools. The village is a mass of color—the façades are terra cotta, bright pink, yellow, and cream, and the gardens full of brightly colored flowers and shrubs. Portmeirion was the realization of a dream for Sir Clough Ellis who bought this wooded hillside plot above the broad sandy river estuary and built the village to show that architecture could be fun and could enhance a beautiful site, not defile it. His architectural model was Portofino and, while there are many Italianate touches to this fantasy village, there are also lots of local recycled houses, for Sir Clough rescued many old buildings and cottages from destruction (he termed Portmeirion "the home for fallen buildings") and had them transported here and erected on the site. Day visitors are charged an admission fee but if you really want to fully enjoy the fantasy (the setting for the BBC television series *The Prisoner*), spend the night at the hotel or in one of the rooms in the village and enjoy it after the visitors have left.

Leave the coast behind you and turn inland to **Blaenau Ffestiniog** where terraced houses huddle together beneath the massive, gray-slate mountain to form a village. Taking the

A470 towards Betws-y-Coed, the road follows terrace upon terrace of somber gray slate up the mountainside to the **Llechwedd Slate Caverns**. Exhibits show the importance of slate mining but the most exiting part of a visit here is to travel underground into the deep mine and follow a walking tour through the caverns. (*Open March–September, tel: 01766-830306.*)

Continuing north (A470), a 15-minute drive takes you over the pass to **Dolwyddlan Castle**, a 13th-century keep built by Prince Llewyn which was captured by Edward I and subsequently restored in the 19th century.

From Betws-y-Coed take the A5 to **Llangollen**, a town that has become the famous scene of the colorful extravaganza, the International Musical Eisteddfod, the contest for folk dancers, singers, orchestras, and instrumentalists. Llangollen's 14th-century stone bridge spanning the salmon-rich River Dee is one of Wales's Seven Wonders.

Leave Llangollen on the A542 and travel over the scenic Horseshoe Pass past the ruins of the Cistercian abbey, Valle Crucis, to **Ruthin**. Nestled in the fertile valley of Clwyd and closed in by a ring of wooded hills, Ruthin is an old, once-fortified market town whose castle is now a very commercialized hotel complete with medieval banquets.

From here a fast drive on the A494 returns you to England and motorways that quickly take you to all corners of the realm. But before leaving the area, visit the charming, medieval city of **Chester**. The Romans settled here in 79 A.D. and made Chester a key stronghold. Much of the original Roman wall survives, although many towers and gates seen today were additions from the Middle Ages. Chester is a fascinating city with a 2-mile walk around its **battlements**—the best way to orient yourself. It is fun to browse in **The Rows,** double-decker layers of shops—one layer of stores at street level and the other stacked on top.

London Hotel Map

Hotels

1 The Abbey Court
2 25 Dorset Square
3 Dorset Square Hotel
4 Brown's Hotel
5 22 Jermyn Street
6 The Stafford
7 Dukes Hotel
8 Knightsbridge Green Hotel
9 L'Hotel
10 Durley House
11 The Beaufort
12 The Franklin
13 Eleven Codogan Gardens
14 The Pelham Hotel
15 Number Sixteen

Places of Interest

A Natural History Museum
B Victoria & Albert Museum
C Buckingham Palace
D Houses of Parliament
E Horse Guards Parade
F National Gallery
G British Museum
H Covent Garden
I Royal Festival Hall
J Museum of the Moving Image
K St. Paul's Cathedral
L Tower of London
⊖ Underground station

111

From the outside, The Abbey Court appears to be nothing extraordinary—just one of the many similar houses along Pembridge Gardens: one would never guess the delightful surprise awaiting within. The lobby is intimate and lovingly renovated with carefully chosen antique furniture, mirrors, wall sconces, and elaborate bouquets of flowers accentuating the fabric-covered walls. Breakfast and afternoon tea are served in the conservatory. Every room offers maximum comfort and charm—three sport lovely four-poster beds.

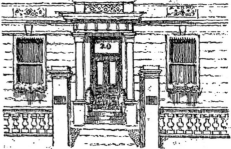

THE ABBEY COURT
Manager: J. M. Berner
Pembridge Gardens
London W2 4DU, England
Tel: (0171) 2217518 Fax: (0171) 7920858
22 rooms
Double: from £120 Suite: from £141
Credit cards: all major
Nearest underground: Notting Hill Gate

The Beaufort is an alluring example of the small luxury hotels that have sprung up in London in recent years. Privately owned and run, the emphasis is very much on treating guests as individuals and making them feel at home. It is newly decorated and carpeted throughout in warm pastel shades and displays 400 original English watercolors. Each room has a Walkman, VCR (they have a huge library of videos), brandy, shortbread, and chocolates—all included in the price, as is a glass of champagne on arrival. There's even a teddy bear. Breakfast is served in the rooms: fresh, hot rolls and croissants. The sitting room has plump sofas and chairs, books, and the company of Harry, the resident cat!

THE BEAUFORT
Manager: Jane McKevitt
Beaufort Gardens
London SW3 1PP, England
Tel: (0171) 5845252 Fax: (0171) 5892834
28 rooms
Double: from £192 Suite: £298
Credit cards: all major
Nearest underground: Knightsbridge

LONDON   BROWN'S HOTEL   Map: 4

Brown's Hotel is terribly British. An old-fashioned, even Victorian, rather stuffy elegance prevails, from the paneled lounge with comfortable sofas, where guests enjoy London's best cup of tea, to the guestrooms with their traditional decor. It is no wonder that Brown's has so much character—it was founded by Byron's valet, James Brown, and was a favorite of Kipling. Brown's is a superb choice for those who want a hotel with a very British atmosphere in the heart of the theatre district.

BROWN'S HOTEL
Manager: Reto Grass
Albermarle & Dover Streets
London W1A 4SW, England
Tel: (0171) 493 6020 Fax: (0171) 493 9381
117 rooms
Double: from £264
Credit cards: all major
Nearest underground: Piccadilly Circus

Dorset Square Hotel is in the area of London made famous by Sherlock Holmes. If you stay in one of the hotel's smallest, least expensive rooms, you find yourself enjoying the fabulous ambiance of a lovely hotel at a good-value-for-money price. The more expensive rooms are absolutely gorgeous. Staying here is like being a guest in an exquisite English home with intimate lounges filled with flowers, lovely oil paintings, and antique furnishings.

DORSET SQUARE HOTEL
Owners: Kit & Tim Kemp
Manager: Jeanette Cox
39–40 Dorset Square
London NW1 6QW, England
Tel: (0171) 7237874 Fax: (0171) 7243328
37 rooms, Double: from £130 Suite: from £188
Credit cards: all major
Nearest undergrounds: Marylebone & Baker Street

There is no sign that this Victorian townhouse in a quiet part of Chelsea is a hotel. You ring the doorbell, step into the paneled hall, sign the visitors' book, and are enveloped by the refined atmosphere of days gone by. It is rather like a discreet private club: Victorian wing chairs, guests daintily sipping afternoon tea, whispered conversations, a chauffeured Mercedes at your bidding. There is no restaurant, though light meals and breakfast are available to you through room service. All but one of the larger bedrooms are at the back of the hotel. Quite a contrast to the sedate hotel is its health club, Synergy, (situated in an adjacent house) where you can be pampered with beauty treatments, work out in the gym, swim, sauna, and steam.

ELEVEN CADOGAN GARDENS
Manager: Mark Fresson
11 Cadogan Gardens
London SW3 2RJ, England
Tel: (0171) 7303426 Fax: (0171) 7305217
61 rooms
Double: from £190 Suite: from £275
Credit cards: MC, VS
Nearest underground: Sloane Square

LONDON   25 DORSET SQUARE   Map: 2

If you are traveling with family or friends, and are not on a strict budget, you will adore 25 Dorset Square, a handsome Georgian building transformed into a marvelous, apartment-style hotel. The suites are truly scrumptious, each individually decorated, and abound with lovely antiques, country English chintzes, and stately, tall French windows. Several have grand pianos and all have open fireplaces. Although the suites are not inexpensive, if two couples were to take one together, each could have a private bedroom and bath and live in greater grandeur for much less money than two comparable rooms would cost in one of London's fine hotels.

25 DORSET SQUARE
Manager: M. Hangari
Dorset Square
London NW1 6QN, England
Tel: (0171) 2627505 Fax: (0171) 7230194
12 suites
Suite: from £170
Reductions for longer stays
Credit cards: all major
Nearest undergrounds: Marylebone & Baker Street

Dukes is a very special little hotel—one of our favorites. Conveniently located only steps from St. James's Street, Dukes is tucked into its own little gas-lit courtyard. Just off the lobby is a snug lounge and beyond is a paneled bar famous for its selection of cognacs where Salvatore, undoubtedly one of the most delightful barmen in London, holds court with a twinkle in his eye. The restaurant is elegantly traditional. The guestrooms are unfussy in their decor, each decorated in light colors with fine fabrics and furniture. Dukes is a superb, luxury category hotel, but if you love cozy elegance without an air of stuffy formality, this hotel is for you.

DUKES HOTEL
Manager: Andrew Phillips
St. James's Place
London SW1A 1NY, England
Tel: (0171) 4914840 Fax: (0171) 4931264
84 rooms
Double: from £188 Suite: from £247
Credit cards: all major
Nearest underground: Green Park

The suites at Durley House on Sloane Street are for those who want to have their own pied-à-terre in the heart of Knightsbridge. Kit and Tim Kemp (who also own the Dorset Square Hotel and the exquisite Pelham) have spared no expense in outfitting the suites in the most luxurious country-house style. Besides a bedroom and separate living room, all have a well stocked kitchen. If requested, a waiter will bring you dinner and serve it to you in your apartment. Across the road you can enjoy a game of tennis in Cadogan Park. A short walk brings you to Sloane Street's sophisticated shops.

DURLEY HOUSE
Owners: Kit & Tim Kemp
Manager: Kirsty Paton
115 Sloane Street
London SW1X 9PJ, England
Tel: (0171) 2355537 Fax: (0171) 2596977
11 suites
Suite: from £229
Credit cards: all major
Nearest underground: Sloane Square

LONDON   THE FRANKLIN   Map: 12

The Franklin is three houses in a mansion terrace knocked into one, just off the bustle of Brompton Road, an intimate hotel of the home-away-from-home genre. An elegant, traditional drawing room opens up to a tranquil oasis of green garden, the communal backyard for the mansions that abut it. There is no dining room but you can enjoy a traditional English tea. Rooms come in all shapes and sizes, the premier ones being the large poster rooms overlooking the gardens. David Naylor-Leyland owns a similar hotel, The Egerton House, just down the street where the rooms are smaller and more uniform in size.

THE FRANKLIN
Owner: David Naylor-Leyland
Manager: Karen Marchant
28 Egerton Gardens
London SW3 2DB, England
Tel: (0171) 5845533 Fax: (0171) 5845449
41 rooms
Double: from £176 Suite: from £223
Credit cards: all major
Nearest undergrounds: Knightsbridge & S. Kensington

Henry Togna's grandfather opened 22 Jermyn Street in 1915 as residential chambers— that is, in-town accommodation for country squires. Now it's a gracious townhouse hotel on an upscale street in close proximity to West End theatres and Piccadilly. A long hallway leads from the street to the desk at the foot of the stairs (there are no public rooms) and from here you are escorted to your luxurious room or elegant suite. A kitchen provides room service and bread for feeding the ducks in St. James's Park. Guests are welcome to join Henry Togna or Annette on their 5-mile jogs before breakfast.

22 JERMYN STREET
Owner: Henry Togna
Manager: Annette Foster
22 Jermyn Street
London SW1Y 6HL, England
Tel: (0171) 734 2353 Fax: (0171) 734 0750
13 suites, 5 studios
Studio: £222.85 Suite: from £281.60
Credit cards: all major
Nearest underground: Piccadilly Circus

Close to Harrods and Hyde Park and just a few yards from the Knightsbridge tube station, the Knightsbridge Green Hotel stands out as a hotel where the staff is friendly, the location superb, and the price reasonable. It is located in a tall, narrow building where an old-fashioned lift takes you from the tiny, street-level lobby to the five floors of bedrooms. Rooms are spacious and suites have a separate sitting room. The decor is sunny, with pastel-washed walls and pretty fabrics. Bathrooms are sparkling and modern. An English or Continental breakfast is served in the rooms. Coffee and tea are available in the small lounge during the day.

KNIGHTSBRIDGE GREEN HOTEL
Manager: Ann Thomson
159 Knightsbridge
London SW1X 7PD, England
Tel: (0171) 5846274 Fax: (0171) 2251635
25 rooms
Double: £110 Suite: £125
Credit cards: all major
Nearest underground: Knightsbridge

LONDON   L'HOTEL   Map: 9

The sister property of the adjacent Capital Hotel, this sophisticated bed and breakfast is decorated in a delightfully simple French country style with pine furniture. There are no public rooms but room service is available and the basement wine bar, Le Metro, has good-value lunches and dinners. The bedrooms, which vary in size, all have small, efficient bathrooms. If you book well in advance, you may be able to secure one of the three bedrooms that has a fireplace.

L'HOTEL
Manager: Debbie Eade
28 Basil Street
London SW3 1AT, England
Tel: (0171) 5896286 Fax: (0171) 2250011
12 rooms
Double: £145 Suite: £165
Credit cards: all major
Nearest underground: Knightsbridge

Number Sixteen provides the atmosphere of staying in town with friends—there is even a secluded, award-winning garden and conservatory. Guests are given front-door keys and encouraged to treat this deluxe pension as their home-away-from-home. Bedrooms are individually designed and several have a terrace onto the garden. Ornate plaster ceilings, individual decor, and antique furniture further enhance the feel of a private house. There is no restaurant but there are a great many close by. The location is convenient—just around the corner from South Kensington tube station.

NUMBER SIXTEEN
Manager: Jean Branham
16 Sumner Place
London SW7 3EG, England
Tel: (0171) 5895232 Fax: (0171) 5848615
36 rooms
Double: from £130
Credit cards: all major
Nearest underground: South Kensington

You might well pass by The Pelham thinking this is a private club, for only a classy brass plaque signifies that a hotel is within. Inside, no expense has been spared to create a romantic, inviting atmosphere. It has a lovely, small, paneled lounge and an attractive basement restaurant and bar. Sumptuous bouquets of flowers and gorgeous antiques set the mood of a fetching English country house hotel. Accommodations range from large suites to smaller rooms with twin, queen, or king beds. You are close to Christies and the Victoria and Albert Museum and surrounded by the interesting boutiques and restaurants of South Kensington..

THE PELHAM HOTEL
Owners: Kit & Tim Kemp
Manager: Sally Holt
15 Cromwell Place
London SW7 2LA, England
Tel: (0171) 5898288 Fax: (0171) 5848444
37 rooms
Double: from £170 Suite: from £264
Credit cards: all major
Nearest underground: South Kensington

LONDON   THE STAFFORD   Map: 6

The bustle of London seems far away from this quiet, refined hotel in historic St. James's just a short walk from Piccadilly. Ornate plaster ceilings grace the elegant lounge and excellent dining room. The amiable, private-club atmosphere is enhanced by an attractive small restaurant and a colorful little bar with a delightful patio. The most deluxe bedrooms are found in The Carriage House, a 350-year-old converted stable building. A longtime, friendly professional staff takes pride in offering the kind of personal service that makes loyal clients return to their "home" in London again and again.

The Stafford
Manager: Terry Holmes
16–18 St. James's Place
London SW1A 1NJ, England
Tel: (0171) 4930111 Fax: (0171) 4937121
74 rooms
Double: from £243 Suite: from £416
Credit cards: all major
Nearest underground: Green Park

Hotels in England

Rothay Manor is an exceptionally enjoyable hotel with the feel of a refined, old-fashioned British resort hotel where everything is done with kindness and without fuss. Waitresses in ankle-length, black dresses with white mop caps graciously take your dinner order and in the afternoon an array of trim little sandwiches, decorated cakes, and biscuits tempts you to partake of tea. Bedrooms are decorated in a more modern style, are comfortable and spotlessly kept—those at the front have balconies opening up to the garden and are preferable to those at the rear where a busy main road can disturb a quiet night's sleep during the summer when you are likely to have your windows open at night. A most attractive downstairs bedroom is available for those who use a wheelchair or have difficulty with stairs. The weather report is posted in the hallway so you can be prepared for the fickle Lake District weather. The Lake District's picturesque villages and stunning scenery are easily reached by car or explored on foot. Dove Cottage, Wordsworth's home, now a museum, is nearby. *Directions:* From Ambleside follow signs for Coniston (A593) and you will find the hotel in the middle of the one-way system on the outskirts of town.

ROTHAY MANOR
Owners: Nigel & Stephen Nixon
Rothay Bridge
Ambleside
Cumbria LA22 0EH, England
Tel: (015394) 33605 Fax: (015394) 33607
18 rooms
Double: from £113 Suite: from £161
Closed January & first two weeks February
Credit cards: all major
Children welcome

Just off the main A6 between the delightful market town of Bakewell and the Victorian spa town of Buxton is the peaceful, sleepy village of Ashford-in-the-Water. In the center of the village, next to the ancient Sheepwash bridge, with a walled garden that borders the River Wye, Sue and Roger Taylor have their country house hotel. Riverside has a cozy, Victorian ambiance and I always expect to see an Agatha Christie heroine like Miss Marples perched in the drawing room sipping afternoon tea. The center of the house is the golden-oak-paneled bar where a log fire burns brightly when needed. Here, before and after dinner, drinks are served. In the adjacent dining rooms the five-course dinner is from a set menu which changes monthly. Bedrooms in the old house vary in size, and a recent visit found them in need or refurbishment, while those in the "new" (albeit traditionally designed) wing are uniform in size, individually decorated, and have the advantage of immaculate modern bathrooms. Off the beaten tourist track, Derbyshire is an area of unsurpassed beauty. Long country walks in the Peak District National Park, visits to neighboring village pubs, and explorations of the stately Chatsworth estate, Haddon Hall, and Hardwick Hall are pursuits to be recommended. *Directions:* Ashford-in-the-Water is 4 miles northwest of Bakewell on the Buxton road (A6).

RIVERSIDE COUNTRY HOUSE
Owners: Sue & Roger Taylor
Ashford-in-the-Water
Near Bakewell
Derbyshire DE4 1QF, England
Tel: (01629) 814275 Fax: (01629) 812873
15 rooms
Double: from £104
Open all year
Credit cards: all major
Children over 10

Blagdon Manor is a spacious 17th-century farmhouse tucked away at the heart of the gently undulating northwest Devon countryside. Like our favorite romantic hideaways, it is very remote and sits in a landscape of fields and quiet country lanes. The manor was built as a large farmhouse in 1600, with an addition of a spacious Georgian drawing room adding elegance. Tim and Gill Casey moved to Devon after living for many years in Hong Kong and run their little hotel almost single-handedly so that guests really feel they are staying in the countryside with friends. Gill prepares a set, three-course dinner which is served on an elegant dining table especially made for the low-ceilinged, beamed room. After dinner guests often enjoy a game of billiards in the bar, or relax by the fire in the library lounge—rooms reached by going up the narrow winding staircase, past the bedrooms, and down again. Most of the country-cozy bedrooms are decorated in bright, sunny colors. All are accompanied by an immaculate white bathroom. To the west lies Boscastle Harbor and the ruins of Tintagel Castle while to the south you find Llanhydrock, a not-to-be-missed stately home. *Directions:* Leave Launceston on the Holsworthy road. Pass Chapman's Well and the first sign to Ashwater. Turn right at the second Ashwater sign and first right, signposted Blagdon. Blagdon Manor is on the right.

BLAGDON MANOR   **NEW**
Owners: Gill & Tim Casey
Ashwater
Devon EX21 5DF, England
Tel: (01409) 211224 Fax: (01409) 211634
7 rooms
Double: from £90
Open all year
Credit cards: all major
Children over 16

This former inn is now an intimate hotel with a renowned restaurant alluringly decorated with murals depicting the seasons: winter, summer, autumn, and spring. The restaurant serves delectable French food and there is a long and tempting wine list. The hotel delights in a friendly welcome from Michael and Patsy Harris and their staff. The only reminders that this was once a traditional pub are the flagged-stone bar with its Windsor chairs and a portrait of Michael's father with pint in hand in the drawing room. Six bedrooms are found within the walls of the original 17th-century inn. The remainder of the bedrooms surround a flower-filled brick courtyard in a converted brewery opposite the main building. Several of these rooms have access to the lovely walled gardens. Most of the parking is across a very busy main road by the pavilion which is used for weddings and conferences. The heart of nearby Aylesbury with its Tudor lanes and courtyards is very picturesque. If you are staying for some time, you can explore Oxford, Henley, and other Thames-side towns. London is about an hour away. *Directions:* The hotel is in an urban location, in Aston Clinton, on the A41, the main London to Aylesbury road.

THE BELL INN
Owners: Patsy & Michael Harris
Aston Clinton, near Aylesbury
Buckinghamshire HP22 5HP, England
Tel: (01296) 630252 Fax: (01296) 631250
21 rooms
Double: from £95 Suite: from £115
Open all year
Credit cards: AX, VS
Children welcome

There can be no better fate for a rundown country estate than to fall into the hands of Historic House Hotels who have meticulously restored Hartwell House which opened its doors as a luxurious country house hotel in 1989. The Great Hall with its ornate fireplace and decorative ceiling sets the scene for the grandeur of the place, yet this is no stuffy hotel—there is a comfortable air of informality. To the left is the oak-paneled bar which leads to the morning room and the library. The dining room is composed of several adjoining rooms which overlook the garden. The second-floor bedrooms, named after the members of the exiled King of France Louis XVIII's court who occupied them, are the largest and several have four-posters. Cozier, and less expensive, are the attic bedrooms, some of which open out onto a sheltered roof terrace where rabbits were reared and vegetables grown by the French émigrés. More bedrooms are found in the stable building adjacent to the conference center and Hartwell Spa with its spacious indoor swimming pool, gym, and beauty salon. A path leads into the walled garden which houses two tennis courts. The surrounding parkland with its ruined church, pavilion, and lake is perfect for long country walks. Oxford is just 20 miles away and Heathrow airport is less than an hour's drive. *Directions*: Hartwell House is 2 miles from Aylesbury on the A418, Oxford road.

HARTWELL HOUSE
Manager: Jonathan Thompson
Aylesbury
Buckinghamshire HP17 8NL, England
Tel: (01296) 747444 Fax: (01296) 747450
Toll-free fax from USA: 1-800-260-8338
47 rooms
Double: from £150 Suite: from £195*
*Breakfast not included
Open all year
Credit cards: all major
Children over 8

The Cavendish Hotel sits at the edge of the Chatsworth estate which surrounds one of England's loveliest stately houses, the home of the Duke and Duchess of Devonshire. Eric Marsh, the owner, has restored and expanded what was originally an 18th-century fishing inn into a fine hotel. The Garden Room (perfect for lunch and informal dinners) frames a panoramic view of the River Derwent meandering through green fields across the estate; comfy sofas and chairs in the adjacent lounge invite you to linger and relax. The bar is a cozy gathering spot for drinks before dinner in the highly commended dining room (you can request a table in a corner of the kitchen if you are anxious to peek at what happens behind the scenes). Bedrooms in the oldest part of the hotel have a lovely feel to them: I particularly enjoyed the spaciousness and old-world ambiance of the superior rooms. An adjoining wing of bedrooms with a more contemporary feel has been built to match the original building and called the Mitford Rooms after their designer, the Duchess of Devonshire, and her Mitford family. A pathway leads you on a beautiful walk through the Chatsworth estate to Chatsworth House. Explorations farther afield reveal unspoilt villages set in beautiful rolling countryside of stone-walled fields, green valleys, and spectacular dales. *Directions*: Exit the M1 motorway at junction 29 and follow signs for Chatsworth through Chesterfield to Baslow.

CAVENDISH HOTEL
Owner: Eric Marsh
Baslow
Derbyshire DE45 1SP, England
Tel: (01246) 582311 Fax: (01246) 582312
* Toll-free fax from USA: 1-800-235-5845*
24 rooms
Double: from £99 Suite: from £130*
*Breakfast not included
Open all year
Credit cards: all major
Children welcome

Fischer's at Baslow Hall is a dream place for a relaxed getaway, with delightful cooking, especially friendly service, and the delights of the Peak District National Park on your doorstep. This superb house with its lead-paned windows set in stone frames, dark-oak paneling, and wide-plank wooden floors has the feeling of a Tudor manor, yet it was built only in 1907 as a home for the Reverend Jeremiah Stockdale and continued to be a home until 1988 when Susan and Max Fischer purchased it to house their successful restaurant Fischer's, relocated from nearby Bakewell, and also provide the most tasteful of accommodation. The house is furnished and decorated with imagination and flair, with a delightful use of soft yet quite vivid colors to create a feeling of warmth. Max is a dedicated chef, offering traditional English dishes as well as more elaborate fare on his mouthwatering menus. Café Max is a simpler, less expensive, dining alternative to the restaurant. The surrounding countryside offers plenty to keep you busy for a week or longer—Chatsworth House, Haddon Hall, and (farther away) Hardwick Hall; mellow stone villages, the spa town of Buxton, and glorious Peak District scenery. *Directions:* Exit the M1 motorway at junction 29 and follow signs for Chatsworth through Chesterfield to Baslow where you follow the A623, Manchester road. Baslow Hall is on the right as you leave the village.

FISCHER'S AT BASLOW HALL
Owners: Susan & Max Fischer
Calver Road
Baslow
Derbyshire DE4 1RR, England
Tel: (01246) 583259 Fax: (01246) 583818
6 rooms
Double: from £95 Suite: from £120
Open all year
Credit cards: all major
Children over 10

From the moment you enter through the rustic porchway into the long, low, whitewashed Pheasant Inn, you are captivated by its charms: a front parlor all decked in chintz with an old-fashioned, open fire; a dimly lit, Dickensian bar with tobacco-stained walls and ceiling, oak settles, and clusters of tables and chairs; a long, low-beamed dining room, its tables covered with crisp damask cloths; dramatic fresh and dried flower arrangements; a blazing fire in the hearth beneath a copper hood in the sitting room, a large, airy room, once the old farm kitchen. Bedrooms are simply yet invitingly decorated, each neat as a new pin with equally attractive modern bathrooms. One has a half-tester bed with floral bed-ruffle and drapes—look carefully and you can see silhouettes of Albert and Queen Victoria incorporated into the design. Behind the inn a garden, with benches lining its pathways, tumbles into the beechwoods which belong (as does the inn) to Lord Inglewood's estate. The Pheasant Inn sits on a quiet country lane just out of sight of Bassenthwaite Lake. This is a quiet part of the Lake District with beautiful views round every corner. Sailing, boating, fishing, bird watching, and, of course, walking are available nearby. *Directions:* The Pheasant Inn is signposted on the A66, at the head of Bassenthwaite Lake, between Keswick and Cockermouth.

PHEASANT INN
Managers: Mary & Barry Wilson
Bassenthwaite Lake
near Cockermouth
Cumbria CA15 9YE, England
Tel: (017687) 76234 Fax: (017687) 76002
20 rooms
Double: from £75
Open all year
Credit cards: MC, VS
Children welcome

We welcome the Priory Hotel back to the pages of the guide. Its new owners have injected the capital necessary to refurbish the rooms and see the Priory return once again to being Bath's premier hotel. Happily, the excellent management team and friendly staff have remained with the hotel throughout the changes. Bedrooms and bathrooms have received a major face lift, bringing them into line with luxury country-house standards. By the time you arrive, the new restaurant, with its lovely view of the garden, may well have been completed and the hotel extended into the adjacent home. Because the Priory was once a grand private home, to the rear of the building is a large garden of rolling lawns and summer flowerbeds—a quiet oasis in this bustling city. Here you find a sheltered outdoor pool, which on hot summer days gives you the perfect excuse to forsake your sightseeing agenda. The Priory is located in a residential district towards the outskirts of Bath. *Directions:* Exit the M4 at junction 18, take the A46 into the center of Bath, then follow the A4 signposted Bristol. Pass Victoria Park on your right and at the end of this very large grassy park turn right into Park Lane then left into Western Road. The hotel is on your left after 300 yards.

PRIORY HOTEL   **NEW**
Manager: Tom Conboy
Weston Road
Bath
Avon BA1 2XT, England
Tel: (01225) 331922 Fax: (01225) 448276
28 rooms
Double: £175
Open all year
Credit cards: all major
Children welcome

If you want a fancy city hotel, then The Queensberry Hotel is not for you, but if you want a small, very friendly, good-value-for-money hotel in the heart of Georgian Bath, on a quiet side street, then this is the place to stay. The ladies who run the front desk are very helpful and friendly and have lots of information on Bath which you can peruse in the adjacent comfortable drawing room. Guestrooms that were at one time enormous drawing rooms with their tall and often decorative plaster ceilings command the highest tariff. Snug attic rooms with windows looking out across the rooftops are well priced to compensate for the inconvenience of climbing the stairs (there is a small lift if you need it). All the bedrooms are simply yet very tastefully appointed, with artistically draped fabrics as bedheads. A Continental breakfast is served in your bedroom or a full breakfast in the basement restaurant, the Olive Tree. Decorated in a casual Mediterranean style, the restaurant offers diners food that has received rave reviews, so it's best to make dinner reservations. *Directions:* When you make your reservation, ask the hotel for the very specific directions on how to find The Queensberry, just a few minutes' walk from the Royal Crescent, to be sent to you. On arrival, double park in front of the hotel while you unload your bags and receive parking advice.

THE QUEENSBERRY HOTEL
Manager: David Brooks
Russel Street
Bath
Avon BA1 2QF, England
Tel: (01225) 447928 Fax: (01225) 446065
22 rooms
Double: from £102
Closed for one week over Christmas
Credit cards: all major
Children welcome

Two hundred years ago, when the gentry came to Bath to "take the waters," the Royal Crescent was the most prestigious address. Two townhouses in the center of this famous cobbled crescent have been restored and incorporated into an elegant hotel complex with the Dower House and the Pavilion buildings reached by way of the garden. On a recent visit we had several concerns about the maintenance of the decor and the high prices charged for mediocre food. Furnished with period furniture and valuable works of art, the hotel recreates the atmosphere of Georgian Bath which was the social center of England for many years. The elegant, high-ceilinged drawing room sets the very sedate, formal atmosphere of the hotel. An additional drawing room and the restaurant are found in the Dower House. On warm summer evenings you can eat in the garden, choosing your meal from a short menu of classic summer dishes. The sweeping central staircase or the book-lined "library" lift give access to the elegant bedrooms and sumptuous suites in the main house—many of these high-ceilinged rooms have ornate plasterwork ceilings. Equally grand suites and rooms are found across the garden. To one side of the garden is a small plunge pool where you can swim against various-strength currents. *Directions:* The Royal Crescent is prominently marked on any detailed map of Bath.

THE ROYAL CRESCENT HOTEL
Manager: Simon Coombe
16 Royal Crescent
Bath
Avon BA1 2LS, England
Tel: (01225) 319090 Fax: (01225) 339401
42 rooms and suites
Double: from £170 Suite: from £305
Open all year
Credit cards: all major
Children welcome

As a result of the Battle of Hastings in 1066, England's history took an unexpected course and the town of Battle earned recognition on its map. On a hillside outside of town, the troops of King Harold and William of Normandy fought over the rightful succession to the throne. To celebrate his victory, William, henceforth named "the Conqueror," had Battle abbey built on the site of the battlefield. Three miles from this historic site is Netherfield Place, an attractive, Georgian-style, 1920s country house personally run by Helen and Michael Collier. They have created a very relaxed country house hotel where everything is done with a friendly smile. A comfortable bar adjoins the lounge where you can enjoy afternoon tea or a pre-dinner drink. The paneled dining room is popular with the locals at weekends—the food is traditional country-house fare incorporating many of the fruits, vegetables, and herbs grown in the walled acre-and-a-half vegetable garden. Bedrooms vary in size, with what were the principal bedrooms of the house being the largest and most comfortable. Around Battle there are Bodiam Castle, Rye, Winchelsea, and gardens at Great Dixter and Sissinghurst. Farther afield lies Canterbury. *Directions:* Battle is 6 miles north of Hastings. Leave town on the A2100 (Tunbridge Wells road) and take the first left (Netherfield road) for 2½ miles. Netherfield Place is on your left.

NETHERFIELD PLACE
Owners: Helen & Michael Collier
Battle
East Sussex TN33 9PP, England
Tel: (01424) 774455 Fax: (01424) 774024
14 rooms
Double: from £130
Closed for two weeks at Christmas
Credit cards: all major
Children welcome

Photographers find perfect compositions everywhere they turn in Bibury: Arlington Row, a cluster of early 17th-century cottages in the meadow by the River Coln, the Saxon/Norman village church, and The Swan Hotel with its trout ponds and pretty gardens facing the slowly flowing river by the bridge. For hundreds of years a simple hostelry—stables, a tap room, and a few simple bedrooms for travelers—stood on this site until the turn of the century when the landlord built capacious new quarters that were frequented by fashionable people who drove out in their motors to lunch or dine and stay overnight. Elizabeth and Alex Furtek recently refurbished the hotel and went to great pains to capture the spirit of the 1920s and 30s and combine it with the more traditional feel so you have, for example, a ballroom-sized, glittering dining room just steps from a cozy, chintzy parlor that was at one time the village post office. The old stables are a crayon-box-bright brassiere joined to the hotel by a bar where a contemporary-style mural depicts everyone involved in the hotel's recent refurbishment. Bedrooms are country-house style, each with a luxurious bathroom. From Bibury you may visit Bath with its Roman spa, Oxford with its spires and colleges, and Cheltenham. *Directions:* From Oxford take the A40 to 1 mile beyond Burford where you turn left on the B4425 towards Cirencester for 9 miles to Bibury.

THE SWAN HOTEL
Owners: Elizabeth & Alex Furtek
Bibury
Gloucestershire GL7 5NW, England
Tel: (01285) 740695 Fax: (01285) 740473
18 rooms
Double: from £115 Suite: from £190
Open all year
Credit cards: all major
Children welcome

Arriving in Blanchland gives one a sense of achievement, for it is far from the beaten path, nestling in a little valley amidst moors and forests. With little cottages, a church, and The Lord Crewe Arms set round a cobbled square, it is a fascinating village which has changed little since it was bequeathed by the Crewe family, in 1721, to a trust which administers the village. Public rooms are intriguing: the abbey kitchen is now the reception-lounge with two elegant old sofas drawn round its fire; the adjacent room has a gigantic fireplace with a "priest's hole," where General Forester hid after his band of Royalist Jacobites was defeated by Cromwell in 1715; the bar with its barrel-vaulted ceiling was once an abbey storeroom. Stairs twist up and around to the bedrooms: Number 17 is the most spacious, with large windows overlooking the garden, and Dorothy's Room comes complete with resident ghost, as well as a tiny shower room and a washbasin in the room. Across the cobbled square an additional ten bedrooms occupy The Angel, a former rival temperance hotel. September is the biggest bedroom with a large attic window looking across the cobbled square. The Lord Crewe Arms is an ideal base for explorations of Hadrian's Wall. *Directions:* From Newcastle take the A69 to Hexham and turn left in the center of town for the 10-mile drive to Blanchland.

LORD CREWE ARMS
Owners: Alex Todd, Peter Ginlell & Ian Press
Blanchland
near Durham
County Durham DH8 9SP, England
Tel: (01434) 675251 Fax: (01434) 675337
18 rooms
Double: from £80
Open all year
Credit cards: all major
Children welcome

The Devonshire Arms, previously a fishing inn, is now a traditional country house hotel resplendent with swimming pool and health spa. A wing of what were originally contemporary rooms has received a country-house-style refurbishment, though our favorite rooms are the ten in what was the original fishing inn. Rooms are identically priced with traditional (the hotel calls them themed) rooms commanding a small additional supplement. Mitford is feminine, Crace has an elegant four-poster, and Chatsworth with its fireplace is especially spacious. The Duke and Duchess of Devonshire's family portraits add a richness to the Long Lounge with its many groupings of comfortable chairs. Dinner in the Burlington restaurant is a formal affair: request a table in the pretty conservatory. For a change of pace you might want to frequent the adjacent Dukes pub, reached by a covered flagstone passageway, which is filled with fishing memorabilia celebrating the life of Percy Braithwaite, a famous local fisherman. Fast roads lead to York and Harrogate. Upper Wharfedale, one of the most scenic Yorkshire Dales, begins at your back door, the ruins of Bolton Abbey are across the fields, and a short drive brings you to Haworth and the Brontë sisters' parsonage. The hotel offers a variety of package holidays. *Directions:* The hotel stands on the B6160, 250 yds north of its roundabout junction off the A59, Skipton to Harrogate road.

THE DEVONSHIRE ARMS
Owners: Duke & Duchess of Devonshire
Manager: Martin Harris
Bolton Abbey near Skipton
North Yorkshire BD23 6AJ, England
Tel: (01756) 710441 Fax: (01756) 710564
40 rooms
Double: from £135 Suite: from £185
Open all year
Credit cards: all major
Children welcome

Woolley Grange, a gracious, 17th-century manor just outside Bradford-on-Avon, is the only listing in this guide that actively encourages families: Heather and Nigel Chapman have a very relaxed attitude towards children—they have four of their own (and a springer spaniel called Birdie). The old coach-house has been converted to a nursery (there is also a huge games room for older children) where children can spend an hour or a day. Little ones can have lunch and tea in the nursery and be tucked up in bed or watch a video in the library while parents enjoy the most excellent of dinners in the lovely dining room—the essence of a stay at Woolley Grange is eating the most delicious food. The bedrooms are scattered throughout the rambling house and the large cottage across the courtyard. Many have old fireplaces, most have creaking old floorboards, and all have sturdy antiques and old-brass or Victorian beds topped with goose-down duvets. There is a large heated swimming pool in the grounds and bikes are available for guests' use. The area is packed with interesting things to do and places to go: historic Bath and Wells, inviting Bradford-on-Avon and Lacock, Longleat House and Safari Park, and Stourhead House and Gardens. *Directions:* Woolley Grange is 8 miles from Bath at Woolley Green, off the B3109 north of Bradford-on-Avon.

WOOLLEY GRANGE
Owners: Heather & Nigel Chapman
Woolley Green
Bradford-on-Avon
Wiltshire BA15 1TX, England
Tel: (01225) 864705 Fax: (01225) 864059
20 rooms
Double: from £97 Suite: from £140
Open all year
Credit cards: all major
Children welcome

Farlam Hall is a superb place to hide away for a relaxed holiday and be thoroughly spoiled, enjoying the pampering attentions of this family-run hotel. Mum and dad, son and daughter and spouses make up the friendly team of one of only a handful of British hotels admitted to the French Relais et Chateaux group. You enter directly into the reception lounge which is full of sofas and chairs—a perfect spot for afternoon tea. The quality of everything, from the abundant antique furniture to the sumptuous food, is a delight. The same quality and good taste continue in the bedrooms which vary greatly in shape and size. My favorite larger rooms are the Garden Room, a grand, high-ceilinged room with an enormous four-poster bed, and the former maids' dormitory, a bright, light, flowery room whose large bathroom sports a Jacuzzi tub and separate shower. While Farlam Hall is a perfect place to break your journey if you are traveling between England and Scotland, it would be a shame to spend only one night in this charming hotel. Nearby sightseeing includes Carlisle and Hadrian's Wall. Day trips can be made to the Lake District and the Scottish border towns. *Directions:* Leave the M6 motorway at junction 43 and take the A69 towards Newcastle for 12 miles to the A689. The hotel is on your left after 2 miles (not in the village of Farlam).

FARLAM HALL
Owners: Joan & Alan Quinion
 Lynne & Barry Quinion
 Helen & Alastair Stevenson
Brampton
Cumbria CA8 2NG, England
Tel: (016977) 46234 Fax: (016977) 46683
12 rooms
Double: from £212 Dinner, B & B
Closed December 26 to 30
Credit cards: all major
Children over 5 (no reduction for children)

Set in the popular, tourist-thronged Cotswold village of Broadway, The Lygon Arms has been an inn since the 14th century. Its numerous little nooks include "the Gin Corner," the original snug with its old log fire; the Inglenook lounge, the inn's ancient kitchen, its huge fireplace hung with blackened spits and hooks; and the domed-ceiling drawing room, all chintz and elegance. The main wing with its creaking floors, heavy beams, and charming rooms furnished with grand antique pieces has the least expensive rooms with bathrooms down the hall and the most expensive: the Great Chamber whose ceiling soars to a thicket of beams and the Charles I Suite whose oak paneling has a secret staircase. A wing of turn-of-the-century rooms leads to the 1960s Garden wing with numerous contemporary-style rooms. Old adjoining properties have been taken over: the 18th-century Great Hall with its minstrels gallery is now the Lygon's restaurant; across the courtyard is a "country club" where residents can enjoy a game of billiards, use the weight room, or swim in the luxurious heated pool; an adjacent house is an up-market wine bar. Broadway is the most appealing of the mellow Cotswold stone villages, its street lined with antique shops and picture galleries. *Directions:* The Lygon Arms is on the main street in Broadway, which is between Stratford-upon-Avon and Cheltenham on the B4632.

THE LYGON ARMS
Manager: Kirk Ritchie
Broadway
Worcestershire WR12 7DU, England
Tel: (01386) 852255 Fax: (01386) 858611
65 rooms
Double: from £165 Suite: from £260
Open all year
Credit cards: all major
Children welcome

Two miles from the hustle and bustle of Broadway is the pretty, small village of Buckland where adjacent to the village church sits Buckland Manor surrounded by acres of gorgeous gardens. Wisteria hugs the walls, blowzy roses fill the flowerbeds, and a rushing stream tumbles beside the woodland walk. The exterior sets the tone for an interior where everything is decorated to perfection. Add masses of flowers and enviable antiques and you have the perfect country house hotel. Relax and enjoy a drink before the huge fireplace in the richly paneled lounge, curl up with a book in the sunny morning room, and relish the sense of occasion in the refined dining room. Bedrooms are elegant and every attention has been paid to every luxurious detail—some have wood-burning fireplaces and four-poster beds. From the moment Gilbert, the hall porter, greets you at the door you will be enveloped in the atmosphere of hushed gentility that pervades this gracious Cotswold manor. Warm weather enables you to enjoy the swimming pool, tennis court, and croquet lawn. Surrounding Buckland are other Cotswold villages with such appealing names as Chipping Campden, Upper and Lower Slaughter, Stow-on-the-Wold, and Upper and Lower Swell. Stratford-upon-Avon, Worcester, Bath, and Oxford are all within an hour's driving distance. Garden lovers will enjoy Kiftsgate, Hidcote Manor, and Batsford. *Directions* Buckland is 1½ miles from Broadway on the B4632.

BUCKLAND MANOR
Owners: Daphne & Roy Vaughan
Manager: Nigel Power
Buckland near Broadway
Worcestershire WR12 7LY, England
Tel: (01386) 852626 Fax: (01386) 853557
14 rooms
Double: from £165
Open all year
Credit cards: all major
Children over 12

The clomp of hooves as horses pulled carriages down the main street of Burford has long disappeared, but the inns that provided lodging and food to weary travelers remain and if you are in search of a simple, quaint hostelry, you can do no better than to base yourself at The Lamb for the duration of your Cotswold stay. A tall upholstered settle sits before the fireplace on the flagstone floor of the main room, the hall table displays gleaming brass jelly-molds, and an air of times long past pervades the place, particularly in winter when the air is heavy with the scent of woodsmoke and a flickering fire burns in the grate. Little staircases and corridors zigzag you up and down to the little bedrooms, all simply decorated in a charming, cottagey style. In the dining room chose from the short à la carte menu or enjoy the set three-course dinner which offers three choices for starters and main courses. The homey little bar with its stone-flagged floor and wooden settles has an indefinable mixture of character and atmosphere. Burford's main street is bordered by numerous antique, gift, and tea shops. There are mellow Cotswold villages to explore and Blenheim Palace and Oxford are less than an hour's drive away. *Directions:* Burford is midway between Oxford and Cheltenham (A40). The Lamb Inn is on Sheep Street, just off the village center.

THE LAMB INN
Owners: Caroline & Richard De Wolf
Manager: Paul Swain
Sheep Street
Burford
Oxfordshire OX8 4LR, England
Tel: (01993) 823155 Fax: (01993) 822228
15 rooms
Double: from £85
Open all year
Credit cards: MC, VS
Children welcome

Burnham Market is the most attractive of the Burnhams which encompass the little villages of Burnham Deepdale, Burnham Overy, Burnham Norton, and Burnham Market. Among the tidy cottages that surround the village green you find a delightful 17th-century pub, the Hoste Arms. It soon becomes apparent that this is not a run-of-the-mill old-world pub, for beyond the beamed public bar with its locals supping pints you find a piano-bar where jazz is played (Mondays and Fridays from April to September), the village shell collection, a guest sitting room that is also an art gallery, and a convivial staff of young Australians, New Zealanders, and South Africans taking a break from their round-the-world travels. Dining options range from tasty pub grub to sophisticated dining in the old-world restaurant. Bedrooms are found in the inn and a quiet stable extension to the rear which overlooks a grassy garden. I particularly liked the spaciousness of room 1, the decor and private patio of room 18, and the luxurious bathroom of room 17—well worth the few extra pounds. Smaller doubles have shower rooms, while larger doubles and twins have bathrooms with showers over the tubs. *Directions:* From King's Lynn take the A1491 around Hunstanton and continue on this road to Burnham Deepdale where you turn left for Burnham Market.

HOSTE ARMS **NEW**
Owner: Paul Wittome
The Green
Burnham Market
Norfolk PE31 8HD, England
Tel: (01328) 738777 Fax: (01328) 730103
21 rooms
Double: £60–92
Open all year
Credit cards: MC, VS
Children welcome

Set amidst a row of grand Georgian townhouses fronting a broad square, Twelve Angel Hill is a delightful upscale bed and breakfast operated with great professionalism by Bernadette (Bernie) and John Clarke. Breakfast is the only meal served in the formal dining room where little tables are topped with crisp linen cloths and surrounded by lovely antique chairs. In the evening guests often gather in the bar-cum-sitting room to discuss which of the 40 nearby restaurants or pubs they are going to dine at. Upstairs the bedrooms range from enormous to snug and all but the four-poster room and the suite are priced the same. I especially enjoyed the two large front bedrooms with spacious seating areas (the four-poster room overlooks the back of the house). Light sleepers be aware there may be a little late-night noise from the square on Fridays and Saturdays. On the square you have the 16th-century cathedral, the church of St. Mary's (even older than the cathedral), and nearby two museums. If you are there on a Wednesday or Saturday, do not miss the street market. Lavenham and Cambridge are popular places to visit. *Directions:* Follow the A14 to the Bury St. Edmunds ring road. Take the second exit (Bury St. Edmunds central) then at the next roundabout turn into Northgate Street. At the T-junction turn right into the square and Twelve Angel Hill is on your right—parking is to the rear. If arriving by train, take a taxi from the station.

TWELVE ANGEL HILL   **NEW**
Owners: Bernadette (Bernie) & John Clarke
12 Angel Hill
Bury St. Edmunds
Suffolk IP33 1UZ, England
Tel: (01284) 704088 Fax: (01284) 725549
6 rooms
Double: from £65
Closed January
Credit cards: all major
Children over 16

With its wrap-around verandah the Danescombe Valley Hotel looks as though it should be an ante-bellum home along the Mississippi rather than in Cornwall overlooking the broad reaches and looping curves of the River Tamar. Built in 1856, it is now the home of Anna and Martin Smith who invite you to share its allure and welcome. Dinner consists of four courses but since there are no choices, discuss any dietary needs you might have with Anna before arrival. Three bedrooms have French windows that open onto a broad verandah. Two of these rooms have small bathrooms tucked into the corner, while the third has its large bathroom across the hall (robes are provided). My favorite room is at the top of the house: though it does not have a verandah it does have a very large bathroom and a window seat for watching the ebb and flow of the river. A local boatman will take you for excursions on the river. A 15-minute walk brings you to Cotehele House with its original furniture and delightful gardens and Cotehele Mill with its adjoining cider press restored to working order. *Directions:* From Tavistock take the A390 to Gunnislake. At the top of the hill turn left to Albaston then left to Calstock. Go under the viaduct, turn sharp right, and follow the river for half a mile to the hotel.

DANESCOMBE VALLEY HOTEL
Owners: Anna & Martin Smith
Lower Kelly
Calstock
Cornwall PL18 9RY, England
Tel & fax: (01822) 832414
5 rooms
Double: from £125
Open April to November & Christmas
Closed every Wednesday & Thursday
Extra charge for payment by credit card
Children over 12

Paul and Kay Henderson have achieved their goal of providing one of the finest small hotels and restaurants in England. Guests have come to expect the best and this is what they receive. Prices are high but so are the standards of luxury and the attention to detail. There are only 16 lovely bedrooms: 14 in the beautiful, Tudor-style home and a 2-bedroom suite in a quaint, thatched cottage overlooking the croquet lawns. The largest bedrooms are on the second floor and those at the front of the house offer lovely views across the valley. The public rooms are paneled in oak with open log fires burning throughout the year. Chef Michael Caines professionally designs the evening meal, considering the fresh produce available each day from local farmers, the hotel's own garden, and the catch from local fishermen. Paul is particularly proud of his extensive wine list, one of the finest in Britain. Chagford is a delightful country town on the edge of Dartmoor. The wild beauty of Dartmoor, with its sheltered villages and towns beneath the looming moor, has a magic all its own—country rambles and cream teas are *de rigueur* when visiting this area. *Directions:* From Chagford Square turn right (at Lloyds Bank) into Mill Street. After 150 yards fork right and go downhill to Factory Crossroad. Go straight across into Holy Street and follow the lane for 1½ miles to the end.

GIDLEIGH PARK
Owners: Kay & Paul Henderson
Chagford
Devon TQ13 8HH, England
Tel: (01647) 432367 Fax: (01647) 432574
14 rooms, 1 suite:
Double: from £275 Dinner, B & B
Suite: from £325 Dinner, B & B
Open all year
Credit cards: all major
Children welcome

Cheltenham was a fashionable destination during the Regency period and today the classical squares and terraces built in delightful garden settings are the town's pride. A fine Regency villa on the edge of Pittville Park has been beautifully restored and opened as a most attractive hotel by Darryl Gregory. Guests share the comfortable library-sitting room with Emily the cat and enjoy drinks and after-dinner coffee in the high-ceilinged drawing room-cum-bar. While there are several restaurants within walking distance, you can do no better than to dine in the hotel, choosing your meal from the short à la carte menu or enjoying the meal of the day. The elegant, smartly decorated bedrooms are named after historic figures associated with the house. I especially enjoyed the Duke of Gloucester room, richly decorated in shades of dark red, and Mead with its sunny yellow decor. Billed as the capital of the Cotswolds, Cheltenham offers excellent shopping and lots of specialist antique shops. Horse-racing takes place at Cheltenham during the autumn and winter months. A ten-minute drive finds you in the midst of the honey-colored stone Cotswold villages. *Directions:* Arriving in Cheltenham, follow signs for city center onto the one-way system then follow signposts for Evesham. The Hotel on the Park is on the left, just as you reach Pittville Park (right) after passing a row of Regency town houses.

HOTEL ON THE PARK   **NEW**
Owner: Darryl Gregory
Evesham Road
Cheltenham
Gloucestershire GL52 2AH, England
Tel: (01242) 518898 Fax: (01242) 511526
12 rooms
Double: from £85 Suite: from £115
Open all year
Credit cards: all major
Children over 8

Though we would not normally include an 86-room hotel in this book, Chester is such a fascinating city that I decided to suggest the Grosvenor as a place to stay with a particular recommendation that you go there on a weekend when it is much more affordable than on weekdays. This palatial, Victorian establishment has in recent years undergone a complete refurbishment and now offers a book-lined library lounge where afternoon tea is served, a street-front, trendy brasserie, and the Arkle restaurant with its Michelin-starred food. Up the grand staircase are the commodious, elegant suites and smaller and more plainly decorated bedrooms. I found Abbotsford, a four-poster room with a Jacuzzi tub in the bathroom, to be the most outstanding "ordinary" bedroom. A small leisure center offers a sauna, sunbed, and exercise equipment. Begin your explorations of Chester by climbing to the top of the adjacent walls at Eastgate Arch crowned by the much-photographed clock commemorating the Diamond Jubilee of Queen Victoria in 1897. From here a 2-mile circuit of the city's ancient walls will give you a look at the city. The Rows are double-decker layers of shops—one layer of stores at street level and the other above. *Directions:* The Chester Grosvenor is half a mile from the railway station. If arriving by car, follow signs for the city center and park on floor 2A of Newgate car park. then ring the doorbell for access to the hotel.

CHESTER GROSVENOR HOTEL
Manager: Jonothan Slater
Eastgate Street
Chester CH1 1LT, England
Tel: (01244) 324024 Fax: (01244) 313246
86 rooms
Double: from £140 weekend
Double: from £170 weekday (breakfast not included)
Open all year
Credit cards: all major
Children welcome

What sets this country house hotel apart are the outstanding facilities offered by its luxurious indoor pool, saunas, steam rooms, solariums, and billiard room. Coincidentally, it is one of only a handful of hotels where I found families with young children in residence. This old Cotswold manor has two lounges (one all cozy with heavy beams and a welcoming fireplace and the other smart and formal) and a restaurant that extends into several cozy, low-ceilinged rooms. The majority of bedrooms are in adjacent converted farm buildings that have been cleverly connected to the main house by long corridors. I especially enjoyed Corbet, a most attractive room in the original house, and Stafford, a superior room in the one-time farm buildings. Children are welcomed into the dining room at breakfast but in the evening it is preferred that they are served an early supper and tucked into bed so that dinner is an adult occasion. Within 2 miles of Charingworth are Hidcote and Kiftsgate Gardens and Chipping Campden, an adorable 14th-century wool village peppered with heavily thatched cottages. Hidcote Manor Gardens is a series of alluring gardens each bounded by sculpted hedges with linked paths and terraces. Next door, another outstanding garden, Kiftsgate Court, has exquisite displays of roses. *Directions:* From Chipping Campden take the B4035 towards Shipston on Stour and Charingworth Manor is on the left-hand side after 3 miles.

CHARINGWORTH MANOR
Manager: Colin Heaney
Chipping Campden
Gloucestershire GL55 6NS, England
Tel: (01386) 593555 Fax: (01386) 593353
24 rooms
Double: from £120 Suite: from £220
Open all year
Credit cards: all major
Children welcome

If you want to stay in an idylically pretty Cotswold town that has changed little over the centuries, opt for the Cotswold House Hotel in Chipping Campden. Step into the impressive hallway with its stone-paved floor from which a grand staircase spirals up the ornate, trompe l'oeil stairwell. Opening up from the hallway are the handsome, high-ceilinged sitting rooms decked out in traditional country-house finery. Bedrooms by and large are in the country house vein (Honeysuckle is a particularly restful room). However, you can also opt for more non-traditional decor such as that in the Indian room with its onion-dome headboards and tiger's head over the bed. For dinner choose either the elegant restaurant where ceiling-high French windows frame views of the garden or the casual bistro. Chipping Campden has an ancient Market Hall where sheep from the surrounding farms were sold, and there are many interesting little shops, two old churches, and lots of pubs. A short distance away lies Hidcote, a series of alluring gardens each bordered by sculptured hedges and linked with paths and terraces. Next door, Kiftsgate has exquisite displays of roses. *Directions:* From Broadway take the A44 towards Stow-on-the-Wold up the hill and turn left for Chipping Campden. At the T-junction turn right into High Street, and Cotswold House Hotel is on your left in the main square. Parking is in the square or behind the hotel in a small private parking lot.

COTSWOLD HOUSE HOTEL   **NEW**
Owners: Louise & Christopher Forbes
The Square
Chipping Campden
Gloucestershire GL55 6AN, England
Tel: (01386) 840330 Fax: (01386) 840310
15 rooms
Double: from £104
Closed Christmas
Credit cards: all major
Children over 8

Situated in the middle of the pretty red-brick village of Cuckfield is Ockenden Manor, in part Tudor, with Victorian and contemporary additions. Viewing the manor from the garden, you appreciate that this combination of building styles is a very pretty one. The spacious sitting room overlooks the garden and the adjacent dining room, with its dark-oak paneling and low, decorative-plasterwork ceiling, is most attractive. A maze of winding corridors and stairs leads to the smallish bedrooms in the older wings: opt for the easier-to-locate rooms in the Garden wing with its new rooms made to look old. They offer spacious quarters and most attractive decor. The four-poster room here is particularly attractive—I did not enjoy the four-poster in the main house where the bedroom windows open to a view of a wall and drainpipes. Less than a half-hour drive finds you in Brighton where seaside honky-tonk contrasts with the vivid spectacle of the onion domes of the Royal Pavilion, the Prince Regent's extravaganza of a home. Enjoy browsing in Brighton's Lanes where old fishermen's cottages are now antique and gift shops. Farther afield, along the coast, lie the massive keep and towers of Arundel Castle. *Directions:* From Gatwick Airport take the M23/A23 to the B2115 signposted Cuckfield. In Cuckfield turn right into Ockenden Lane and the manor is at the end of the lane.

OCKENDEN MANOR   **NEW**
Manager: Kerry Turner
Ockenden Lane
Cuckfield
West Sussex RH17 5LD, England
Tel: (01444) 416111 Fax: (01444) 415549
22 rooms
Double: from £100 Suite: from £165
Open all year
Credit cards: all major
Children welcome

Dorchester, made famous as Casterbridge in native son Thomas Hardy's novels, still has a great deal of character, even though it is not as prosperous as it used to be. John and Stuart Turner (who own the Priory in nearby Wareham) recognized the potential of their grandparents' home, a lovely 1790 Georgian house on the High Street, and converted it into a townhouse hotel. While John runs the luxurious Priory, Stuart and his wife, Rita, concentrate on this more modest hotel. Breakfast is the only meal served in the little conservatory or snug breakfast room but menus of local restaurant are on hand in the traditionally furnished front parlor to help with where to go for dinner. Bedrooms are found both in the house and just a few steps across the courtyard in a modern townhouse. While the new rooms are most attractively decorated and two of the ground-floor rooms have private terraces, I much preferred the ambiance of the rooms in the main house which vary in size from snug doubles tucked under the eaves to the more spacious quarters offered by room 4, a most attractive twin-bedded room. Favorite sightseeing includes Hardy's cottage, Maiden Castle, and Corfe Castle, and Salisbury and Shaftesbury are within touring distance. Other attractions include the Dorset coast at Lulworth Cove, Durdle Door, and Ringstead Bay. *Directions:* The Casterbridge Hotel is on High East Street (A35) in the center of Dorchester.

THE CASTERBRIDGE HOTEL   **NEW**
Owners: Rita & Stuart Turner
49 High East Street
Dorchester
Dorset DT1 1HU, England
Tel: (01305) 264043 Fax: (01305) 260884
16 rooms
Double: from £55
Open all year
Credit cards: all major
Children welcome

One of England's most elegant small country house hotels, Gravetye Manor maintains the warmth and friendliness of a private club. The staff is absolutely dedicated to making all guests feel very special. All the ingredients are on hand to ensure that those who visit have a wonderful experience: a magnificent Elizabethan manor isolated by acres of woodlands and set in glorious gardens landscaped by onetime owner William Robinson who pioneered the natural look in English gardens. Inside, the manor lives up to every expectation: the rooms are elegantly yet comfortably furnished with soft-toned fabrics which contrast warmly with intricately carved wood paneling. Fine antiques blend comfortably with this lovely old house. The dining room is beautiful and the food exceptional. Throughout the southeast corner of England are an abundance of glorious gardens and stately homes: Chartwell (Churchill's home), Hever Castle, Penshurst Place, and Sheffield Gardens. *Directions:* Exit the M23 at junction 10 onto the A264, signposted East Grinstead. After 2 miles, at the roundabout, take the B2028 (Haywards Heath and Brighton) and after Turners Hill watch for the hotel's sign.

GRAVETYE MANOR
Owner: Peter Herbert
General Manager: Mark Yates
Near East Grinstead
West Sussex RH19 4LJ, England
Tel: (01342) 810567 Fax: (01342) 810080
18 rooms
Double: from £135 to £223*
*Breakfast & VAT not included
Open all year
Credit cards: all major
Babes in arms & children over 7

Nestling up to the little village of Evershot deep in Thomas Hardy country, Summer Lodge was built by the Earl of Ilchester in 1789. Thomas Hardy (who was an architect before he became a writer) designed the Lodge's first addition, the elegant high-ceilinged drawing room. More recently Margaret and Nigel Corbett have added their changes with the conversion of the stables into luxurious bedrooms and the building of a swimming pool and tennis court. The result is a house of contrasts where you walk from cozy-cottage sitting room (complete with resident cat) to gracious, high-ceilinged drawing room with floor-to-ceiling windows. It's a similar situation with the bedrooms which vary from cottage-cozy to the expansive spaciousness of room 1 (I particularly enjoyed rooms 17 and 18 with their private patios bordering the swimming pool). Whatever room you choose, you will enjoy the mellow tranquillity of this hotel with its exquisite restaurant and delightful decor enhanced by beautiful flower arrangements— but, most of all, what makes this hotel stand out from others is the dedicated caring of owners Margaret and Nigel. *Directions:* From Dorchester take the A37 towards Yeovil for 10 miles and turn left for Evershot. When you arrive at the village turn left into Summer Lane and the hotel is on your right after 100 yards.

SUMMER LODGE   **NEW**
Owners: Margaret & Nigel Corbett
Evershot
Dorset DT2 0JR, England
Tel: (01935) 83424 Fax: (01935) 83005
16 rooms
Double: from £125
Junior suite: from £225
Open all year
Credit cards: all major
Children welcome

The heart and soul of a successful country house hotel are its owners and at Stock Hill House Nita and Peter Hauser fill the bill perfectly, with the ebullient Nita presiding over the front of house and Peter being the chef. Prior to opening, Nita and Peter spent several years restoring and furnishing this nine-bedroom Victorian home. The result is a pleasing eclectic decor: step in the front door to be greeted by two 6-foot prancing wooden Indian horses cavorting in front of a floor-to-ceiling French mirror. The mood is that of a luxurious private residence where you can stroll through the acres of garden to work up an appetite. At dinner vegetables from the garden and local Dorset produce are the order of the day, but remember to save room for one of Austrian-born Peter's decadent desserts. Bedrooms are delightful, but I was particularly drawn to room 4 and the opportunity to repose in an elegant, extra-large, ornate wrought-iron bed that once belonged to a Spanish princess. Stock Hill is an ideal base to visit Sherbourne Abbey, Stourhead Gardens, Wells Cathedral, Glastonbury with its King Arthur connections, and the Saxon town of Shaftesbury. *Directions:* Leave the M3 at junction 8 and take the A303 towards Exeter for 4 miles, turning onto the B3081 for Gillingham and Shaftesbury. Stock Hill is on your right after 3 miles.

STOCK HILL HOUSE   **NEW**
Owners: Nita & Peter Hauser
Gillingham
Dorset SP8 5NR, England
Tel: (01747) 823626 Fax: (01747) 825628
9 rooms
Double: £190–220
Open all year
Credit cards: MC, VS
Children over 7

High on the hillside above the popular Lake District village of Grasmere, isolated by 3 acres of secluded gardens, sits Michael's Nook, a grand Victorian house now run as a superlative country house hotel by Elizabeth and Reg Gifford. You enter into a large wood-paneled, antique-filled entrance hall which leads to the drawing room with its large windows framing gorgeous green views of the garden, soft damask sofas, Oriental carpets, and on either side of the grand fireplace massive flower arrangements. Guests gather in the homely, old-world-hostelry-style bar before dinner. The heart of Michael's Nook is the restaurant whose deep-red walls and gleamingly polished tables set with silver and crystal form an elegant backdrop for an evening-long, five-course dinner. Bedrooms come in all shapes and sizes (and all price ranges) from the least expensive, small but pretty room to the grandest suite which has a sitting room upstairs, a spiral staircase leading down to the bedroom, and French doors which open onto a garden terrace. Personal favorites are the twin, Woodpecker, and the four-poster room, Chaffinch. Just down the lane is Dove Cottage, poet William Wordsworth's cottage from 1799 to 1808. Also nearby is Rydal Mount, his home from 1813. *Directions:* Take the A591 to Grasmere: do not go into the village but turn uphill off the A591 beside the Swan Hotel.

MICHAEL'S NOOK
Owners: Elizabeth & Reg Gifford
Grasmere near Ambleside
Cumbria LA22 9RP, England
Tel: (015394) 35496 Fax: (015394) 35645
14 rooms
Double: from £190 Dinner, B & B
Suite: from £340 Dinner, B & B
Open all year
Credit cards: all major
Children by arrangement

This cozy little hotel tucked in a garden off the Ambleside to Grasmere road has (like so many places hereabouts) associations with poet William Wordsworth who lived just down the road at Rydal Mount—it was lived in by his descendants until the 1930s. Now it is owned by Susan and Peter Dixon who, while giving guests their personal attention, give the same attention to detail that you find at much fancier establishments. Peter exercises his culinary talents in the five-course dinners which are freshly prepared and served in the cottage-style dining room. The small adjacent lounge guarantees conviviality amongst the guests. Each bedroom has its own character—No.1 is a particularly attractive twin with a ribbon-and-bow-motif running through the bedspread fabric and also has a small grassy patio. Two additional bedrooms are in nearby Brockstone Cottage. Guests can fish on nearby Rydal Water and have free use of a local leisure club. Lakeland scenery is glorious whether you come in spring when the famous daffodils bloom, in summer with the crowds, or in autumn when the bracken and leaves turn golden-brown. You can stroll to Rydal Mount and Dove Cottage, Wordsworth's famous homes. *Directions:* White Moss House is on the A591 between Ambleside and Grasmere.

WHITE MOSS HOUSE
Owners: Susan & Peter Dixon
Rydal Water
Grasmere
Cumbria LA22 9SE, England
Tel: (015394) 35295 Fax: (015394) 35516
7 rooms
Double: from £73 Suite: from £100
Open March to November
Credit cards: MC, VS
Children over 8

A French name for the loveliest of English country house hotels is appropriate because this heavenly hotel is owned by a Frenchman, one of the top chefs in England, Raymond Blanc. Before you are seduced by its luxurious charms and exquisite food, it is only fair to mention that this hotel is incredibly expensive. Yet for a hotel that blends captivating surroundings with beautiful decor and exquisite food it is worth every penny. The bedrooms themselves are reason enough to come and stay—each offers the ultimate in luxury without overdoing it: beautiful antique furniture, coordinated carpets, curtains and walls, plump beds topped by crisp, white lace pillows, and welcoming glasses of Madeira. There are large bathrooms, several with gracious oval tubs, soft robes, and fluffy towels—no expense has been spared to offer the most luxurious of everything. But it is Raymond Blanc's exceptional cuisine that really makes the place—the food is outstanding (rated two stars by Michelin). Oxford is a 15-minute drive away, Heathrow 30 minutes, and London 45. *Directions:* Le Manoir is in the village of Great Milton, a mile from the M40 (exit 7).

LE MANOIR AUX QUAT' SAISONS
Owner: Raymond Blanc
Church Road
Great Milton
Oxford OX44 7PD, England
Tel: (01844) 278881 Fax: (01844) 278847
19 rooms
Double: from £175 Suite: from £325
Open all year
Credit cards: all major
Children welcome

Congham Hall is a splendid Georgian country house hotel in the pretty Norfolk countryside set in 40 acres of parkland just 6 miles from the historic port of King's Lynn. Congham Hall has paddocks, a small swimming pool, a tennis court, a glorious kitchen garden full of veggies, fruits, and over 300 varieties of herbs, vast lawns, and the village cricket pitch. The inside is as attractive as out: suites are large and divine with king-sized beds and magnificent marble bathrooms and each pretty bedroom has a lovely bathroom. Peach-colored walls, crisp white linens, and a lovely view enhance the restaurant. Dinner is a divine, evening-long occasion with either a three- or four-course or a gourmet dinner where the courses are a series of starters in the manner of the tasting menus of France. The atmosphere is quiet and serene—either Christine or Trevor Forecast is always there to offer friendly assistance. Nearby places of interest include the Queen's retreat, Sandringham, miles of quiet beaches, the historic port of King's Lynn from which George Vancouver set out to explore the northwest coast of America, and Caley Mill where sweet-scented lavender is grown. *Directions:* Take the A149 from King's Lynn towards Cromer, then at the second roundabout turn right on the Sandringham/Fakenham road. After 100 yards turn right to Grimston and Congham Hall.

CONGHAM HALL
Owners: Christine & Trevor Forecast
Grimston
near King's Lynn
Norfolk PE32 1AH, England
Tel: (01485) 600250 Fax: (01485) 601191
14 rooms
Double: from £115 Suite: from £165
Open all year
Credit cards: all major
Children over 12

Near the center of England lies Oakham, the once-proud capital of what was England's smallest county, Rutland. Close by is Rutland Water where you drive onto a spit of land stretching out into the middle of the lake. At its end is the quiet village of Hambleton and a jewel of a hotel, Hambleton Hall. The staff is caring, anxious above all else to please. The motto over the front door echoes the relaxed, happy atmosphere: "Fay Ce Que Voudras" or "Do As You Please"—I cannot imagine anyone leaving Hambleton Hall discontented. The garden tumbles towards the vast expanse of water with rolling hills as a backdrop and behind a wall is a sheltered, heated pool. The interior is decorated with great flair and complemented by enormous flower arrangements. The lounge with its large inviting windows provides glorious water views. In fine weather enjoy lunch and tea on the terrace. Delicious smells will tempt you to the award-winning restaurant. The bedrooms are adorable, the decorations varying from soft English pastels to the vibrant rich colors of India. Tim Hart produces a witty booklet, "Things to do around Hambleton Hall" which covers shopping in Oakham and Stamford; visits to the country houses of Burghley and Belton; and trips to Cambridge and Lincoln. *Directions:* From the A1 take the A606 (Oakham road) through Empingham and Whitwell and turn left for Hambleton and Hambleton Hall.

HAMBLETON HALL
Owners: Stefa & Tim Hart
Hambleton near Oakham
Leicestershire LE15 8TH, England
Tel: (01572) 756991 Fax: (01572) 724721
15 rooms
Double: from £135
Open all year
Credit cards: all major
Children welcome

On the banks of the River Avon slipping slowly through green fields sits The Mill at Harvington, converted from the bakery served by the original mill downstream. This is an unpretentious, very welcoming hotel run with great enthusiasm by Jane and Simon Greenhalgh and Sue and Richard Yeomans. Several small rooms have been combined into a sitting room where heavy bakehouse oven doors decorate the fireplace mantle, small Victorian-style parlor chairs in shades of burgundy and jade are arranged into little conversation groups, and French windows open to a broad expanse of lawn that slopes down to the river. Oatcake, Bannock, Porcupine, and Flowerpot are some of the bedrooms named after types of loaves of bread. All are prettily decorated in very soft shades of pink, blue, and peach. If you stay for two nights, ask for the well priced dinner, bed, and breakfast rate. From Harvington a half-hour drive brings you to the china factories at Worcester, the magnificent castle at Warwick, Shakespearean Stratford, and Cotswold villages such as Chipping Campden and Broadway. *Directions:* Take the A435 from Evesham towards Alcester for 2 miles, ignoring all signs for Harvington, and turn right on the B439 (signposted Bidford). The Mill is signposted on your right after ¾ mile.

THE MILL AT HARVINGTON
Owners: Jane & Simon Greenhalgh
 Sue & Richard Yeomans
Anchor Lane
Harvington, Evesham
Worcestershire WR11 5NR, England
Tel & fax: (01386) 870688
15 rooms
Double: from £85
Closed last week of December
Credit cards: all major
Children over 10

Hawnby is a quiet little village in the heart of the North York Moors with a few houses, a shop, a Wesleyan chapel, and a drovers' inn. The Countess of Mexborough, whose estate the village is on, decided in the 1980s to convert her hostelry to a small hotel while still keeping the lively public bar. Sofas and chairs are grouped round the fire at one end of the sitting room and at the other end little tables are set for dinner or breakfast. Dinner is good home cooking with choices in each of the three courses, but I did not like the glass-topped tables and paper napkins. The decor throughout is soft and pretty, with soft, flowery drapes, attractive bedspreads, and pretty wallpapers. The bedrooms are named after their most predominant color, with Cowslip a favorite in soft yellows, Jade very attractive with jade-green wallpaper, and Rose a smaller room of soft pinks with roses. The manager, Dorothy Allanson, finds that guests love visiting the traditional open-air markets so prevalent in the area. *Directions:* Helmsley is on the A170 midway between Thirsk and Pickering. Turn along the side of the market place and follow B1257 signposted Stokesley out onto the moor. Hawnby is signposted to your left after 3 miles. Please note that guests are not able to check in between 3 and 6 pm.

HAWNBY HOUSE HOTEL:
Owner: Countess of Mexborough
Manager: Dorothy Allanson
Hawnby near Helmsley
N. Yorks Y06 5QS, England
Tel: (01439) 798202 Fax: (01439) 798417
6 rooms
Double: from £70
Closed January and February
Credit cards: MC, VS
Children over 10

Helmsley, a collection of gray-stone houses grouped round a traditional market square, lies at the edge of the glorious North York Moors, an area of wild and magnificent scenery where webs of little roads cross vast stretches of heather-covered moorlands joining hamlets and villages nestling in snug green valleys. Bordering the market square, a traditional old Yorkshire coaching inn has served travelers for well for over 150 years in this beautiful town. Old adjoining properties have been taken over—a Georgian house and a black-and-white Tudor rectory. A large new wing of rooms has been built next to the lovely back garden where old-fashioned wicker chairs are set on the lawns amongst beds of scented flowers. But The Black Swan is little changed: its higgledy-piggledy maze of little low-beamed rooms gives it a snug feeling, and its traditional furniture, lounges with old-fashioned chintzy chairs, and attentive staff all add to its charms. Eating and drinking is a great joy at The Black Swan. The chef knows how to satisfy Yorkshire tastes and appetites with traditional roasts, fillets, and chops. Fresh fish and vegetarian dishes are always on the menu. The most popular places to visit are Rievaulx Abbey, York, Castle Howard, Robin Hood's Bay, Whitby, and the folk museum at Hutton-le-Hole. *Directions:* Helmsley is on the A170 midway between Thirsk and Pickering.

THE BLACK SWAN
Manager: Steve Maslen
Helmsley
North Yorks Y06 5BJ, England
Tel: (01439) 770466 Fax: (01439) 770174
44 rooms
Double: from £100
Open all year
Credit cards: all major
Children welcome

Hintlesham Hall is a serene country house hotel that you will soon come to love. The grand Georgian façade is well matched inside, with the grand salon sumptuously decorated in soft pastels highlighting its lofty ceiling. More intimate in their proportions are the pine-paneled dining room and the book-lined library lounge with its Regency-red walls and soft-green sofas. There is an array of bedrooms varying in size from opulent, two-story affairs, through grand, traditional four-poster rooms to small, snug bedrooms. The warm, pine-paneled bar with its comfortable sofas and chairs grouped round a large fireplace and the large book-lined library with its magnificent old billiard table are particularly inviting. Bedrooms have lovely fabrics, antiques, sparkling modern bathrooms with a profusion of toiletries, and views over miles of peaceful countryside. Just a few yards from the hotel is a magnificent 18-hole golf course which is very popular with guests. Hintlesham Hall is handily located for visiting Norwich with its beautiful cathedral and castle, Flatford Mill, the area where Constable painted several of his most famous paintings, and the medieval wool towns Lavenham, Kersey, and Long Melford with their majestic churches and timber-framed buildings. *Directions:* Just before reaching Ipswich on the A12 take the A1071 (signposted Hintlesham and Hadleigh)—Hintlesham Hall is on your right after 3 miles.

HINTLESHAM HALL
Manager: Tim Sunderland
Hintlesham near Ipswich
Suffolk IP8 3NS, England
Tel: (01473) 652268 Fax: (01473) 652463
33 rooms
Double: from £110 Suite: from £210
Open all year
Credit cards: all major
Children welcome

Langshott Manor is a beautiful Elizabethan house which, with just seven bedrooms, retains the intimate feeling of a home. The interior, warmed by blazing log fires, more than exceeds the promise of the historic exterior: at every turn you admire low-ceilinged, beamed rooms, polished oak paneling, and stained-glass windows where the motifs of flowers in bloom and birds in flight are over 400 years old. Crisp Egyptian cotton sheets are the order of the day in the bedrooms. I especially enjoyed Christopher, a most spacious room whose windows frame the rose garden, and The Nursery with its private staircase leading under the eaves to an attractive bedroom with a spacious, whimsical bathroom. Two smaller bedrooms (the Cook's and the Butler's Rooms) are found on the ground floor. The manor, run by friendly owners Patricia and Geoffrey Noble (along with son Christopher) is just 2½ miles from Gatwick airport, but do not fear aircraft noise—it is not on the flight path. Churchill's home, Chartwell, the Royal Horticultural Society Gardens at Wisley, and Brighton are amongst the most popular visitor attractions. *Directions:* From Gatwick take the A23 north towards Redhill for 2½ miles to the large roundabout with a garage in the middle and bordered by the Chequers pub. Take the Ladbroke Road exit from the roundabout and follow the country lane to the hotel, which borders on a suburban area.

LANGSHOTT MANOR   **NEW**
Owners: Patricia, Geoffrey & Christopher Noble
Horley
Surrey RH6 9LN, England
Tel: (01293) 786680 Fax: (01293) 783905
7 rooms
Double: from £114
Open all year
Credit cards: all major
Children over 10

Several miles of winding, single-track country lanes lead you deep into the south Devon countryside to Buckland Tout Saints, an elegant Queen-Anne manor house isolated by miles of rolling countryside. The beautifully proportioned house was built in 1690 and so impressed Tove and John Taylor that they were tempted out of retirement to purchase it and run it with their son, George, and a small friendly staff. In the evening Tove mans the bar, George serves the wine, and John ensures that guests feel at home. Dinner is eaten either in the grand pine-paneled dining room or the more intimate green dining room. The grand staircase curves up to the three principal bedrooms. These very spacious suites (one of them with a four-poster) enjoy lovely countryside views. Tucked under the roof you find more ordinary, smaller double or twin-bedded rooms. Beyond the old market town of Kingsbridge lies Salcombe, Devon's southernmost resort, and certainly her most beautiful one. Salcombe estuary is very popular for sailing, gardeners come to see Sharpitor, and walkers make for Bolt Head. In the opposite direction lies picturesque Dartmouth. *Directions:* From Totnes take the A384 and A381 towards Kingsbridge. Before Kingsbridge pass through Halwell and The Mounts and continue 2 miles more to a left-hand turn for Goveton. Go through the village and Buckland Tout Saints is on your left after a mile.

BUCKLAND TOUT SAINTS **NEW**
Owners: Tove & John Taylor
Goveton, Kingsbridge
Devon TQ7 2DS, England
Tel: (01548) 853055 Fax: (01548) 856261
10 rooms, 3 suites
Double: £110–130 Suite: from £150
Open all year
Credit cards: all major
Children welcome

The magnificent scenery of the Lake District, the Yorkshire Dales, and Hadrian's Wall are within easy driving distance of Hipping Hall, so visitors can easily justify a stay of several days in Jocelyn Ruffle and Ian Bryant's comfortable home. Guests help themselves to pre-dinner drinks from the honesty bar in the conservatory which links the main part of the house to the Great Hall where dinner is served. A soaring, beamed ceiling and a broad-plank oak floor provide an impressive setting for the excellent five-course meal served around one large table where guests are looked after by Ian while Jos creates in the kitchen. Ian selects wine to complement each course. The bedrooms are named after local hills and dales, and all are comfortably and very tastefully furnished, often with lovely old pieces bought at local auctions. Each has its own sparkling new, well equipped bathroom. The 3 acres of garden are a delight and feature a large expanse of lawn set up for croquet and a kitchen garden which provides many of the vegetables enjoyed at dinner. Two suites, named Emily and Charlotte after the Brontë sisters who attended school in Cowan Bridge, occupy a courtyard cottage. They each have a kitchen and living room downstairs, bedroom and bathroom upstairs. *Directions:* Leave the M6 at junction 36 and follow the A65 through Kirkby Lonsdale towards Skipton. Hipping Hall is on the left, 3 miles after Kirkby Lonsdale.

HIPPING HALL　　**NEW**
Owners: Jocelyn Ruffle and Ian Bryant
Cowan Bridge
Kirkby Lonsdale
Cumbria LA6 2JJ, England
Tel: (015242) 71187 Fax: (015242) 72452
5 rooms & 2 suites
Double: from £79 Suite: from £89
Open March to November
Credit cards: MC, VS
Children over 12

At The Sign of The Angel is a black-and-white timbered inn at the heart of the well preserved National Trust village of Lacock. This 15th-century wool merchant's house is easy to spot as it contrasts strikingly with its neighboring stone buildings. The main dining room is a mixture of antique tables clustering around a large fire. A smaller, adjacent dining room is perfect for private parties. Dinner is always by candlelight and centers around a traditional English roast main course (with a fish or vegetarian alternative) and choices being given for starters and desserts. Heavy old beams, low ceilings, and crooked walls add to the rustic elegance of the inn. The bedrooms are small and cozy with low doors, uneven creaking floors, and ancient timbers. If you have difficulty with narrow stairs and uneven floors, you may prefer the ground-floor double-bedded room. Nestled among the bedrooms on the first floor is a comfortable, inviting residents' lounge. Three additional country-style bedrooms are found in the old farmhouse at the bottom of the garden. Be sure to leave time to visit the Fox Talbot Museum of early photographs and Lacock Abbey. Lacock is just 12 miles from Bath. *Directions:* If you are arriving from London, exit the M4 at junction 17 and take the A350 Melksham road south to Lacock.

AT THE SIGN OF THE ANGEL
Owners: The Levis family
Church Street
Lacock
near Chippenham
Wiltshire SN15 2LB, England
Tel: (01249) 730230 Fax: (01249) 730527
9 rooms
Double: from £75
Closed last week of December
Credit cards: all major
Children over 8

The village of Lastingham is unhurried and peaceful, an oasis of green surrounded by the rugged, untamed beauty of the North York Moors National Park. Lastingham Grange preserves a 1950s style—everything is in apple-pie order, with such things as flowery wallpapers, patterned carpets, and candlewick bedspreads giving an old-fashioned air. I love the long lounge crowded with intimate groupings of sofas and chairs where in the morning the smell of furniture polish mixes with fresh-brewed coffee as you enjoy your morning coffee and homemade biscuits. The charm of the house extends outside where a broad terrace leads to the rose garden and acres of less formal gardens which give way to fields and the distant moor. Guest of all ages and their dogs are welcome—there are listening devices for babies and a large adventure playground tucked beyond the formal garden where older children can romp and play. The village church dates back to 1078 when a group of monks built a crypt to house the sacred remains of St. Cedd which now remains a church beneath a church. Thirty miles distant lies medieval York and, closer at hand, narrow roads lead you to the coast with its fishing villages and long sandy beaches. *Directions:* Take the A170 from Thirsk towards Pickering. Just after Kirbymoorside turn left to Hutton-le-Hole where you turn right and cross the moor to Lastingham. The hotel is on your left in the village.

LASTINGHAM GRANGE
Owners: Jane & Dennis Wood
Lastingham
York Y06 6TH, England
Tel: (01751) 417345/417402
12 rooms
Double: from £119.75
Closed December, January & February
Credit cards: none
Children welcome

Lavenham with its lovely timbered buildings, ancient guildhall, and spectacular church is the most attractive village in Suffolk. The Great House on the corner of the market square, a 15th-century building with an imposing 18th-century façade, houses a French restaurant-with-rooms run by Regis and Martine Crepy. Dinner is served in the oak-beamed dining room with candlelight and soft music and is particularly good value for money from Monday to Friday when a fixed-price menu is offered. On Saturday you dine from the à-la-carte menu and on Sunday evenings the restaurant is closed. In summer you can dine al fresco in the flower-filled courtyard. There are four large bedrooms, all with a lounge or a sitting area. Architecturally the rooms are divinely old-world, with sloping plank floors, creaking floorboards, little windows, and a plethora of beams. Enjoy them for their size and age, not for their decor which is eclectically homey and not particularly spiffy. The bathrooms are small and somewhat dated. Enjoy the village in the peace and quiet of the evening after the throng of daytime summer visitors has departed. Next door Little Hall is furnished in turn-of-the-century style and is open as a museum. Farther afield are other historic villages such as Kersey and Long Melford, and Constable's Flatford Mill. *Directions*: Lavenham is on the A1141 between Bury St. Edmunds and Hadleigh.

THE GREAT HOUSE   **NEW**
Owners: Martine & Regis Crepy
Market Place
Lavenham
Suffolk CO10 9QZ, England
Tel: (01787) 247431 Fax (01787) 248007
4 rooms
Double: from £68 per person
Closed January
Credit cards: all major
Children welcome

Lavenham is the epitome of an old-world English village with many half-timbered houses, and a 16th-century cross and Guildhall, an impressive structure built in the 1520s which now contains a museum tracing 700 years of wool trade. The Swan is now a sophisticated hotel, but was once several houses—the town's ancient Wool Hall and humbler weavers' dwellings. The hotel is the flagship of the Forte Heritage group who have tastefully joined these lovely old buildings round a courtyard garden, preserving ancient beams and whitewashed plaster and timbered walls. The delightful galleried entrance leads you to quaint, beamed lounges that beckon you to partake of a traditional afternoon tea. The hub of the hotel is its snug bar whose floor is made of bricks brought to Lavenham after being used as ships' ballast and which is full of World War II paraphernalia from the time it was the local for American airmen. Narrow corridors and steep staircases wind you to 47 beamed bedrooms tucked into nooks and crannies. The restaurant offers a set three-course dinner with lots of choices. As a dining alternative consider the Great House (01787-247431), a country-French restaurant on the Market Square. A few miles from here are other delightful Suffolk villages, Kersey, Long Melford, and Constable's Flatford Mill. *Directions*: Lavenham is on the A1141 between Bury St. Edmunds and Hadleigh.

THE SWAN
Manager: Michael Grange
High Street
Lavenham
Suffolk CO10 9QA, England
Tel: (01787) 247477 Fax: (01787) 248286
47 rooms
Double: from £110 Suite: from £140*
*Breakfast not included
Open all year
Credit cards: all major
Children welcome

As you walk directly into the oak-paneled hall, you catch the spirit of this lovely house with its enormous stone fireplace, ornate, stone mullioned windows, and plump sofas enticing you to sit and relax. The adjacent paneled dining room has the same comfortable, inviting atmosphere. The dark-oak paneling, the carvings, and the ornate plasterwork ceilings are embellishments added by Lewtrenchard Manor's most famous owner, the Reverend Sabine Baring Gould, who composed many well-known hymns. The bedrooms are all different, named after the melodies of the Reverend's tunes—Melton and Prince Rupert are four-poster rooms. Sue and James run the house themselves and guests appreciate the homelike atmosphere. You do not see many hotel keepers making tea for guests, serving drinks in the bar, and chatting in front of the fire with guests as Sue does. You cannot beat this hotel for friendliness and hospitality. Within a short drive are Castle Drogo, a fanciful Lutyens house, Lydford Gorge, an outstanding beauty spot, Dartington Glass, wild Dartmoor, and the north and south coasts of Devon. *Directions:* From Exeter (the M5) take the A30 for Okehampton and Bodmin and after 25 miles take the A386 slip road off the highway. Immediately turn right and left onto the old A30 for Bridestowe and Lewdown. After 6 miles of single carriageway (just after Jethro's) turn left at the sign marked Lewtrenchard ¾ mile.

LEWTRENCHARD MANOR
Owners: Sue & James Murray
Lewdown
near Oakhampton
Devon EX20 4PM, England
Tel: (01566) 783256 Fax: (01566) 783332
8 rooms
Double: from £100 Suite: from £140
Open all year
Credit cards: all major
Children over 8

The Arundell Arms is a traditional fishing inn that provides its guests the opportunity to fish for salmon, trout, and sea trout in miles of river and a 3-acre lake. Owner Anne Voss-Bark, an expert fisherwoman ably assisted by head bailiff Roy Buckingham and instructor David Pilkington, offers a variety of residential fishing courses. Fisherfolk gather in the morning in the hotel garden's 250-year-old cock pit (a long-since retired cock-fighting arena), now the rod-and-tackle room. In the evening the catch of the day is displayed on a silver platter on the hall table. The traditional fishing inn has been extended over the years to encompass the village assembly rooms—now the tall-ceilinged dining room—and the courthouse and jail—now the adjacent village pub. Cozy bedrooms, all but two of which face the garden, are found in a converted stable block and the main house. Non-fisherfolk can enjoy walking, riding, golf, and, of course, traditional cream teas of scones, clotted cream, and jam. Sightseers head for Dartmoor and the north Cornish coast with the ruins of Tintagel Castle and the ancient fishing villages of Boscastle and Port Isaac. *Directions:* Exit the M5 at Exeter and take the A30 (signposted Bodmin) for approximately 40 miles to the Tavistock exit. Once off the dual carriageway turn right for Lifton and the hotel is on your left in less than a mile.

ARUNDELL ARMS   **NEW**
Owner: Anne Voss-Bark
Lifton
Devon PL16 0AA, England
Tel: (01566) 784666 Fax: (01566) 784494
29 rooms
Double: from £97
Closed Christmas
Credit cards: all major
Children welcome

This elegant Georgian townhouse was built in 1770 and designed by Sir James Gibbs of Radcliffe Library (Oxford) and St. Martins in the Fields (Trafalgar Square) fame. Michael and Guy have decorated their home with great flair, and added the most enviable collection of paintings and antique furniture. A great deal of effort is put into the evening meals. Breakfast is ordered the night before and served promptly at the time of your choosing. Stairs wind up to the sitting rooms and up again to the bedrooms (there are lots of stairs and no lift). While the principal bedroom sports a decorative, wrought-iron-and-brass bed, I preferred the adjacent spacious twin-bedded room. Farther up the house is a double-bedded room with brass half-tester and another standard twin-bedded room. All these rooms overlook the walls and gardens of Ludlow Castle, while a sweet little bedroom under the eaves looks south towards the river. Guests are not given door, or room keys, and the house is no-smoking. Ludlow, its castle, marketplace, and antique and second-hand bookshops are on your doorstep. Stokesay Castle and Powys Castle and garden are great attractions as are the nearby towns of Worcester and Shrewsbury. *Directions:* Take the one-way system through Ludlow almost to the castle gates. With the walls on your right, turn left down Dinham and look for the three burgundy-colored doors. There is unrestricted parking on the street.

NUMBER ELEVEN **NEW**
Owners: Guy Crawley & Michael Martin
Dinham
Ludlow
Shropshire SY8 1EJ, England
Tel: (01584) 878584
5 rooms
Double: from £56
Open all year
Credit cards: none
Children over 12

Lower Slaughter Manor sits beside the church tucked behind a high stone wall in the heart of one of England's prettiest villages. The style of the house is grand and the furnishings are elegant, but the friendly, down-to-earth hospitality of owners Audrey and Peter Marks saves the hotel from being too formal. One of the most attractive rooms is the cream-paneled drawing room with its magnificent ornate palsterwork ceiling and attractive blue-and-peach decor. Upstairs the window seat in the galleried landing overlooks the garden and a 15th-century dovecote. The bedrooms are large and attractively decorated with quality fabrics. Splurge and request Antoinette, with its ornate 19th-century four-poster bed and views across the front lawn. I preferred the rooms in the house to the luxurious suites in the adjacent stable block. Extras include sherry, toffees, biscuits, and bathrobes which are handy for crossing the cellars to the indoor heated swimming pool and sauna. Peter is justifiably very proud of his stupendous wine list. Amongst the more popular (crowded) nearby Cotswold villages are Bourton-on-the-Water, Stow-on-the-Wold, Chipping Campden, and Broadway. On the quieter side, consider the hamlets of Lower and Upper Swell, Stanton, Stanway, and Snowshill. *Directions:* From the A429 on the outskirts of Bourton-on-the-Water a small signpost indicates "The Slaughters." Follow the lane and the manor is on your right.

LOWER SLAUGHTER MANOR   **NEW**
Owners: Audrey & Peter Marks
Lower Slaughter
Gloucestershire GL54 2HP, England
Tel: (01451) 820456 Fax: (01451) 822150
14 rooms
Double: from £230 Dinner B & B
Suite: from £320 Dinner B & B
Closed January
Credit cards all major
Children over 10

On a secluded hillside stands the small gray Elizabethan manor house that is Riber Hall. The hall is found beyond the town of Matlock, overlooking the small hamlet of Riber. This attractive mansion has been carefully restored from a ruin by Gill and Alex Biggin and Alex's mother. Riber Hall opened first as a restaurant and is now also a luxury hotel. Crackling logs blaze in the enormous, ornate, dark-wood fireplace which dominates the cozy lounge where guests gather for drinks before dinner. The candlelit dining rooms are a blend of polished wood, gleaming silver, and sparkling crystal. On a rainy or cold evening it must be difficult to stir from the warm, intimate rooms for the walk across the courtyard to the converted stables which house the bedrooms. The big attraction of the bedrooms is that all but one have beautiful, antique Jacobean and Elizabethan four-poster beds. These gorgeous beds are doubles, their footboards restricting the sleeping room for tall people. When I arrived, the receptionist was enthusiastically describing each of the bedrooms to a gentleman making a reservation by phone. Nearby are the jewels of Derbyshire—rolling green dales and lovely stone villages, medieval Haddon Hall, and the Chatsworth estate. *Directions:* Exit the M1 at junction 28 (Chesterfield) and take the A38 and the A615 (Matlock road) to Tansley where you turn left at the Murco petrol station, up Alders Lane to Riber Hall.

RIBER HALL
Owners: Gill & Alex Biggin
Matlock
Derbyshire DE4 5JU, England
Tel: (01629) 582795 Fax: (01629) 580475
11 rooms
Double: from £99
Open all year
Credit cards: all major
Children over 10

Nansidwell is in the center of the sheltered south Cornish coast between the Helford and Fal river estuaries overlooking a green valley that slopes gently to the sea. In early summer cascades of wisteria drape the house which dates from the turn of the century when it was built as a grand home. Owner Jamie Robertson is the most colorful of hosts—by contrast to his extrovert outfits the hotel seems very quiet in its decor. The ambiance is luxuriously comfortable, making you feel more like a house guest than a paying guest. Wellington boots in the entrance porch set a homey tone. Off the room-sized entrance hall is the spacious sitting room where a window seat set in the broad bay window offers spectacular views down the garden to the sea. The dining room shares the same impressive view. The chef places great emphasis on fresh local seafood. Bedrooms, and their bathrooms, vary greatly in size from large to tiny. Two ground-floor rooms are available. Boats can be chartered on the nearby Fal or Helford rivers. The Helford river—famous for its Duchy of Cornwall Oyster Farm—was immortalized by Daphne du Maurier's *Frenchman's Creek*. An hour-and-a-half's drive brings you to Land's End in one direction and to the Devon border in the other. *Directions:* From Truro take the A39 for 8 miles, then follow signs to Mabe and Mawnan Smith. At the Red Lion pub, bear left and Nansidwell is on the right after half a mile.

NANSIDWELL
Owners: Felicity & Jamie Robertson
Mawnan Smith
near Falmouth
Cornwall TR11 5HU, England
Tel: (01326) 250340 Fax: (01326) 250440
12 rooms
Double: from £145 (Continental breakfast)
Closed January
Credit cards: MC, VS
Children welcome

This peaceful little corner of Norfolk boasts miles of flat sandy and shingle beaches backed by salt marshes lined with quaint villages of gray-flint houses trimmed with red brick. One of these is Morston with its pub, 13th-century church, and Morston Hall. Fortunately for visitors, Galton and Tracy Blackiston and Justin Fraser forsook the Miller Howe in the Lake District to open Morston Hall as a small country house hotel. Being seduced by Galton's exquisite dinners is a large part of your stay here—fortunately, there are plenty of opportunities for exercise, so you can afford to repeat the divine experience. Bedrooms are extremely large and beautifully decorated. Four have inherited the former owner's exuberant decor: she spared no expense on bathroom fixtures and tile, but her taste for the exceedingly ornate means that the bathrooms are definitely not of the country-house genre. Birdwatchers will find nearby marshes a paradise. Guests often take a boat from Morston's little quay to visit the seal sanctuary at Blakeney Point. Nearby Holkham Hall, an imposing Palladian mansion, contains grand paintings and items of bygone days. Blickling Hall is elegantly furnished. *Directions:* Morston Hall is situated on the A149 King's Lynn to Cromer road between Wells-next-the-Sea and Cley-next-the-Sea.

MORSTON HALL
Owners: Tracy & Galton Blackiston,
  Justin Fraser
Morston
near Holt
Norfolk NR25 7AA, England
Tel: (01263) 741041 Fax: (01263) 740419
6 rooms
Double: from £140 Dinner, B & B
Closed January & February
Credit cards: all major
Children welcome

The peaceful, steep-sided Newlands valley which stretches from Buttermere towards Derwentwater is the location of 19th-century Swinside Lodge. Graham Taylor bought the house in 1990 and has completely revamped it, decorating in coordinating soft pastel tones and giving the entire house a fresh and welcoming ambiance which shines through even on the dreariest of days. Lilac is a particularly attractive large bedroom whose bay window is large enough for two armchairs and whose zip-link beds can be either twins or one king-sized. Graham prefers that guests dine in, but he is happy to negotiate on this matter, so do insist if you want to leave your dinner plans flexible. In this part of the world fell (hill) walking is very popular and one of the delights of staying here is that walks begin almost on your doorstep. A favorite walk takes you up the Catbells fell, which rises behind the house, and leads you to Grange where you take a motor launch across Derwentwater to the dock which is five minutes from the hotel. Take the launch in the other direction and you are in Keswick, a delightful, bustling, tourist-packed town. *Directions:* Leave the M6 at junction 40 and follow the A66 past Keswick towards Cockermouth. Turn left through Portinscale on the road towards Grange. You will find Swinside Lodge Hotel on your right after 2 miles (ignore all signposts for Swinside and Newlands as the hotel is nowhere near the village of Newlands).

SWINSIDE LODGE HOTEL   **NEW**
Owner: Graham Taylor
Newlands, near Keswick
Cumbria CA12 5UE, England
Tel & fax: (017687) 72948
7 rooms
Double: from £60
Open mid-February to mid-November
Credit cards: none
Children over 12

Wander across the fields to the sea or explore the lovely surrounding area and return to Chewton Glen for tea in the garden ablaze with flowers—this is a heavenly way to pass the fading afternoon hours. When the chill of the evening starts to stir, it is wonderful to know that Chewton Glen provides a comforting warmth, which in turn beckons you indoors to the beauty and privacy of your own room. Chewton Glen is an outstanding luxury hotel which is continuously improving. Now Martin Skan's dream of perfection has 58 rooms (in the main house and adjacent converted stables). With a hotel this size it is hard to keep a feeling of warmth, but the Skans have done it. There are several attractive bars and lounges decorated with bright print fabrics. Chewton Glen is famous for its award-winning food and has one of the finest wine lists in Britain. There are tennis courts, croquet, a beautiful heated swimming pool set beneath a balustraded terrace, and a health club complex with pool, gym, tennis, and various treatments. The New Forest where wild deer and ponies roam on miles of moorland is nearby. Stonehenge, Salisbury and Winchester cathedrals, and Kingston Lacy House are prime attractions. *Directions:* From the A35 follow signposts for Highcliffe (not New Milton), go through Walkford, then turn left down Chewton Farm Road—the hotel is on your right.

CHEWTON GLEN
Owners: Brigitte & Martin Skan
New Milton
Hampshire BH25 6QS, England
Tel: (01425) 275341 Fax: (01425) 272310
* Toll-free from USA: 800-344-5087*
58 rooms
Double: from £195 Suite: from £295*
*Breakfast not included
Open all year
Credit cards: all major
Children over 7

Between Keble and Somerville colleges you find The Old Parsonage Hotel, a mellow, golden-stone building draped with wisteria that dates back to 1660. In 1989 it was purchased by Jeremy Mogford (owner of the adjacent, very popular Brown's restaurant) and completely remodeled to become an upmarket small hotel. In years past the Old Parsonage grew like Topsy with a higgledy-piggledy of rooms and corridors added to the rear. Jeremy has done his best to give the rambling warren a cohesive feel. For the main sitting room several small rooms have been combined into one, giving the feeling of space while still keeping some walls to provide cozy seating nooks for coffee, lunches, afternoon teas, and bar suppers. The bedrooms are all priced the same and tend to be on the compact size with just enough room for the bed, a couple of chairs, and all the extras of a mini-bar, TV, and phone. Bathrooms are small. The most attractive of the newer rooms are those that overlook the little garden. The largest rooms, and certainly our favorites, are the four rooms in the original house. Reached by going through a pretty little sitting room and up narrow flight of stairs, they have slanting doors, uneven floors, and little windows peeking out through the wisteria. The location is perfect: park your car at the hotel and walk to everything in Oxford. *Directions:* The Old Parsonage is situated just beyond St. Giles Church on the A423, Banbury Road.

OLD PARSONAGE HOTEL
Owner: Jeremy Mogford
Manager: Michael Thompson
1 Banbury Road
Oxford OX2 6NN, England
Tel: (01865) 310210 Fax: (01865) 311262
30 rooms
Double: from £140 Suite: from £180
Open all year
Credit cards: all major
Children welcome

Padstow is an extremely pretty fishing port on the north coast of Cornwall. Narrow, twisting lanes lead to the harbor where attractive little houses surround the quay. Rick Stein's popular seafood restaurant is just a few steps from the spot where fishing boats unload their catch—fish go straight from boat to kitchen. Dinner reservations are essential in summer. Above the Seafood Restaurant are ten bedrooms: two small, inexpensive rooms (9 and 10) with no view, and two rooms (5 and 6, double the price of 9 and 10) with magnificent sea views of harbor and coastline and floor-to-ceiling sliding glass doors opening to spacious terraces. Room 3 has no terrace but enjoys a lovely harbor view. If you cannot secure accommodation at the Seafood Restaurant, opt for St. Petroc's House just around the corner. Here the Bistro restaurant doubles as a breakfast room. The bedrooms I was able to see were decorated attractively but lacked views. There are several outstanding buildings in the village, among them the Court House where Sir Walter Raleigh used to pass judgment. While the north coast of Cornwall is less touristy than the south, be aware that pretty little villages such as Padstow attract throngs of summer tourists. *Directions:* From Exeter take the A30 to Bodmin, the A389 to Wadebridge, and the A39/389 to Padstow. The restaurant and hotel have designated parking in the pay-and-display car park on the quay.

SEAFOOD RESTAURANT   **NEW**
Owners: Jill & Rick Stein
Riverside,
Padstow
Cornwall PL28 8BY, England
Tel: (01841) 532485 Fax: (01841) 533344
10 rooms, 8 at St. Petroc
Double: £61–120
Closed mid-December to end of January
Credit cards: all major
Children welcome

In the oldest part of Penzance, on a narrow street overlooking the harbor, is The Abbey Hotel. With their penchant for house restoration and her love of antiques, Michael and Jean Cox purchased and restored the hotel, turning it into the gem it is today. Soft blues and pinks throughout provide a background for the old pine furniture, country antiques, and interesting old knickknacks. The ambiance is informal: on arrival you are given a key to the front door. There are no bedroom door keys. The second floor contains the three choice bedrooms. Room 1 is especially attractive, with its large patchwork-quilt-covered bed, fireplace, comfy chairs, and huge, pine-paneled bathroom with large antique tub. Room 3 has a delightful sitting nook and a bathroom hidden behind a bookcase door. Room 4 has twin beds covered with hand-embroidered covers and inviting window seats providing views of the harbor and its dry dock: a shower and WC are tucked into a large closet. A two-bedroom apartment offers the most spacious accommodation. Penzance is a lively town with a mishmash of architectural styles. Nearby are St. Michael's Mount, Mousehole, and Land's End (very commercialized). *Directions:* On entering Penzance stay on the seafront road. Just before the bridge (across the harbor) turn right and immediately left up the slipway—The Abbey Hotel is at the top of the hill.

THE ABBEY HOTEL
Owners: Jean & Michael Cox
Penzance
Cornwall TR18 4AR, England
Tel: (01736) 66906 Fax: (01736) 51163
7 rooms
Double: from £85 Suite: from £130
Open all year except Christmas
Credit cards: all major
Children over 5

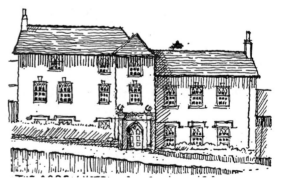

This tall, skinny Edwardian house sits high above the pretty village of Porlock and was designed as a home where almost every room has views of the distant sea across the roofs and chimneys of the village. When Anne and Tim purchased The Oaks several years ago it had already been converted to a hotel and while they have worked wonders in the decoration and bathroom departments, they have not been allowed to do anything about the ugly fire-safety partitions surrounding the stairway. Downstairs, guests have a little bar, snug hallway parlor with just a couple of chairs drawn round a log fire, and a spacious sitting room full of old-fashioned velvet chairs. The dining room has been extended and picture windows added so that, no matter where you sit, you have sea views across the rooftops of the village. Upstairs, the bedrooms enjoy similar sea views. As all the rooms are identically priced, I suggest you request the more spacious quarters offered by room 2 (an Edwardian-style, double-bedded room) and room 7 (set under the eaves). Stroll around the village with its attractive houses and shops and drive the short distance to the nearby harbor of Porlock Weir. Just inland is Lorna Doone Country—the church at Oare was the scene of her wedding. *Directions:* Arriving from the Dunster direction, as you enter down the hill on the one-way system, turn left into the hotel just as the road becomes two-way.

THE OAKS   **NEW**
Owners: Anne & Tim Riley
Porlock
Somerset TA24 8ES, England
Tel & fax: (01643) 862265
9 rooms
Double: from £80
Closed February
Credit cards: all major
Children over 8

The Burgoyne family were people of substance hereabouts for they secured the premier building site in this picturesque Swaledale village and built an impressive home which dwarfs the surrounding buildings. Gone are the days when one family could justify such a large home—now it's a welcoming hotel run by Derek Hickson and Peter Carwardine. Derek makes guests feel thoroughly at home while Peter makes certain that they live up to their motto "'Tis substantial happiness to eat." Peter prepares a fixed-price, four-course meal every evening with plenty of choices for each course. The handsome lounge is warmed by a log fire in winter and is full of inviting books on the area. There's abundant scope for walking and driving in this rugged area using Reeth as your base, though you'll be hard pressed to find a lovelier Dales view than that from your bedroom window of stone-walled fields rising to vast moorlands. One bedroom faces the back of the house. Redmire and Marrick are the premier rooms, being larger and more spacious. Robes and slippers are provided for the occupants of Keld and Thwaite who have to slip across the hall to their bathrooms. Eskeleth is a lovely, wheelchair-accessible, ground-floor room. Richmond with its medieval castle and the Bowes Museum are added attractions. *Directions:* From Richmond take the A6108 towards Leyburn for 5 miles to the B6270 for the 5-mile drive to Reeth.

THE BURGOYNE HOTEL
Owners: Derek Hickson and Peter Carwardine
Reeth
North Yorkshire DL11 6SN, England
Tel & fax: (01748) 884292
9 rooms
Double: from £65
Closed January
Credit cards: MC, VS
Children welcome

Romaldkirk epitomizes a traditional north-of-England village with honey-colored stone cottages set spaciously round the large village green where the old pump and even older stocks (for punishing wrongdoers) still stand. The surprisingly sophisticated Rose and Crown pub bordering the village green has a pretty sitting room (where guests can escape the hubbub of the bar) and a paneled dining room serving four-course dinners. However, like all great pubs, the Rose and Crown also has an excellent traditional bar where beams are decorated with horse brasses and locals gather for a pint in the evenings. Delectable bar meals are served here or in the adjacent Crown Room. Up the narrow stairs you find four attractive bedrooms (room 10 is a lovely large double-bedded room overlooking the village green) and two suites which are especially suitable for families as the sofas in the sitting rooms make into beds for children. Five additional, more modern bedrooms are in the courtyard behind the hotel. Walking is a popular pastime hereabouts and a few minutes' drive brings you into empty Pennine countryside. Barnard Castle is a lively local market town where the Bowes Museum merits an all-day visit. A 40-minute drive finds you at Beamish Museum, a turn-of-the-century mining town hosted by costumed "staff." *Directions:* Romaldkirk is 6 miles northwest of Barnard Castle on the B6277 in the direction of Middleton in Teesdale.

THE ROSE & CROWN   **NEW**
Owners: Alison & Christopher Davy
Romaldkirk, Barnard Castle
Co Durham DL12 9EB, England
Tel: (01833) 650213 Fax: (01833) 650828
12 rooms
Double: from £75
Suite: from £84
Closed Christmas
Credit cards: MC, VS
Children welcome

Stone House, the manor house for Rushlake Green, has belonged to the Dunn family for over 500 years. Built in 1432 with an addition in 1778, this glorious house is filled with wonderful antique furniture and old English china which is complemented by chintzes and family memorabilia. There is a croquet lawn and an antique, full-size billiard table. Bedrooms vary in size from small and cozy to large and spacious. Almost all have old beams and are furnished with care and provided with practically everything you might need from TV to hot-water bottles, sewing kits, books, and tempting biscuits. Two rooms are gorgeous, with four-poster suites with equally lovely bathrooms—one of the bathrooms is decorated with antique samplers. Dinner and breakfast are served in the oak-paneled dining room and Continental breakfast is available in your bedroom. Nearby is the Glyndebourne Opera house, where from May to September great singers and conductors perform. Nearby, Churchill's home, Chartwell, and Rudyard Kipling's home, Batemans, are very popular. Glorious gardens include Sissinghurst, Great Dixter, Scotney Castle, and Sheffield Park. *Directions:* From Heathfield take the B2096 towards Battle and then the fourth turning on the right to Rushlake Green. Turn left in the village (with the green on your right) and Stone House is on the far left-hand corner of the crossroads.

STONE HOUSE
Owners: Jane & Peter Dunn
Rushlake Green
near Heathfield
East Sussex TN21 9QJ, England
Tel: (01435) 830553 Fax: (01435) 830726
7 rooms
Double: from £95 Suite: from £165
Open May to October
Credit cards: none
Children over 9

Rye is beautiful—once a busy port, it became marooned 2 miles inland when the sea receded. As a port, it was the haunt of smugglers who smuggled wool to France and returned with brandy, lace, and salt. Climb the narrow cobbled streets to one of the smugglers' favorite haunts, The Mermaid Inn. This ancient, timbered inn is a historic delight—traces of lovely oil paintings remain on the dark-wood paneling. You will find yourself spending time in the popular, inviting bar warmed by a fireplace which is large enough to stand in, and even longer hours enjoying dinner in the restaurant. Creaking staircases lead to beamed bedchambers and secret passages which add validity to the tales of pirates and smugglers. Less expensive bedrooms are bland and characterless. A bedroom to request is Dr. Syn's bedchamber. Spacious, with two grand wooden beds, leaded-glass windows, a beamed ceiling, and a sunken small bathroom, it also has a hidden staircase, to be found—where else?—behind the bookcase and leading down to the bar. Places to visit in the town include the Town Hall, the church, the town model, Lamb House (home of author Henry James), and the Ypres Tower and museum. Inland lies Bodiam Castle. Birdwatchers enjoy the nature reserves at Romney Marsh and Rye Harbour. *Directions:* Rye is on the A259 between Folkestone and Hastings.

THE MERMAID INN
Owners: Judith Blincow & Robert Pinwill
Mermaid Street
Rye
East Sussex TN31 7EU, England
Tel: (01797) 223065 Fax: (01797) 225069
28 rooms
Double: from £126
Open all year
Credit cards: all major
Children welcome

I was actually thankful for the rainstorm which drove me inside to the shelter and warmth of The Greenway's beautiful drawing room and lounges. (Having noticed the inviting drawing room on arrival, I found any excuse to retire to it very welcome.) A peaceful afternoon reading before a crackling log fire happily took the place of an abandoned walk in the hillsides. What bliss to listen to the gentle rainfall! An equally delightful evening was spent in the conservatory dining room overlooking the lily pond and, in the far distance, the Cotswold hills: lit by dancing candles, it set the mood for an intimate, delicious dinner. Upstairs, the luxurious, handsomely furnished bedrooms overlook the surrounding countryside. Another block of equally luxurious bedrooms is located beside the house in a converted 19th-century coach house. Situated on the edge of the Cotswolds and not far from the Welsh Marches, The Greenway is an ideal spot for exploration. If you are a devoted sightseer, I might almost recommend you bypass The Greenway, as it is so hard to leave and might upset your scheduled itinerary. The lovely Georgian spa town of Cheltenham is just a few minutes' drive away. *Directions:* The Greenway is nestled under the Cotswold Hills, protected from the somewhat suburban location by acres of parkland and gardens. The hotel is 2 miles south of Cheltenham on the A46, Cheltenham to Stroud road.

THE GREENWAY
Owners: Valerie & David White
Shurdington
near Cheltenham
Gloucestershire GL51 5UG, England
Tel: (01242) 862352 Fax: (01242) 862780
19 rooms
Double: from £120
Open all year
Credit cards: all major
Children over 7

Farmer John Shapland and his wife Mary purchased Whitechapel Manor from a Harley Street doctor who had rescued it from the wrecker's ball. The dark-oak paneling that divides the front hall from the drawing room is Jacobean, several of the ornate plasterwork ceilings are William and Mary, and the terraced garden with its tall yew hedges is Edwardian. Surprisingly for a house that is over 400 years old, there have been only ten previous owners to leave their mark on this Elizabethan building. Handily, there are also ten bedrooms, so each previous owner has a room named for his family. Smaller, less expensive bedrooms are found at the back of the house and do not enjoy the lovely views of the more desirable (hence more expensive) bedrooms at the front of the house. Guests enjoy forays down country lanes that take you across the wild moorlands of Exmoor National Park to Lorna Doone country where R. D. Blackmore used the little church just outside the village of Oare for Lorna Doone's marriage. From Oare you can take a 3-mile walk along the river to Badgworthy Valley, the home of the Doone family. *Directions:* Exit the M5 at junction 27 on the A361 towards Barnstaple. After about 30 minutes (at the second roundabout) turn right onto a country lane signposted Whitechapel then after 1 mile turn right onto the private lane which leads to Whitechapel Manor.

WHITECHAPEL MANOR   **NEW**
Owners: Patricia & John Shapland
South Molton
Devon EX36 3EG, England
Tel: (01769) 573377 Fax: (01769) 573797
10 rooms
Double: from £110
Open all year
Credit cards: all major
Children welcome

The gallows sign outside The George stood as a warning to highwaymen not to rob coaches departing from the Stamford inn. The waiting room for London coaches is now an oak-paneled private dining room, while the adjacent York waiting room serves as a friendly bar. History positively oozes from this place and the staff are always happy to enliven your stay with tales of resident ghosts and secret passages. Do not be put off by the hotel's austere façade being directly on the busy Great Northern road (now bypassed) because most bedrooms face a peaceful inner courtyard and you are not aware of the road once you are inside the hotel. Horses once clip-clopped across the cobbled courtyard where overflowing tubs of flowers paint a pretty picture and tables and chairs are set beneath umbrellas for traditional afternoon tea. Most the bedrooms face this pretty courtyard and I particularly enjoyed the historic ambiance of room 29 (a standard double) with its dark-oak paneling—apparently Princess Anne has slept here. Traditional roast dinners are the hallmark of the dining room—be sure to save room an old-fashioned pud—while lighter, more casual fare is served in the indoor Garden Lounge. A short walk brings you to Stamford's antique shops and Burghley House is just down the road. *Directions:* From Peterborough take the A1 north for 14 miles to the first roundabout where you take the B1081 to Stamford. The George is on the left by the traffic lights.

THE GEORGE OF STAMFORD　　**NEW**
Manager: Chris Pitman
71 St. Martins
Stamford
Lincolnshire PE9 2LB, England
Tel: (01780) 55171 Fax: (01780) 57070
47 rooms
Double: £105–160
Open all year
Credit cards: all major
Children welcome

Ston Easton Park is one of the most elegant country house hotels in England. Decoration of the grand, Palladian-style rooms has been supervised by an acknowledged authority on 18th-century decor and sumptuous period antiques are found in all the rooms. The most impressive room is the grand salon with its high, ornate plaster ceiling, intricate carved pediments over the doorways and fireplace, carefully arranged groups of chairs and sofas around a lovely circular table, and an attentive maid hovering just out of sight. I enjoyed the less formal atmosphere of the snug library where comfortable chairs are grouped around a blazing log fire and the walls are lined with books in their mahogany bookcases. Explorations downstairs show the other side of life in the 18th century—the old servants' hall, kitchen, linen room, wine cellar, and billiard room—all restored and in use on a day-to-day basis. Upstairs, the principal bedrooms have lovely four-poster beds with matching hangings and curtains. Outside you can stroll through the park-like grounds (created by Humphry Repton in 1793) or play croquet on the lawn of this serene mansion. Ston Easton is a perfect touring base for forays to Bath, Bristol, Wells, Salisbury, Glastonbury, Longleat, and Stonehenge. *Directions:* Ston Easton Park is on the A37, 6 miles northeast of Wells.

STON EASTON PARK
Owners: Christine & Peter Smedley
Ston Easton
near Bath
Somerset BA3 4DF, England
Tel: (01761) 241631 Fax: (01761) 241377
21 rooms
Double: from £160 Suite: from £280
Open all year
Credit cards: all major
Children over 12

Just 50 miles south of London, Tim and Pauline Ractliff have created a small luxury hotel of such warmth that you feel as though you are staying in an elegant private home. Little Thakeham is a fine example of a Lutyens, Tudor-style mansion, with tall brick chimneys and small diamond-paned windows. Deep, comfortable armchairs and sofas grouped round the fireplace welcome you to the large two-storied sitting room in the center of the house. To one side is the comfortable bar and to the other the gracious, oak-furnished dining room. Beautiful pieces of Art Deco glassware are displayed throughout the house. The bedrooms are particularly appealing, with views out of the little stone-mullioned windows across the garden to acres and acres of orchards. Stroll along the flagged paths through the garden before dinner or, if inclined to more energetic pursuits, take advantage of the heated outdoor swimming pool. During the cricket season you may well see Mr Ractliff and his team demonstrating their skills on their pitch—the large lawn that separates the gardens from the orchards. Guests head for Petworth House to see Turner's paintings, the Weald and Downland Museum of Rural Life, and Arundel Castle. *Directions:* Take the B2139 from Storrington towards Thakeham. After 1¼ miles turn right into Merrywood Lane—Little Thakeham is 400 yards down on the left.

LITTLE THAKEHAM
Owners: Pauline & Tim Ractliff
Merrywood Lane
Storrington
West Sussex RH20 3HE, England
Tel: (01903) 744416 Fax: (01903) 745022
9 rooms
Double: from £150 Suite: from £200
Closed over Christmas
Credit cards: all major
Children welcome

Plumber Manor has been a country home of the Prideaux Brune family since the early 17th century. Portraits hanging in the upstairs gallery hint at the grandeur of the family's past. (There is also a portrait of Charles I, which he personally presented to his mistress, a member of the family.) Billed as a "restaurant with bedrooms," Plumber Manor is under the personal supervision of the family. Richard and Alison Prideaux Brune look after guests; Brian Prideaux Brune, the chef, conscientiously provides a high standard of cuisine and wine. Six comfortable, spacious bedrooms are in the main house and just across the garden ten rooms surround a courtyard. Our favorites are 14, 15, 16, and 17— spacious, two-level rooms with luxurious modern bathrooms. Ten miles away lies Milton Abbas, a picture-perfect village of thatched cottages built in 1770 by the Earl of Dorchester who had the old village razed because it interfered with his view. Another pretty village is Cerne Abbas with thatched and Tudor cottages, 7 miles north of Dorchester (Hardy's Casterbridge). Within reach are Salisbury, Longleat, and the many attractions in and around Bath. *Directions:* In Sturminster Newton turn left from the A352 onto the road leading to the village of Hazelbury Bryan. Plumber Manor is 1¼ miles beyond on the left.

PLUMBER MANOR
Owners: The Prideaux Brune family
Hazelbury Bryan
near Sturminster Newton
Dorset DT10 2AF, England
Tel: (01258) 472507 Fax: (01258) 473370
16 rooms
Double: from £84
Closed February
Credit cards: all major
Children over 12

Swaffham folklore tells of John the pedlar who dreamed that if he went to London he would be told where to find treasure. On the road he met a stranger who told him of the great treasure buried beneath a certain tree in Swaffham. John dashed back, found his fortune, and used it to build the north aisle of the church. His generosity to this attractive market town is remembered by a monument in the market-place and carvings in the church. Behind the market-place, secluded by a high stone wall and a pretty garden lies Strattons, a substantial house that began life as a country villa in the 1720s. Now it's home to Vanessa and Les Scott and their family and run more as a stylish country home than a formal hotel. From the overstuffed chairs in the living room to the sweet bedrooms, the house brims with a melange of country-style antique furniture, books, magazines, pictures, and knickknacks. A few miles to the east lies Castle Acre, a ruined Norman castle considered to be one of the finest examples of castle earthworks in England. Close by is an interesting ruined Clunic priory. Moated Oxburgh Hall shows the development of the Bedingfield's family home from medieval austerity to Victorian comfort. *Directions:* Swaffham is on the A47, between Norwich and King's Lynn. Ash Close, the narrow lane that becomes Strattons' driveway, runs between two shops on the northern end of the market place.

STRATTONS
Owners: Vanessa & Les Scott
Ash Close
Swaffham
Norfolk PE37 7NH, England
Tel: (01760) 723845 Fax: (01760) 720458
7 rooms
Double: from £75
Open all year
Credit cards: all major
Children welcome

Midway between the outstandingly pretty Cornish fishing villages of Looe and Polperro, Talland Bay Hotel sits in a quiet cove offering unobstructed views of headlands and the sea. Parts of this lovely Cornish manor date back to the 16th century and Annie and Barry Rosier were immediately drawn to it as it reminded them of Brittany where Annie grew up. The interior is comfortably furnished and the Rosiers are working very hard on a program of total refurbishment. A great many of the bedrooms are freshly decorated and have sparkling new bathrooms. I especially enjoyed room 9 with its large balcony and room 12 set under the eaves (up lots of stairs) with its spectacular sea view. If you need a single room, opt for room 18 on the ground floor with a private garden. If you are traveling with a young family, or want total privacy, consider one of the four little cottages in the grounds (without sea view). The swimming pool on the back patio is heated during the summer months. Gardens terrace down towards the headland where the coastal path takes you to either Polperro or Looe, avoiding the tourist-congested roads. If you are looking for a scrumptious Cornish cream tea, you can do no better than to visit Tencreek farmhouse nearby. *Directions:* From Plymouth take the A38 towards Truro then turn left on the A387 towards Looe and Polperro. At the T-junction turn towards Polperro and turn first left for Talland. The hotel is on your left.

TALLAND BAY HOTEL   **NEW**
Owners: Annie & Barry Rosier
Talland-by-Looe
Cornwall PL13 2JB, England
Tel: (01503) 272667 Fax: (01503) 272940
18 rooms, 2 suites
Double: from £110 Suite: from £150
Closed January
Credit cards: all major
Children welcome

Teffont Evias is an estate village of honey-colored stone cottages strung along a quiet country lane beside the tumbling baby River Teff with its church and grand manor house hidden behind a tall wall. Across the road from the manor, the estate's dower house was rescued from years of neglect by Paul Firmin and Jonathan Ford who took the plunge to remodel, renovate, and become hoteliers after running a successful restaurant, The Garden Room, in nearby Tisbury. Because of their culinary background dinner is a most important part of a stay here: plenty of choices are offered on their three-course dinner menu. Bedrooms are decorated in quiet, restful colors in a most attractive blend of traditional and contemporary—all but one (a twin) have king-sized beds. The sitting room offers a large stone fireplace and French windows which open to a long expanse of lawn bordered by well-tended flowerbeds. The Chilmark stone that built this village also built Salisbury cathedral some 10 miles distant. Salisbury with its cathedral and close is a great draw for visitors as are Stonehenge, Old Sarum, and Stourhead House and Gardens. An hour's drive will bring you to the hustle and bustle of Georgian Bath or the Dorset coast. *Directions:* From Salisbury take the A36 to Wilton and the A30 (Shaftesbury), after 3 miles turn right (B3089) signposted Mere and Teffont Mere, then after 4½ miles turn left at the Black Horse and the hotel is on your right.

HOWARD'S HOUSE HOTEL
Owners: Jonathan Ford & Paul Firmin
Teffont Evias
near Salisbury
Wiltshire SP3 5RJ, England
Tel: (01722) 716392 Fax: (01722) 716820
9 rooms
Double: from £107.50
Open all year
Credit cards: all major
Children over 16

Tucked away at the edge of the small town of Thornbury is Thornbury Castle and from the moment you see it you will be enchanted. Construction began in 1510 at the order of the 3rd Duke of Buckingham, but ceased when he was beheaded in 1521 at the Tower of London. Carol and Maurice Taylor, in keeping with their status as owners of a castle, have purchased the title of Baron and Baroness of Portlethen. They continue the upkeep of this partially restored castle, leaving other areas as a romantic ruin. Dinner in the baronial dining rooms is a leisurely affair. Softly carpeted hallways lead to the bedrooms—this is no longer a castle of drafty stone passages. The guestrooms are elegantly decorated as befits their castle surroundings, several with four-poster beds, all with lovely bathrooms. The large octagonal tower room has a four-poster bed and its own turret staircase. Nearby Slimbridge Wildlife Trust was founded by Sir Peter Scott (son of the explorer) in 1946. Just south of Slimbridge is Berkeley and Berkeley Castle where Edward II was murdered in the dungeon in 1327. Also in the grounds is the Jenner museum, a tribute to Edward Jenner, discoverer of the smallpox vaccination. *Directions*: At the junction of the M4 and M5 motorways take the A38 north to Thornbury. At the bottom of the hill in the High Street fork left down Castle Street and the entrance to the castle is on the left of the parish church.

THORNBURY CASTLE
Owners: Baron & Baroness of Portlethen
Thornbury near Bristol
Avon BS12 1HH, England
Tel: (01454) 281182 Fax: (01454) 416188
18 rooms
Double: from £110 Castle rooms: from £200
Closed 2 days in January
Credit cards: all major
Children over 12

Claiming the honor of being King Arthur's legendary birthplace, the ruins of Tintagel Castle cling to a wild headland exposed to the coastal winds. It's a place of myths that attracts visitors who come to soak up its past and enjoy its rugged scenery. While the village of Tintagel is a touristy spot, just a mile away lies the quiet hamlet of Trenale, a cluster of cottages, and the delightful Trebrea Lodge. Behind the impressive, tall Georgian façade lies a much older building of cozy, comfortable rooms. Upstairs the drawing room is full of splendid antiques but you will probably find yourself downstairs toasting your toes by the fire enveloped by a large armchair, enjoying drinks and coffee after a delicious dinner in the paneled dining room with its views across stone-walled fields to the distant sea. We particularly liked our room (4) furnished, as are all the rooms, with lovely antiques and enjoying a large bathroom. Guests help themselves from a tempting array of hot breakfast dishes on the buffet. Walkers enjoy spectacular clifftop paths along rugged headlands that lead to hidden beaches and sheltered inlets such as picture-perfect Boscastle harbor. To the north lies Clovelly with its whitewashed cottages tumbling down cobblestone lanes to the harbor below. *Directions:* From Tintagel take the road towards Boscastle. At the edge of the village turn right at the church, right at the top of the lane, and Trebrea is on your left.

TREBREA LODGE
Owners: John Charlick, Fergus Cochrane,
* Sean Devlin*
Trenale, Tintagel
Cornwall PL34 0HR, England
Tel: (01840) 770410 Fax: (01840) 770092
7 rooms
Double: from £70
Closed January 8 to 31
Credit cards: MC, VS
Children over 6

Touching the water's edge, the Sharrow Bay Hotel has one of the most glorious views in England—a panorama of Ullswater mirroring the surrounding mountains. Francis Coulson and Brian Sack bought the hotel in 1948 armed with a vision of a country house hotel and for many years Sharrow Bay has been the yardstick by which other luxury country house hotels are measured. From the warmth of welcome from Brian, Francis, and their staff to the divine, five-course dinner where portions are large and you have to pace yourself to complete your meal, a visit to Sharrow Bay Hotel is a wonderful experience. Bedrooms are furnished with antiques and come with absolutely everything, even though they are of very cozy proportions. Twelve lovely bedrooms are in the main house, the remainder in cottages nearby or just down the road at Bank House where guests enjoy breakfast in the beamed refectory dining room, larger bedrooms, and stunning views of the lake from this hillside location. Idyllic Lake District scenery is on your doorstep, tempting you to go no farther than the terrace patio. Close by are plenty of good walks, fishing, and boating. *Directions:* Exit the M6 at junction 40 onto the A66 towards Keswick. At the roundabout take the A592 towards Lake Ullswater. Turn left at the lake then go through Pooley Bridge where you turn right at the church, following signs for Howtown to Sharrow Bay.

SHARROW BAY HOTEL
Owners: Francis Coulson & Brian Sack
Co-Directors: Nigel Lawrence & Nigel Lightburn
Ullswater near Penrith
Cumbria CA10 2LZ, England
Tel: (017684) 86301 Fax: (017684) 86349
28 rooms
Double: from £260 Suite: from £300*
*Includes dinner, bed & breakfast
Closed December, January & February
Credit cards: none
Children over 13

Upper Slaughter, just down the lane from its sister village, Lower Slaughter, is a quiet, tranquil collection of idyllic cottages surrounded by bucolic Cotswold countryside. At its edge lies the former home of the Witts family, "lords of the manor" hereabouts for over 200 years—a massive portrait of the Reverend Witts sitting regally on his stallion graces the landing on the main staircase of the hotel. Facing lush, rolling countryside, the main house with its well proportioned, high-ceilinged rooms oozes country-house charm and peacefulness—three of the five largest bedrooms have four-posters. Cleverly blended into this large home is a curving wing of rooms built to appear like other farm buildings that overlook the narrow lane. Smaller than the grander rooms of the main house, these rooms are smartly outfitted and have well equipped bathrooms. A walk leads through the fields to the old mill at Lower Slaughter. It is a perfect location for forays through the Cotswolds: nearby Lower and Upper Swell are very picturesque; Broadway and Bourton-on-the-Water are best visited early in the morning to avoid the crowds. The Cotswold Farm Park with its rare farm animals is nearby. *Directions:* From the A429 on the outskirts of Bourton-on-the-Water a small signpost indicates "The Slaughters." Follow the lane through Lower to Upper Slaughter.

LORDS OF THE MANOR HOTEL
Manager: Richard Young
Upper Slaughter
Cheltenham
Gloucestershire GL54 2JD, England
Tel: (01451) 820243 Fax: (01451) 820696
29 rooms
Double: from £115 Suite: from £190
Open all year
Credit cards: all major
Children welcome

Veryan, with its thatched circular houses built so that the devil had nowhere to hide, is one of several particularly attractive Cornish villages hereabouts connected by narrow, winding country lanes. Just a mile beyond the village you find the Nare Hotel sitting beside the quiet sandy stretches of Carne beach. What was once an old-fashioned seaside hotel has been extended over the years to become an upmarket family resort. I was struck by the spaciousness of the public rooms with their large windows framing a broad expanse of ever-changing seascape. The styles of the rooms vary from the gaiety of the sun lounge whose walls are hung with the owner's collection of modern art to traditional sitting rooms filled with antiques. The vast majority of the most attractive bedrooms face the sea and a great many have private terraces and balconies. The indoor heated pool is a popular feature. Porthscatho and Portloe are nearby fishing hamlets that have not been overrun with tourists, while the beauty of Mevagissey attracts writers, artists, and throngs of tourists. *Directions:* From St. Austell take the A390 towards Truro for 5 miles and turn left on the B3287 for Tregony. At the bottom of Tregony turn right on the A3078 towards St. Mawes then after 1½ miles turn left for Veryan. Go through the village and straight on to the sea (leave Veryan with the New Inn on your left).

NARE HOTEL   **NEW**
Manager: Daphne Burt
Carne Beach
Veryan, Truro
Cornwall TR2 5PF, England
Tel: (01872) 501279 Fax: (01872) 501856
34 rooms, 2 suites
Double: from £138
Closed January 3 to mid-February
Credit cards: MC, VS
Children welcome

Standing on the River Frome on the edge of the very attractive town of Wareham, this 16th-century building was once the priory of Lady St. Mary, a former Benedictine monastery, and is now a particularly lovely hotel. The entrance, through a little walled courtyard, sets the ambiance for this most delightful hotel. Decorated in soft pinks, the dining room is most inviting. Lovely furniture and a grand piano highlight the beamed living room whose French windows lead under the wisteria-laden trellis to a broad expanse of lawn which slopes down to the lazily flowing river. Up the narrow staircase a blackboard has room numbers and guests write their requests for early-morning tea and newspapers. A narrow maze of corridors and stairs winds amongst the rooms which are on the small side but very smartly outfitted. If you are looking for the most deluxe of quarters, request one of the suites in the riverside boathouse. The gardens are a delight, full of roses in the summer, with a series of small sheltered walled gardens. Wareham is an interesting mix of architectural styles encircled by earth banks built by the Saxons. Lawrence of Arabia's home is open to the public at nearby Clouds Hill. There are many wonderful places to visit, such as Lulworth Cove, Corfe Castle, Poole Harbor, Wool, Bindon Abbey, and Durlston Head. *Directions:* Wareham is on the A351 between Poole and Swanage.

THE PRIORY
Owners: Ann & John Turner
Church Green
Wareham
Dorset BH20 4ND, England
Tel: (01929) 551666 Fax: (01929) 554519
19 rooms
Double: from £80 Suite: £185
Open all year
Credit cards: all major
Children by arrangement

I was very pleased to find a hotel in this lovely part of Northumberland. The Waren House Hotel was more or less derelict when Anita and Peter Laverack bought it but they undertook a major renovation program, taking care to retain all the lovely old architectural features of this traditional, Georgian country house. The decor is a little too fussy for my taste: Anita and Peter love swags, frills, knickknacks, and glossy brocades. The hallway grand piano is home to several dolls (Anita has an extensive collection around the house), while a pink-brocaded sofa sits center stage in the ornately decorated drawing room. By contrast, the large dining room, decorated in soft peach, is much more restful on the eye, with family portraits and pictures decorating the walls. Bedrooms are decorated in different styles: Maria is very French while the Gray suite is all gray silk. This is a particularly attractive part of Northumberland: Bamburgh Castle commands a rocky outcrop high above the dunes with the stone cottages of the village in its shadow. A short drive brings you to Holy Island, historically known as Lindisfarne. The island is surrounded by water only at high tide, so careful attention must be paid to tide tables. *Directions:* Forty-five miles north of Newcastle on the A1, turn right to Waren Mill and the hotel is on your right at the far end of the village.

WAREN HOUSE HOTEL
Owners: Anita & Peter Laverack
Waren Mill, Belford
Northumberland NE70 7EE, England
Tel: (01668) 214581 Fax: (01668) 214484
9 rooms
Double: from £104 Suite: from £134
Open all year
Credit cards: all major
Children over 14

Just steps away from Winchester cathedral sits the most attractive Hotel du Vin and Bistro in an elegant townhouse designed by Christopher Wren (of St. Paul's fame). The hotel's theme is wine, with each bedroom named for its sponsoring winery that provided the photos and memorabilia decorating the walls. The rooms' overall decor is very similar—smart striped curtains, a duvet-topped king-sized bed, television, and bathroom with oversized tub and Victorian shower. I particularly enjoyed the most expensive and very large Courvoisier room with its ornate plasterwork ceiling, large window framing the garden, and two-part bathroom. Beringer's view of the car park was more than compensated for by its spaciousness and attractive photos of the famous winery. Trompe l'oeil plasterwork is an interesting feature of the spacious drawing room. The bistro's menu is fun and varied, offering rib-eye steak with bubble and squeak, taleggio skins, and pan-fried fillet of seabass with Mediterranean vegetables and pesto. *Directions:* Turn off the M3 at Winchester and follow signposts for the city center along the one-way system. Turn left at the top of George Street and first left into Southgate Street. The Hotel du Vin is on the right with lots of parking to the rear.

HOTEL DU VIN   **NEW**
Owners: Gerard Basset & Robin Hutson
14 Southgate Street
Winchester
Hampshire SO23 9EF, England
Tel: (01962) 841414 Fax: (01962) 842458
19 rooms
Double: from £65*
*Breakfast not included
Open all year
Credit cards: all major
Children welcome

The Wykeham Arms is a very extraordinary Victorian pub: over 600 pictures decorate the walls, 1,400 tankards hang from beams, walls, and windows, and Winchester memorabilia abound—many of the tables are old desks from nearby Winchester College. The menu, posted on the board in the bar, offers choices ranging from elaborate fare to tasty pub grub. (Breakfast is the only meal served on Sundays.) Quieter tables can be reserved in the Bishop's Bar or the Watchmaker's Room with its pictures of an old-time watch mender. A family bible sits atop a lectern outside the breakfast room. Up narrow stairways, the pretty bedrooms are not elaborate; several have views across the chimney tops. Small refrigerators are stocked with very reasonably priced drinks. Because The Wykeham Arms is located in a pedestrian zone, all is peace and quiet (except on Friday morning when barrels of beer are rolled across the cobbles at 6:30 am). You can wander the lovely old streets, stroll through the King's Gate and across the lawns to Winchester Cathedral with its seven chapels, medieval wall paintings, and royal tombs, and walk to everything in Winchester. *Directions:* Winchester is between junctions 9 and 10 on the M3. The Wykeham Arms is located near the cathedral. Graeme will send you a map which will enable you to navigate your car through the pedestrian zone to the pub's car park.

THE WYKEHAM ARMS
Owners: Anne & Graeme Jameson
75 Kingsgate Street
Winchester
Hampshire SO23 9PE, England
Tel: (01962) 853834 Fax: (01962) 854411
7 rooms
Double: from £75
Open all year
Credit cards: all major
Children over 14

Windermere is one of the most popular and most crowded Lake District towns, but Holbeck Ghyll is set far from the traffic-clogged streets high above Lake Windermere in a rhododendron-filled garden overlooking the lake and the peaks of the Langdale fells—idyllic scenery that has made the Lake District such a magnet for visitors. Mellow, golden-oak paneling in the entrance hall extends up the staircase of Holbeck Ghyll and heavy beams create a nook just large enough for comfortable chairs on either side of the blazing fire in the large sitting room which makes it very popular in winter. In summer guests prefer the smaller sitting room whose window seat offers a magnificent view of the lake and the distant mountains. Dinner is delicious: there are lots of choices for each course and vegetarian dishes are available. Bedrooms come in all shapes and sizes, the premier rooms, of course, being those that offer lake views. Room 7, in the tower, has its own private, narrow staircase and is worth the climb for its view from the four-poster bed. Room 11, tucked under the eaves, has a sitting alcove that enjoys the same spectacular view. Enjoy a game of billiards or tennis on the hard court. Within a 20-minute drive are Dove Cottage, Rydal Mount, Brockhole Visitors' Center, and the villages of Hawkshead and Grasmere. *Directions:* From Windermere take the A591 (Ambleside road) for 3 miles, turn right on Holbeck Lane, and the hotel is on your left after half a mile.

HOLBECK GHYLL
Owners: Patricia & David Nicholson
Holbeck Lane
Windermere
Cumbria LA23 1LU, England
Tel: (015394) 32375 Fax: (015394) 34743
14 rooms
Double: from £130 Suite: from £190 Dinner, B & B
Open all year
Credit cards: all major
Children welcome

A cozy refuge in stormy winter weather, a marvelous spring, summer, or autumn base for exploring Somerset by car or on foot, Langley House is truly a lovely hotel for all seasons. Relish its log fires and cozy comfort in inclement weather and its lovely decor, beautiful garden, and superb food after a day's sightseeing. At Langley House you feel relaxed, at home, and cushioned from the outside world. Peter used to work for Lygon Arms and Ston Easton and his professionalism and Anne's flair for people and decor ensure their hotel its success. "Oohs" and "ahs" all round for the decor in general and especially for the bedrooms, furnished with care, decorated in warm, soft pastels accompanied by exquisite fabrics, and provided with almost everything you might need. After the initial tail-wagging welcome from Paddington, the family's golden retriever, Anne makes certain that guests are well cared for while Peter makes certain that they are well fed. Peter designs the menu on a daily basis, offering choices in all courses and making use of the excellent local fresh produce. A short drive brings you to the rolling hills of Exmoor, Dunster with its old yarn market, and the pretty villages of Selworthy and Porlock. *Directions:* Leave the M5 at junction 25. At the center of Wiveliscombe turn right, signposted Langley Marsh: the hotel is on your right after 1 mile.

LANGLEY HOUSE
Owners: Anne & Peter Wilson
Langley Marsh
Wiveliscombe
Somerset TA4 2UF, England
Tel: (01984) 623318 Fax: (01984) 624573
8 rooms
Double: from £85 Suite: from £125
Closed February
Credit cards: all major
Children welcome

Four 17th-century townhouses at the very heart of this delightful Cotswold town have been cleverly interwoven to create this charming hotel, which accounts for the maze of little staircases going seemingly every which way up and around to the bedrooms. Bedrooms are all different: several have high ceilings and all are decorated in soft, muted colors in a most appealing, country-house style. Nightingale, Jay, Swan, and Robin are particularly attractive rooms. Five additional bedrooms are found in the adjacent cottage. The dining room, decked out in vivid blue and yellow, is enhanced by dramatic, large flower arrangements. There is a large drawing room upstairs. A central log fireplace burns a cheery blaze in the bar with its rush-matted floor and peach-washed walls. An especially cozy nook is the tiny flagstone-floored room with its country-style chairs. French windows open up to a small garden where tables, benches, and colorful hanging baskets are encircled by a high stone wall—a lovely sheltered spot to enjoy lunch in the summer. The small town of Woodstock is at its best after the crowds have left. Early mornings or summer evenings are especially good times to stroll through the park-like grounds of the adjacent Blenheim Palace. Oxford is 8 miles away and Stratford-upon-Avon 32 miles. Lovely Cotswold villages are on your doorstep. *Directions:* Market Street is off Oxford Street, which is the A44 Oxford to Stratford-upon-Avon road.

THE FEATHERS
Manager: Tom Lewis
Market Street
Woodstock
Oxfordshire OX20 1SX, England
Tel: (01993) 812291 Fax: (01993) 813158
17 rooms
Double: from £99 Suite: from £185
Open all year
Credit cards: all major
Children welcome

York, where Romans walked, Vikings ruled, and Normans conquered, is a fascinating city, its historical center encircled by a massive stone wall. The Grange, a lovely townhouse hotel, lies just beyond the city walls and five minutes' walk from the Minster (cathedral), making it an ideal spot for exploring this wonderful city. The morning room, which leads directly off the marble lobby, has a rich, traditional feel with its Turkish carpet and Victorian portrait hung over the fireplace. The Ivy Restaurant's dramatic saffron-yellow decor was chosen to enhance the gilt-framed oil paintings of St. Ledger winners on loan from the York Racehorse Museum. The basement brasserie offers simpler, lighter fare. Each of the bedrooms—some with canopied, four-poster, or half-tester beds—has different decor: several are very dramatic. I much prefer the softer, brighter, chintzier-looking bedrooms to the rather somber, dark-colored rooms which appear somewhat gloomy on dark days. York takes several days to explore: attractions include the Minster, Betty's teashop, the Jorvik Viking museum, the Treasurer's House, the medieval streets of The Shambles, the castle and its adjacent museum, walks along the walls, and a boat ride on the River Ouse. *Directions:* The Grange is located along Bootham which is the A19, York to Thirsk road. There is ample, off-street parking to the rear of the hotel.

THE GRANGE
Manager: Andrew Harris
Clifton
York Y03 6AA, England
Tel: (01904) 644744 Fax: (01904) 612453
29 rooms
Double: from £115 Suite: from £145
Open all year
Credit cards: all major
Children welcome

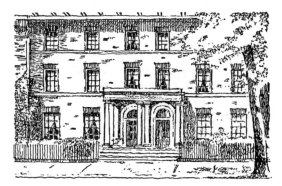

Middlethorpe Hall is an imposing, red-brick William-and-Mary country house built in 1699 for Thomas Barlow, a successful cutler who wished to distance himself from his industrial success and establish himself as a country gentleman. It has been skillfully restored by Historic House Hotels and is now a very grand hotel, but without one iota of stuffiness or snobbishness. The two refined dining rooms have large windows overlooking the grounds. After enjoying elegant, country-house fare you retire to the enormous, graceful drawing room for coffee, chocolates, and liqueurs round the fire watched over by the massive portraits of long-departed gentry. Up the magnificent carved-oak staircase, bedrooms enjoy high ceilings, tall windows (those at the back with views across the grounds), and Edwardian-style bathrooms. Additional, very attractively decorated bedrooms are in the stable block across the courtyard. York (a ten-minute drive away) will keep you busy for at least two days—add Castle Howard, explorations of the dales, moorlands, and the coast, and you can justify a week in this most superlative of country house hotels. *Directions:* The hotel is situated just outside the village of Bishopthorpe, next to the racecourse. Exit the A64, Leeds to Scarborough road, at the A1036, Tadcaster to York road, and follow the hotel's map.

MIDDLETHORPE HALL
Manager: Stephen Browning
Bishopthorpe Road
York Y02 1QB, England
Tel: (01904) 641241 Fax: (01904) 620176
30 rooms
Double: from £141 Suite: from £181*
*Breakfast not included
Open all year
Credit cards: all major
Children over 8

Hotels in Scotland

Farlayer House was built in the 16th century as a croft on the estate of nearby Castle Menzies which is being restored by the clan. Following the 1745 Rebellion, the croft was extensively enlarged and eventually became the main residence of the head of the clan. Now sitting in acres of park-like and wooded grounds, Farlayer House has been refurbished as a lovely country house hotel. Warm golden pine on the doors, the staircase, and paneling gives an atmosphere of coziness and warmth. In the upstairs drawing room rugs cover some of the old wooden floor, sofas and chairs are arranged in inviting groupings, and tall windows frame views across the park-like grounds. Bedrooms vary in size from small attic rooms tucked under the eaves to larger, more elegantly decorated rooms which were the principal bedrooms when this was a home. Guests dine by candlelight in the formal Menzies restaurant or choose something tantalizingly different in The Scottish Bistro, a popular venue with locals. The grounds contain a six-hole golf course and guests are welcome to use the pool at the local country club. Atholl Palace, Cluny Gardens, and Bolfraks Gardens are nearby. *Directions:* From Perth take the A9 (Inverness) to the A827 to Aberfeldy where you take the B846 through Ween. Farlayer House is on your right.

FARLAYER HOUSE
Manager: Nick White
Aberfeldy
Perthshire PH5 2JE, Scotland
Tel: (01887) 820332 Fax: (01887) 829430
11 rooms
Double: from £140
Open all year
Credit cards: all major
Children welcome

Fifteen miles of winding, single-track road lead you through land and sea lochs in some of Scotland's wildest scenery to Achiltibuie, a few cottages straggling along the road overlooking a broad expanse of bay and the Summer Isles, grassy little islands whose name extends to include the five tiny communities on the peninsula of which Achiltibuie is one. Just beyond the post office you find the Summer Isles Hotel run by Mark and Geraldine Irvine: it has been in their family since the '60s. Guests come to enjoy solitude and wild scenery in the daytime and sophisticated food in the evening. Nearly everything you eat is locally grown or freshly caught. Produce often comes from the adjacent large, very unusual building, a hydroponic farm where fruits, vegetables, and flowers are grown in hi-tech growing houses. Accommodation is in three distinct categories: the main house (ask for a room that faces the sea), the turf-roofed log cabins (lots of country charm but no view but priced accordingly), and cottage rooms (very attractively decorated with two rooms that offer views of the sea across the fields). A welcoming cup of tea is served to you on arrival and early-morning tea (extra charge) is brought to you in your room if you wish. You can take a boat round the islands to see seals. *Directions:* Achiltibuie is 85 miles from Inverness. Take the A835 for 10 miles beyond Ullapool and turn left for Achiltibuie.

SUMMER ISLES HOTEL
Owners: Gerry & Mark Irvine
Achiltibuie
Wester Ross IV26 2YG, Scotland
Tel: (01854) 82282 Fax: (01854) 622251
12 rooms
Double: from £70 Suite: from £128
Open Easter to mid-October
Credit cards: none
Children welcome

Steeped in the history of Robert the Bruce and featured in the writings of Scotland's most loved poet, Robbie Burns, this is the first region of Scotland you come to after leaving Carlisle. It is an unspoilt area, not visited much by tourists, which extends from a pretty, rolling coastline, through heather-clad moors to forest. Overlooking the Solway Firth and the distant Cumbrian hills, Collin House is the most amiable of hotels where Pam Hall makes guests welcome and John Wood ensures that they are well fed. Menus are designed on a daily basis, offering choices in all courses and making use of the excellent local fresh seafood and game. Upstairs, the five spacious bedrooms are most attractively decorated and have particularly large modern bathrooms. The sixth bedroom just off the sitting room is equally attractive and has its own entry, making it ideal both for those who have difficulty with stairs and those who like to take their dog on holiday with them. At dinner I chatted with guests who come to Galloway every year to play golf on the many uncrowded courses of which Southerness is their favorite. Interesting nearby towns are Kirkcudbright, Gatehouse of Fleet, and Castle Douglas. Other places of interest include Threave Castle, Threave Gardens, and Port Logan Gardens. *Directions:* Take the A711 from Dumfries towards Kirkcudbright. Six miles west of Dalbeattie and just before Auchencairn turn right to Collin House. (Do not confuse Collin House with the nearby B & B, Collin Hill.)

COLLIN HOUSE
Owners: Pam Hall & John Wood
Auchencairn by Castle Douglas
Kirkcudbrightshire DG7 1QN, Scotland
Tel: (01556) 640292 Fax: (01556) 640276
6 rooms
Double: from £80
Closed January & February
Credit cards: MC, VS
Children welcome

The Reid family, wealthy industrialists who built steam locomotives, had a yen for grandeur when they built Auchterarder in the 1830s as their country residence. It boasts vast rooms with lofty ceilings, lavishly paneled halls and reception rooms, and a winter-garden conservatory leading to an ornate sitting room—a tremendous amount of craftsmanship went into this magnificent house. This is truly a house of the age of Scottish baronial architecture, an era of grandeur which the Browns have gone to great lengths to keep and enhance with the use of ornate wallpapers and elaborate furnishings. Audrey, Ian, and their son Alan concentrate on making guests feel at home. The six very large master bedrooms have high ceilings, tall windows, and very spacious bathrooms. The Graham Room has a particularly impressive array of fitted furniture. The Stuart Room sports a huge Victorian bathroom with marble floor and walls and a large clawfoot tub with a dinner-plate-sized shower head. Turret and courtyard rooms are, by comparison, small rooms with much quieter decor. Perth, the ancient capital of Scotland, is only a few miles away, as are Stirling Castle, Drummond Castle, and Crief. *Directions:* From Perth take the A9 (Stirling road) to Auchterarder where you turn right on the Crief road. The hotel is on your right after 1½ miles.

AUCHTERARDER HOUSE
Owners: Audrey & Ian Brown
Auchterarder
Perthshire PH3 1DZ, Scotland
Tel: (01764) 663646 Fax: (01764) 662939
15 rooms
Double: from £130
Open all year
Credit cards: all major
Children over 10

We were not able to include Braemar in our 1995 visit to Britain, so we have not met the new owners, Edna and Sara Coyne, who assure us that things have changed only for the better. The Braemar Gathering draws thousands to the spectacle of kilted clansmen, pipe bands, caber tossing, and the like. If you book a year in advance, Braemar Lodge can offer you accommodation within walking distance of the games. But do not confine your visit to Braemar to this one famous week, for this area has much beside the Highland games to offer the visitor and Braemar Lodge, a small hotel, provides a delightful place to stay. You enter through a little paneled bar into the hotel. Sink-in-comfortable, chintz-covered chairs are arranged round the fireplace in the living room and beyond lies the dining room. Upstairs the bedrooms are simply decorated and individually furnished. Next to the house is a small, contemporary log cabin which is rented out on a self-catering basis. Walking, fishing, and golf are great attractions for those who visit hereabouts. Craithe church where the Royal Family worship when they are staying across the river at Balmoral is just down the road. Balmoral's gardens are open when the Royal Family is not in residence. *Directions:* Braemar is on the A93, 50 miles northwest of Perth, 47 miles from Aberdeen.

BRAEMAR LODGE
Owners: Edna & Sarah Coyne
Braemar
Aberdeenshire AB3 5YQ, Scotland
Tel & fax: (013397) 41627
6 rooms
Double: from £68
Open all year
Credit cards: MC, VS
Children over 12

Callander is a delightful, small Scottish town, the gateway to the Trossachs, a lovely area of mountains and lochs. Situated just off the town's main street, its large garden bordering the banks of the River Teith, the Roman Camp remains one of my favorite Scottish hotels. The building's pale-pink walls and small, gray-roofed turrets create a charming atmosphere which is continued indoors. It is the feel of this lovely hotel with its stately, dark-paneled library and comfortable sitting room rather than its elegant decor that endears it to me. Eric Brown, who grew up in Callander, his wife, Marion, and their young, friendly staff offer a warm Scottish welcome. Dinner is served in the long, slender dining room under its low, ornately painted ceiling. Long corridors and narrow winding staircases lead to the bedrooms which come in all shapes and sizes, fitting into the rooms of the old house, the adjacent cottage, and extensions which have been added over the years. A walk through woodlands along the bank of the River Teith brings you into Callander with its little shops and gray-stone houses stretched out along the road. Nearby are the Trossachs and their lovely lakes, Loch Katrine, Loch Achray, and Loch Venachar. *Directions:* Callander is only an hour's drive from Edinburgh. Take the M9 to junction 10, beyond Stirling, and the A84 towards Crianlarich. You will find the entrance to Roman Camp on the main street of town.

ROMAN CAMP HOTEL
Owners: Marion & Eric Brown
Callander
Perthshire FK17 8BG, Scotland
Tel: (01877) 330003 Fax: (01877) 331533
14 rooms
Double: from £105 Suite: from £150
Open all year
Credit cards: all major
Children welcome

The tree-lined drive winds through a vast estate to the park-like lawns surrounding Cromlix House. Little rabbits hop gaily around—they're so tame that you can approach within a few yards of them before they disappear into the surrounding woodlands. The heavy, unattractive Victorian exterior of Cromlix House hides a jewel of an interior. Converted in 1981 from the Eden family home, the original Victorian bedroom and reception room furniture has been retained along with the exquisite family porcelain, heavy silver, and glassware that grace the lovely dining rooms. The tone of an elegant Victorian home is set by the stately front hall with its wooden ceiling and richly paneled walls and is carried through into the inviting drawing rooms, peaceful, well-stocked library, and garden conservatory. Unusual features are the private chapel with its organ pipes along one of the staircases, and the way in which the set five-course dinner is offered to you verbally along with choices, should you not care for the meal that is proposed. Upstairs are 14 large and very comfortable bedrooms, 8 of which are suites, all with spacious bathrooms. Within a half-hour drive are the Trossachs and their lovely lakes, Stirling Castle, and Bannockburn. *Directions:* Take the A9 out of Dunblane, turn left onto B8033, go through Kinbuck village and take the second left turn after a small bridge.

CROMLIX HOUSE
Owners: Ailsea & David Assenti
Kinbuck by Dunblane
Perthshire FK15 9JT, Scotland
Tel: (01786) 822125 Fax: (01786) 825450
14 rooms
Double: from £125 Suite: from £170
Open all year
Credit cards: all major
Children welcome

Kinnaird was built in 1770 as a home on the vast Atholl Estate. In 1990 Constance Ward turned her home into a hotel, keeping all its grandeur and the hospitality which characterized her and her late husband's sporting house parties. John Webber, a distinguished chef, joined Mrs Ward in the venture. From a large entrance hall you enter the Cedar Room, an elegant, comfortable, cedar-paneled sitting room with a door opening onto a grand billiard room—your first clue that Kinnaird is a sporting estate as well as a luxury hotel. The quality of everything, from the furniture to gorgeous fabrics and decor (much of it in shades of green), is a delight. The dining room with its delicately painted panelwork and stunning views of the Tay valley is magnificent. The same quality of good taste extends to the spacious bedrooms, many of which are furnished with antiques or copies of furniture originally in the house. Acres of lawns and shrubbery lead to the vast sporting estate. Sportsmen have a comfortable, clubby sitting room below stairs where they can bring their dogs. A short distance away lies Dunkeld with its ruined cathedral, a most attractive town as are Crieff and Bridge of Cally. *Directions:* From Perth take the A9 towards Inverness. Pass the exit for Dunkeld and take the next left, the B898 towards Dalguise. After 4½ miles the gates of Kinnaird are on your right.

KINNAIRD
Owner: Constance Ward
Chef: John Webber, Manager: Douglas Jack
Kinnaird Estate by Dunkeld
Perthshire PH8 0LB, Scotland
Tel: (01796) 482440 Fax: (01796) 482289
9 rooms
Double: from £195 Suite: from £260
Closed February
Credit cards: all major
Children over 12

A brisk, fifteen-minute walk from Princes Street brings you to Channings, a delightful hotel encompassing five large Edwardian townhouses whose front parlors are now quiet sitting rooms. Downstairs is a clubby bar where a blackboard outlines the menu and a brasserie which serves more sophisticated fare at very good-value-for-money prices. Bedrooms are not large but they are all very attractively decorated, usually in soft pinks and blues. Furniture for first-floor (second if you're American) rooms is dark-wood traditional, while rooms tucked under the eaves have pine furniture and sloping ceilings which give them a cottage-cozy ambiance. Room 53 has the most glorious antique bed. If you enjoy fancy toiletries, flowers, and chocolates, your room can be "superiorized" for an additional charge. Edinburgh has a dearth of parking places, so feet are the preferred form of transportation. There are plenty of taxis and a good bus service. A good way to orient yourself is to take one of the conducted bus tours that leave from Waverley Bridge, by the station. There are also some interesting walking tours that highlight ghosts, witches, and crime. *Directions:* Take George Street (parallel to Princes Street) through Charlotte Square (Hope Street) and onto Queensferry Road. Cross the river and take the second right (beside Learmonth Hotel) and follow South Learmonth Gardens to Channings. Double park on arrival and get advice on where to leave your car.

CHANNINGS
Owner: Peter Taylor
Manager: Simon Williams
12–16 South Learmonth Gardens
Edinburgh EH4 1EZ, Scotland
Tel: (0131) 3152226 Fax: (0131) 3329631
48 rooms
Double: from £110
Open all year
Credit cards: all major
Children welcome

The location is absolutely perfect—just a ten-minute stroll from Princes Street in the heart of Georgian Edinburgh, three townhouses have been joined to form this luxury hotel which has the air of a private club. Within, no expense has been spared to create the look and feel of a sumptuous home. Beautiful fabrics, antiques, gorgeous furniture, and lots of flowers set an elegant mood. The drawing room, decked out in dark colors with wing-back chairs and a plump sofa drawn round the fireplace, sets a masculine tone though the hotel is not a dark or dreary place. There is no bar: guests order from the waiter. Each bedroom has a different decor and color scheme. A great many of the bathrooms are especially grand, with clawfoot tubs in the center of the rooms. Either a Continental breakfast is served in your room or a cooked breakfast is available in the restaurant. Edinburgh abounds with restaurants from formal to funky—if the former is to your taste, try Number 36, the hotel's basement restaurant where high-backed, green paisley chairs, red tartan tablecloths overlaid with white linen, paneled walls, and dining nooks create a delightful atmosphere. Park your car in the hotel's off-street car park and explore on foot. The Howard is within strolling distance of Princes Street with its shops and stores and the Castle. *Directions:* From Princes Street (with the castle on your left) turn right on Frederick Street and Great King Street is the fourth road on your left.

THE HOWARD
Manager: Adrian Hanger
32–36 Great King Street
Edinburgh EH3 6QH, Scotland
Tel: (0131) 5573500 Fax: (0131) 5576515
16 rooms
Double: from £180 Suite: from £255
Open all year
Credit cards: all major
Children welcome

A long, tree-lined drive leads to Prestonfield House Hotel, located beyond the city center in a countryside setting just ten minutes' drive from the center of Edinburgh. An elegant mood is set by peacocks strutting gracefully on a circular lawn directly in front of this grand, white stone manor (sometimes they provide unrequested early wake-up calls). The hotel's interior is delightfully dignified and old-fashioned. Its old wood floors are warmed by attractive rugs; oil paintings and tapestries dress the thick walls; archways frame intimate sitting areas; soft lighting and scattered flower arrangements add gentle touches. You dine in the almost circular restaurant watched over by massive portraits of long-dead ancestors. After dinner you climb a worn stone staircase to the dignified tapestry room where, beneath the most ornate of plasterwork ceilings, you enjoy coffee, chocolates, and after-dinner drinks. In keeping with the public rooms, the bedrooms have a very old-fashioned feel to them. Bruce and Cunningham have en-suite bathrooms, while the smaller bedrooms share two bathrooms. A Continental breakfast is served in the bedrooms. In the summer of 1996 25 deluxe rooms will be added to the property, but details on these were not available when we went to press. From April to October a "Taste of Scotland" evening with dinner, song, dance, and, of course, bagpipes is held in the adjacent stables. *Directions:* From the city center take the A68 (A7). Turn left at the lights after passing the Commonwealth swimming pool.

PRESTONFIELD HOUSE HOTEL
Owners: The Stevenson family
Priestfield Road
Edinburgh EH16 5UT, Scotland
Tel: (0131) 6683346 Fax: (0131) 6683976
5 rooms (30 in 1997)
Double: from £75
Open all year
Credit cards: all major
Children welcome

Under the attentive eye of the owner, Grete Hobbs, Inverlochy Castle remains Scotland's premier luxury hotel. This Highland home of the Hobbs family is screened from the main road by a winding driveway and groves of rhododendrons. Surrounded by landscaped gardens overlooking its own private loch, the turreted and gabled house was built to resemble a castle. Its magnificence does not appear to have altered since Queen Victoria visited in 1873. In her diaries she wrote, "I never saw a lovelier nor more romantic spot." Central heating and modern plumbing appear to be the only 20th-century additions. The two-storied Grand Hall with its frescoed ceiling sets the tone of this memorable hotel and the furnishings and decor throughout are luxurious. Dinners in the elaborate dining room are elegant affairs. The staff outnumber the guests and attention to detail ensures that things are done properly. Inverlochy Castle is very grand, very expensive, and the most outstanding hotel. The small number of rooms and the hotel's popularity mean that early reservations are necessary. From Fort William you can take the Road to the Isles, a lovely, dead-end drive that brings you to Mallaig where you can take ferries to the isles of Skye, Rhum, Eigg, Canna, and Muck. *Directions:* The castle is on the A82, Inverness road, 3 miles north of Fort William.

INVERLOCHY CASTLE
Manager: Michael Leonard
Torlundy
Fort William
Inverness-shire PH33 6SN, Scotland
Tel: (01397) 702177 Fax: (01397) 702953
16 rooms
Double: from £220 Suite: from £315
Open mid-March to mid-November
Credit cards: all major
Children welcome

Just a five-minute drive from the center of Glasgow in a fashionable Victorian suburb, three adjacent grand Victorian mansions, once the homes of wealthy industrialists, are now a funky, luxury hotel. The hotel began in number 1 and has since been joined by 2 and 3. The houses are not interconnected, so you pop in and out, under wide umbrellas when it's raining—dining rooms are in 1, reception, drawing room, and bar in 3. Spectacular features of 2 and 3 are the enormous, two-story stained-glass windows half-way up the staircases. Bedrooms are for the most part very large and high-ceilinged. Our attic room—a gorgeously decorated twin room in blue/gray silk—was large enough for a sofa and easy chairs as well as a dining room table and chairs. A great many of the rooms have four-posters swathed in countless yards of striking, dark-colored fabric—one room is done completely in black. Number 3 has the quietest, most traditional decor. Try to stay on a weekend for, at the time of going to press, the hotel was offering a 33% discount off its weekday tariff. The Burrell Collection with its rotating displays of art, furniture, and porcelain is a must. *Directions:* Leave the M8 at junction 17 onto the Great Western Road (A82 Fort William) which you follow to Hyndland Road. Turn left and first right three times which brings you to the hotel.

ONE DEVONSHIRE GARDENS
Owner: Ken McCullough
Manager: Beverly Payne
Devonshire Gardens
Glasgow G12 0UX, Scotland
Tel: (0141) 3392001 Fax: (0141) 3371663
27 rooms
Double: from £145 Suite: from £225
Open all year
Credit cards: all major
Children welcome

Golf players will be enchanted with Greywalls because it is on the very edge of the Great Muirfield golf course founded in 1744. Even if you have no interest in the game, you will love this most beautiful of houses built in 1901 by Sir Edward Lutyens and you will adore the gardens laid out like a series of rooms by Gertrude Jekyll. It was the Weaver family home until 1948 when they turned it into a hotel—family photos and letters decorate the ladies' loo (perhaps they also adorn the gents' too—I did not visit) and photos of famous guests, particularly golfers, are grouped around the reception area. The dining room overlooks the tenth tee. The lounges are especially attractive, particularly the paneled library with its interesting pictures, shelves of books, and open fireplace. The bar is most convivial. Edward VII used to stay here and, because he admired the view, a special outside loo-with-a-view was built for him near the garden wall: now it's a suite called King's Loo. Guests can choose it or from an array of bedrooms which overlook either the flower-filled gardens or the golf course. A Monday or Friday golf package can be arranged in conjunction with a two-night stay, though guests can make their own arrangements at Muirfield as well as at the other ten courses nearby. Eighteen miles to the west lies Edinburgh. *Directions:* From Edinburgh take the city bypass to the A198, go through Gullane, and the hotel is on your left.

GREYWALLS
Owners: Ros & Giles Weaver
Muirfield by Gullane
East Lothian EH31 2EG, Scotland
Tel: (01620) 842144 Fax: (01620) 842241
23 rooms
Double: from £155
Open April to October
Credit cards: all major
Children welcome

Dunain Park Hotel is a lovely country home overlooking the famous Caledonian Canal which joins Loch Ness to the Moray Firth. The large sitting room all decorated in shades of green with its crackling log fire provides a snug retreat on stormy days. Ann Nicoll loves to cook, using vegetables from the garden and lamb, beef, venison, and salmon fresh from local suppliers, and mixing traditional Scottish cooking with modern Continental. The bedrooms are all very attractive. Room 1 overlooks the back garden and has an elegant, four-poster canopy bed and a delicate writing desk tucked into one corner. Room 11 is a particularly pretty upstairs corner suite with lovely views across the garden. A suite consists of a very large bedroom, a small adjacent sitting room where the sofa can be made into a child's bed, and an immaculate, modern bathroom. You find a large heated swimming pool in a log cabin almost hidden by tall bushes in the extensive grounds. A very pleasant drive leads around Loch Ness to Fort Augustus and back on the other bank. The Monster Research Centre is on the north bank near Drumnadrochit. *Directions:* Dunain Park Hotel is just off the A82, 2 miles south of Inverness.

DUNAIN PARK HOTEL
Owners: Ann & Edward Nicoll
Dunain Park
by Inverness
Inverness-shire IV3 6JN, Scotland
Tel: (01463) 230512 Fax: (01463) 224532
14 rooms
Double: from £120 Suite: from £130
Closed January
Credit cards: all major
Children welcome

Set in the Border Country, Sunlaws House Hotel provides visitors driving to or from England with an ideal base for exploring the eastern Scottish Lowlands. The rambling Victorian house with its large sunny rooms is surrounded by a spacious garden of rolling lawns and trees. From his residence at nearby Floors Castle, the owner, the Duke of Roxburghe, supervised the conversion of Sunlaws in 1982 from a private home to a hotel, chose the decor, and provided much of the fine antique furniture that graces this charming country hotel. Sports enthusiasts will enjoy the excellent fishing in the nearby Tweed. Tennis and croquet are available within the grounds. For those who just wish to relax, the large conservatory, inviting lounge, and paneled library (which is also the bar) provide ideal locations. A skylit staircase leads to the large comfortable bedrooms. My favorite bedrooms are room 10 with its large bay window framing a lovely view and room 8 with its large windows and balcony. Floors Castle, a vast, very ornate building, is the largest lived-in home in Scotland. By contrast, Tranquair House is Scotland's oldest home, dating from 950 A.D.—this is a must-visit house and the tour is both educational and fun. *Directions:* From Kelso take the A698 towards Heiton: Sunlaws House is signposted 3 miles out of town.

SUNLAWS HOUSE HOTEL
Manager: David Webster
Sunlaws by Kelso
Roxburghshire TD5 8JZ, Scotland
Tel: (01573) 450331 Fax: (01573) 450611
22 rooms
Double: from £140 Suite: from £175
Open all year
Credit cards: all major
Children welcome

Overlooking the romantic ruins of Kildrummy Castle and surrounded by acres of lovely gardens and woodlands, Kildrummy Castle Hotel is a grand mansion house. The richly paneled and tapestried walls and ornately carved staircase give a baronial feel to this grand house, a feel that is echoed in the lounge and bar whose large windows overlook the romantic castle ruins and the gardens. Yet this is not a stuffy, formal hotel: the smiling, friendly staff do a splendid job, offering people a warmth of welcome that was unsurpassed by any other on my most recent visit to Scotland. Dinner in the richly furnished dining room is a delight. The bedrooms (named after various pools in the hotel's trout stream) are tastefully decorated and traditionally furnished. Their size ranges from a snug attic bedroom with a private balcony to a grand corner room with enormous windows framing the countryside. From Kildrummy you can join the Speyside Whisky Trail and enjoy a wee dram. At Alford lies Craigiever, a fairy-tale castle unchanged since it was built in 1626. Nearby Ballater is a busy resort surrounded by wooded hills. Between Kildrummy and Braemar, home of the September Royal Highland Gathering, lies Balmoral Castle whose grounds are open in July and August when the Royal Family is not in residence. *Directions:* From Aberdeen take the A944 through Alford to the A97 where you turn left for Kildrummy Castle.

KILDRUMMY CASTLE HOTEL
Owners: Mary & Thomas Hanna
Kildrummy by Alford
Aberdeenshire AB33 8RA, Scotland
Tel: (019755) 71288 Fax: (019755) 71345
16 rooms
Double: from £125
Closed January
Credit cards: all major
Children welcome

Ballathie House is a large turreted, Victorian Scottish country estate home on the banks of the River Tay, surrounded by lawns, fields, and woodlands. While the house is imposing, it has a wonderfully warm atmosphere and a homey feel as well as glorious views over the river. A grand sweep of staircase leads up from the enormous hallway where sofas and chairs are grouped around a blazing fire. The drawing room, with its tall windows framing views across the lawn to the river, is made more intimate by cozy groupings of tables and chairs. My favorite accommodations are the spacious bedrooms with turret bathrooms and the smaller bedrooms with river views. Beyond the kitchen there is a ground-floor suite equipped for the handicapped. The bar is a lively place and dinner delicious, with friendly, efficient service. Small wonder that Ballathie was named country house hotel of the year in 1994. Salmon fishing is a big attraction and engraved whisky tumblers are awarded to anglers for catches of over 20 lbs. Nearby is Dunkeld, a delightful town with a ruined cathedral set in expansive lawns. Scone Palace, where Scottish kings were once crowned, has fine furniture, clocks, porcelain, and needlework. *Directions:* From Perth take the A9 towards Inverness for about five minutes to the B9099, Stanley road. Go through Stanley and take a right-hand fork towards Blairgowrie, following signs for Ballathie House.

BALLATHIE HOUSE
Manager: Christopher Longden
Kinclaven near Perth
Perthshire PH1 4QN, Scotland
Tel: (01250) 883268 Fax: (01250) 883396
27 rooms
Double: from £150 Suite: from £200
Open all year
Credit cards: all major
Children welcome

Set at the foot of the Black Isle (a sheltered spit of land just north of Inverness), The Dower House was built as the retirement home for the owners of baronial Highfield House. While Highfield fell into disrepair, The Dower House flourished and was remodeled into a cottage orné, an adorable, single-story doll's house. The cute exterior belies a more spacious interior. The dining room and sitting room open up from the entrance hall where Sweep the springer spaniel adds his tail-wagging greeting to Mena's warm welcome. Mena has played on the interesting architecture and decorated the house in a most appealing, flowery, feminine way, adding attractive, Victorian furniture and all the special touches that make you feel you are staying with friends. While Mena takes care of the front of house, Robyn cooks a four-course dinner, offering choices of starter, main course, and dessert. An enjoyable day trip is to explore the villages of the Black Isle of which the historic port of Cromarty with its fine old buildings is a highlight. You can enjoy magnificent Highland scenery on the train journey from nearby Dingwall to Kyle of Lochalsh. The local distillery at Glen Ord offers tours and samples. Traditional Scottish tweeds and woolens are available in nearby Beauly. *Directions:* Take the A862 from Inverness through Beauly to Muir of Ord. The Dower House is on the left 1 mile beyond the town on the Dingwall road.

THE DOWER HOUSE
Owners: Mena & Robyn Aitchison
Highfield
Muir of Ord
Ross-shire IV6 7XN, Scotland
Tel & fax: (01463) 8700090
5 rooms
Double: from £98 Suite: from £100
Open all year
Credit cards: MC, VS
Children welcome

Clifton House is a unique hotel which reflects the character of its owners, the Gordon MacIntyre family, and their love of the theatre. As a highlight during the winter months, from October to May, a number of plays, concerts, and recitals are staged in the hotel. The overall decor is flamboyantly Victorian, abounding in flowers, masses of pictures, rich colors, and draped curtains. A log fire lures you into the warmth of the main drawing room with its ornate, hand-blocked wallpaper which was used in the robing room of the Palace of Westminster in 1849—it is very elaborate and marvelously Victorian. Each of the 12 bedrooms has its own flavor and personality, and one must appreciate the imagination and interest behind each scheme. The bedrooms tend to be decorated dramatically, so it is as well to ask to see several rooms to decide which suits you best. Small, artistic, and colorful, the Clifton is personally managed by family members and a very conscientious staff, and is interesting and fun to stay in. Nairn is an old fishing/seaside town on the Moray Firth. There are several castles to visit (Cawdor, Brodie, Balvenie, and Grant) and whisky distilleries to tour. *Directions:* From Inverness take the A96 (15 miles) to Nairn, turn left at the only roundabout in town and Clifton House is on your left after half a mile.

CLIFTON HOUSE
Owner: Gordon MacIntyre
Viewfield Street
Nairn
Nairnshire IV12 4HW, Scotland
Tel: (01667) 453119 Fax: (01667) 452836
12 rooms
Double: from £88
Open March to November
Credit cards: all major
Children welcome

This turreted, baronial-style mansion stands on the site of the home of Colonel Alexander Murray who accepted the surrender of Quebec after General Wolfe was killed. A traditional lounge bar is the only ground-floor room, the gracious, paneled drawing room and spacious dining room being found up the dramatic, sweeping staircase. In recent years the Maguires have replaced the worn hallway and stair carpets with an exact match of the old one in a vibrant, bright plum color—some question their decision. Bedrooms are all over the place—in attics, beyond the kitchens, up the main staircase, up the back service stairs. They come in all shapes and sizes, but all have the same tariff and modern bathrooms. The old-fashioned lift is useful for those who have difficulty with stairs. Stanley and son Simon deal with the front of the house (Simon is passionate about hens) while mother Aileen supervises the kitchen with son Paul (who is passionate about beekeeping). The food is especially good and attracts a great deal of local patronage. In the grounds are beautiful, lush, green lawns and flowerbeds leading to a bountiful, walled vegetable garden. The ancient abbeys, remote castles, and small wool towns of the Tweed Valley that lie just a few miles to the south of Edinburgh can easily be explored from Cringletie House Hotel. *Directions:* Cringletie House is on the A703, 3 miles north of Peebles and 20 miles south of Edinburgh.

CRINGLETIE HOUSE HOTEL
Owners: The Maguire family
Peebles
Peeblesshire EH45 8PL, Scotland
Tel: (01721) 730233 Fax: (01721) 730244
13 rooms
Double: from £98
Open March to January 2nd
Credit cards: MC, VS
Children welcome

Surrounded by the peace and quiet of the countryside yet only a few minutes' drive from the center of Pitlochry, Auchnahyle is a complex of cottages and farm buildings set round a farmyard. The largest cottage is Penny and Alastair's home and inside everything is cottage-cozy, brimming with a charming array of antiques. A snug dining room and lounge open off either side of the steep, narrow staircase which leads to two little bedrooms tucked under the eaves with rambling roses peeping in at the windows. If you have difficulty with stairs, ask for the ground-floor bedroom, all bright and cheerful in red and white. Penny cooks as though she is giving a private dinner party and guests are encouraged to bring their own wine. Across the farmyard Rowan Tree Cottage is rented for family vacations: parents often tuck their children in bed and slip across the farmyard for a meal. Goats and three friendly dogs, Daisy, Pixie, and Waggle, complete the rural picture. Pitlochry is a delightful town absolutely stuffed with woolen shops—you can spend a day just choosing a selection of sweaters. The Festival Theatre is a great draw and Blair Castle is only a ten-minute drive away. *Directions:* Enter Pitlochry from the south (A9). Pass under the railway bridge, turn right on East Moulin Road, and take the fourth turning right (by the letter box) down Tomcroy Terrace. Continue right to the end until you reach Auchnahyle.

AUCHNAHYLE
Owners: Penny & Alastair Howman
Pitlochry
Perthshire PH16 5JA, Scotland
Tel: (01796) 472318 Fax: (01796) 473657
3 rooms
Double: from £59
Open all year
Credit cards: MC, VS
Children over 12

Pitlochry developed in the latter half of the 19th century as a Highland health resort and remains today an attractive town of sturdy Victorian houses standing back from the wooded shores of Loch Faskally. Knockendarroch House sits above the rooftops of the town, isolated by its own little hill and surrounding garden. Mary and John, having launched a family of six children, now devote themselves to taking care of their guests with tremendous enthusiasm and warmth. Dinner guests are treated to a glass of sherry as they peruse the three-course menu. Intertwining flowers decorate the stained-glass windows which filter sunlight onto the staircase leading up to the spacious, high-ceilinged bedrooms—two of the snug attic bedrooms have little balconies overlooking the town's rooftops. All are crisply decorated and equipped with color television and coffee and tea makings, and have modern bathrooms with showers. If you have difficulty with stairs, request the ground-floor bedroom. Pitlochry and the surrounding countryside have much to keep visitors occupied for several days. During the summer season the Pitlochry Festival Theatre has a repertoire of plays which makes it possible for you to see as many as four plays in a three-night stay. *Directions:* Enter Pitlochry from the south (A9). Pass under the railway bridge, turn right on East Moulin Road and take the second turning left onto Higher Oakfield (the hotel is on your left).

KNOCKENDARROCH HOUSE
Owners: Mary & John McMenemie
Higher Oakfield
Pitlochry
Perthshire PH16 5HT, Scotland
Tel: (01796) 473473 Fax: (01796) 474068
12 rooms
Double: from £60
Open April to October
Credit cards: all major
Children welcome

The Airds Hotel, a long, low, white ferry inn, looks down on the shore of Loch Linnhe, the Isle of Lismore, and the green Morvern Mountains. Here Eric and Betty with their son Graeme and his wife Anne have created the most delightful, intimate country house hotel that provides a haven of perfect tranquillity in a stunningly beautiful area. Betty and Graeme's food has earned a coveted Michelin star and dining is a divine, evening-long occasion. Betty and Graeme remain behind the scenes while Eric, in his Clan Ranald kilt, is your most congenial host and Anne mans reception and warmly assists guests. The two large lounges have lots of comfortable chairs. All the bedrooms are cottagey in size, but beautifully appointed, with lovely fabrics, quality furniture, and luxury bathrooms. My favorites are the snug attic rooms that look out over the loch, but it is a tight squeeze getting large bags up the final flight of stairs, so you may want to request a main-floor room—with loch view. The suite of two small rooms enjoys loch views both from the bedroom and the sitting room and has an immaculate, large bathroom. The road runs in front of the hotel, but this is not a problem since there is not much traffic in this quiet part of the world. A small passenger ferry sails from Port Appin to the Isle of Lismore. *Directions:* Port Appin is 2 miles off the A828, 25 miles north of Oban.

THE AIRDS HOTEL
Owners: Betty & Eric Allen
* Anne & Graeme Allen*
Port Appin
Argyll PA38 4DF, Scotland
Tel: (0163) 173236 Fax: (0163) 173535
14 rooms
Double: from £150 Suite: from £190
Closed January & February
Credit cards: MC, VS
Children welcome

Viewfield House has always been home to the Macdonald family and there have always been Macdonalds on Skye. At the end of the 19th century this prosperous family remodeled Viewfield House adding a huge extension of large, grand rooms and completing the refurbishment with a baronial tower. Continuing a tradition begun by his grandfather, Hugh and Linda welcome guests to their home. Trophies of hunts and safaris (along with a smattering of British wildlife specimens) decorate the vast entrance hall and guests enjoy the large living room and the grand dining room hung with Macdonald family portraits. Linda produces very attractively priced four-course dinners shared around the long dining room table in a true dinner-party atmosphere. Bedrooms in the Victorian wing are very large—room 3 enjoys the original, very lovely wallpaper of birds and flowers hung over 100 years ago and a large bathroom. Rooms in the Georgian wing are smaller and those in the nursery under the eaves cozy. Portree is the only town on the island, built round a natural harbor where colorful cottages line the port and houses rise steeply up to the main streets of the town. It is a bustling, lively town which hosts Skye week in June, a folk festival in mid-August, Highland Games in August, and a fiddlers' rally in September. *Directions:* From Kyle of Lochalsh take the bridge to Skye, then the A850 to Portree. Just as you enter the town Viewfield House is on your left-hand side.

VIEWFIELD HOUSE
Owners: Linda & Hugh Macdonald
Portree
Isle of Skye IV51 9EU, Scotland
Tel: (01478) 612217 Fax: (01478) 613517
11 rooms
Double: from £70
Open Easter to mid-October
Credit cards: MC, VS
Children welcome

Surrounded by 40 acres of gardens and fields where Highland cattle graze, Rothes Glen Hotel was designed by the architect who built Balmoral, the Scottish royal residence. Its turrets and towers give the hotel the feeling of a baronial castle. Many of the original furnishings, a number of tapestries, high, ornate ceilings, and lovely, rich, wooden doors remain to enhance the residents' lounge, bar, and dining room. The 14 bedrooms are furnished in an eclectic, old-fashioned style. Room 44 is the grandest bedroom, with large windows and ornate French antique furniture. Room 30 is a favorite with its pretty floral fabric and suite of comely Victorian furniture. All rooms have the same price. The Carmichael family have owned the castle for five generations and take great pride in providing a "home away from home" for their guests. They personally supervise the meals which frequently feature freshly caught fish as well as excellent Angus beef. Whisky has been distilled in this area for many years and it seems as though there is a distillery around every corner. Several of the plants are open for tours and sampling of the product. *Directions:* Rothes Glen is 50 miles west of Inverness on the A94, 2 miles before the village of Rothes.

ROTHES GLEN HOTEL
Owners: Elaine & Donald Carmichael
Rothes
Morayshire AB38 7AH, Scotland
Tel: (01340) 831254 Fax: (01340) 831566
14 rooms
Double: from £95 Suite: from £110
Closed January
Credit cards: all major
Children welcome

Shieldaig has an overwhelmingly beautiful location facing a small, tree-covered island on the shores of Loch Torridon. Here single-track roads wind you through spectacular, rugged scenery of mountains rising straight from the sea and sea lochs penetrating far inland. A wonderful place to stay in Shieldaig is Tigh an Eilean, an old pub converted into the most delightful hotel by Elizabeth and Callum Stewart. The decor is quiet and soothing with soft beiges and warm pastels. Dinner is taken in the airy dining room overlooking the loch and there are snug little lounges and an honesty bar. Bedrooms are cozy and very comfortable—be sure to request a loch view. The hotel will pack you a picnic lunch or you can obtain supplies from the Stewarts' little shop next door. Walking, birdwatching, and fishing are popular pastimes with the Beinne Eighe Nature Reserve and the 15,000-acre National Trust estate nearby. Guests often drive around the Applecross peninsula with its awesome, twisting pass of Bealach-nam-Bo and its views of Skye and the Outer Hebrides. Tigh An Eilean is an excellent place to stop if you are traveling between Skye (Kyle of Lochalsh) and Ullapool and do not want to rush through all this magnificent scenery in one day. *Directions:* Shieldaig is 68 miles from Inverness. Take the A832 (Ullapool road) to Kinlochewe where you turn left on the A896 (single-track road) to Shieldaig. The hotel is on the waterfront.

TIGH AN EILEAN (House by the Island)
Owners: Elizabeth & Callum Stewart
Shieldaig by Strathcarron
Wester Ross IV54 8XN, Scotland
Tel: (01520) 755251 Fax: (01520) 755321
11 rooms
Double: from £87
Open Easter to October
Credit cards: MC, VS
Children welcome

On a rocky spit of land almost surrounded by water, the whitewashed Eilean Iarmain hotel, a shop, and a huddle of cottages face Isle Ornsay, a tiny island whose lighthouse was built by Robert Louis Stephenson's grandfather. Across the sound mountains tumble directly into the sea, adding a wild, end-of-the-earth feel. The Eilean Iarmain (pronounced ellen earman) is a hotel with a lot of style. Chintz chairs add a homey touch to the cozy parlor and in the dining room you find that the menu is in Gaelic, thankfully with an English translation (the staff speaks Gaelic and English). A tartan-patterned carpet leads up the pine stairs to six bedrooms. All have the same tariff but there is a great variety of size and decor: room 2 has a half-tester bed that once resided in Armadale castle: the turret room is paneled in mellow pine and has a seating area in the turret; and room 56 has a brass bed. I prefer rooms in the main house to those in the cottage across the road. Step out of the front door and round the side and you find yourself in the old-fashioned pub (bar meals are served) where locals gather—on Thursday evenings they often bring their instruments. Be sure to visit the Clan Donald Center. *Directions:* From Kyle of Lochalsh take the bridge to Skye, then the A850 to the A851, a single-track road with passing places, towards Armadale: turn left to Eilean Iarmain.

EILEAN IARMAIN (Isle Ornsay)
Owners: Sir Iain & Lady Noble
Manager: Effie Kennedy
Sleat
Isle of Skye IV43 8QR, Scotland
Tel: (01471) 833332 Fax: (01471) 833275
12 rooms
Double: from £78
Open all year
Credit cards: all major
Children welcome

Quite the most impressive building that you see for many a mile along the breathtakingly beautiful, rugged coast of Wester Ross is the Loch Torridon Hotel, a grand shooting lodge built by the Earl of Lovelace in 1887. The Earl picked an isolated spot where the mountains descend almost to the lochside, leaving just enough room for this imposing building and its sweep of lawn to the water's edge. The public rooms are huge: an enormous bay window frames the idyllic view of loch and mountains and the pretty pink-and-navy damask sofas and chairs seem almost lost in the vastness of the sitting room. The large pine-paneled entry and the dining-room have a tribute to the 50th anniversary of Queen Victoria's reign painted just below the ceiling as a border encircling the rooms. The principal bedrooms are very large and enjoy magnificent bathrooms—I particularly admired the turret bathroom in room 2 and the grand tub sitting center-stage in room 1. Smaller bedrooms are tucked cozily under the eaves. The area is renowned for its beautiful Highland scenery and you can take a spectacular drive by following the southern shore of Loch Torridon to Applecross, down the hair-raising Pass of the Cattle, and returning to Torridon via the A896. *Directions:* Torridon is 64 miles from Inverness. Take the A832 (Ullapool road) to Kinlochewe where you turn left on the A896 (single-track road) to Torridon. The hotel is on your left by the loch.

LOCH TORRIDON HOTEL
Owners: Geraldine & David Gregory
Torridon by Achnasheen
Wester Ross IV22 2EY, Scotland
Tel: (01445) 791242 Fax: (01445) 791296
21 rooms
Double: from £80 Suite: from £160
Closed January & February
Children welcome

At Ullapool harbor, phone Fred Brown and he will arrange for a small motor launch to come to collect you and your bags (bring walking boots or wellingtons) and ferry you to the Altnarharrie Inn nestling at the foot of rugged hills on the far side of the loch. Fred meets the boat and his warm, easygoing, very professional manner soon makes you feel at home. The simple, whitewashed house yields a most alluring interior, with soft white the predominant color and pine the predominant wood—it is very sophisticated with a Scandinavian ambiance. We prefer rooms in the main house. There is no TV, radio, or phone in the bedrooms but you do have a flashlight and a candle for when the generator is switched off at night. The glorious location with all the attraction of remote places is incentive enough to stay here but THE reason that people come is because of Fred's wife Gunn Eriksen's cooking: dinner includes three savory courses before cheese then a choice of three desserts (or all three). It is an evening-long affair with conversation between adjoining tables the rule rather than the exception. Seals, eagles, deer, and otters are often spotted on walks over the unspoilt, heather-clad hills or by the lochs. Inverewe Gardens is a popular day trip. *Directions:* Ullapool is 60 miles northwest of Inverness. Phone on arrival at Ullapool and you will be directed where to park your car and where the launch will meet you.

ALTNAHARRIE INN
Owners: Gunn Eriksen & Fred Brown
Ullapool
Wester Ross IV26 2SS, Scotland
Tel: (01854) 633230
8 rooms
Double: from £290 Dinner, B & B
Open Easter to October
Credit cards: all major
Unsuitable for children

Ullapool is a popular holiday resort, as well as being a fishing port and ferry terminal, set on the shores of Loch Broom, a broad sea loch. The Ceilidh Place (pronounced *Kaylee,* Scottish for "a party with music and festivity") has a façade of a whitewashed row of fishermen's cottages but the interior is anything but traditional: this is a somewhat Bohemian, very eclectic establishment and the nicest place in town. Jean and Robert Urquhart opened a coffee shop which grew to involve music and the sale of pictures, then along came accommodation, a bookstore, an exhibition hall, and a restaurant. Accommodation is in the hotel which has a modern extension to the rear or dormitory accommodation in the clubhouse across the road. The rooms are 70s modern-looking, with a built-in desk and fitted furniture. A large upstairs sitting room has an eclectic mix of 60s modern sofas, large floor pillows, and Victorian chairs. The adjacent kitchen has tea and coffee makings and an honor bar. The coffee bar is a great place to enjoy a cappuccino or a meal or you might prefer the more up-market conservatory restaurant. Guests often make day trips to the north to visit the Inchnadamph Caves, the ruin of Ardvreck Castle, and Lochinver with its heart-stopping views. *Directions:* Ullapool is 60 miles northwest of Inverness on the A835. West Argyll Street parallels the harbor one street back from the water.

THE CEILIDH PLACE
Owners: Jean & Robert Urquhart
Manager: John Grant
14 West Argyll Street
Ullapool
Wester Ross IV26 2TY, Scotland
Tel: (01854) 612103 Fax: (01854) 612886
13 rooms
Double: from £76
Closed 2 weeks mid-January
Credit cards: all major
Children welcome

If you have a Michelin map of Scotland, you will be able to find not only Whitebridge, but also Knockie Lodge three-quarters of the way down the southern shores of Loch Ness. This lovely home is one of those places that has an ends-of-the-earth feel to it—it is hard to believe that the problems and hustle and bustle of the world exist as you sit in the sun lounge and gaze across Loch Nan Lann at heather-covered hills. It's a lovely view at any time, but especially magnificent when the sun sets, flaming gold and red. A houseparty atmosphere prevails as guests join one another (or sit in separate groups) at polished antique tables whose candlelit patina reflects crystal goblets and silver service. The billiard room draws guests after dinner. Bedrooms are especially nicely decorated, varying in size from small (less expensive: contact the hotel directly for these rates) through medium-sized to Lovat, Grant, and Spruce, large, lovely rooms with exquisite views of the loch and mountains. Guests use Knockie Lodge as a base for touring the Highlands, venturing as far afield as Skye and Ullapool, or stay closer to home with the Culloden Battlefield, and Highland castles and glens. *Directions:* From Edinburgh taking the M90 to Perth and the A9 to Daviot (just south of Inverness) where you turn left towards Fort Augustus. Pass through Whitebridge, and after 2 miles take a right-hand turn to Knockie Lodge.

KNOCKIE LODGE
Owners: Brenda & Ian Milward
Whitebridge
Inverness-shire IV1 2UP, Scotland
Tel: (01456) 486276 Fax: (01456) 486389
10 rooms
Double: from £90
Open May to October
Credit cards: all major
Children over 10

246

Hotels in Wales

The adjoining villages of Aberdyfi and Penhelig nestle beneath the craggy hillside along the Dyfi estuary where the lively Penhelig Arms sits beside the harbor wall, looking towards the distant ocean. Lunchtime bar meals offering omelets, sandwiches, and pizza are a popular feature. Beyond the traditional pub all is peace and quiet in the hotel lobby and the restaurant which serves a set four-course dinner with lots of choices for each course. A narrow staircase and little hallways lead to the bedrooms, the majority of which face the water. The smaller rooms are snug—definitely not for those who bring substantial amounts of luggage. Rooms 1, 3, and 12 offer the most space. Do not be put off by the Penhelig Arms being directly on the road and next to a railway line: trains do not run at night and the road is quiet from evening to morning. Guests receive concessionary rates at the 18-hole championship golf course set in the dunes on the edge of Aberdyfi. Walk along the waterfront to the wharf where you can arrange fishing expeditions, sailing, canoeing, and windsurfing. A walk in the other direction takes you through Penhelig gardens to Picnic Island along a footpath where at high tide the water runs under bridges set into the rocks. Aberdyfi lies at the edge of Snowdonia National Park so you can explore North Wales using this village as your base. *Directions:* Aberdyfi is on the A493 10 miles west of Machynlleth. Pass under the railway bridge and the hotel is on your right. Parking is opposite by the sea wall.

PENHELIG ARMS   **NEW**
Owners: Sally & Robert Hughes
Aberdyfi
Gwynedd LL35 0LT, Wales
Tel: (01654) 767215 Fax: (01654) 767690
10 rooms
Double: from £68 Suite: from £78
Open all year
Credit cards: MC, VS
Children welcome

The Old Bull's Head has a long and interesting history. The walls of its traditional beamed bar are decorated with antique weaponry and the town's ancient ducking chair provides a most unusual curio. Guests have the use of a large sitting room with flowery-chintz-covered chairs. Tasty pub food is served in the daytime in the bar while the upstairs dining room serves more elaborate fare prepared by chef/proprietor Keith Rothwell. On Sundays a traditional roast beef lunch is served. David Robertson, the other owner, takes care of the front of the house. Charles Dickens stayed here, hence most bedrooms are named after Dickens characters. Each room is decorated differently, with matching drapes and bedspread and often coordinating wallpaper and armchair. All have modern bathrooms, television, and phone and either a lovely antique brass or iron bed. Castle Street leads to Beaumaris Castle, a squat, concentric fortification commissioned by Edward I. Nearby the Marquis of Anglesey's house and gardens are open to the public. Past Bangor, on the mainland, is Caernarfon Castle where Prince Charles was invested as Prince of Wales. *Directions:* From Chester take the A55, coast road, to Anglesey and cross on the Britannia Road Bridge, then follow the A545 to Beaumaris.

THE OLD BULL'S HEAD
Owners: David Robertson & Keith Rothwell
Castle Street
Beaumaris
Isle of Anglesey
Gwynedd LL58 8AP, Wales
Tel: (01248) 810329 Fax: (01248) 811294
15 rooms
Double: from £75 Suite: from £85
Open all year
Credit cards: MC, VS
Children welcome

Beryl and Richard Tudhope came here more than 20 years ago and were the second guests to put their name in Ty Mawr's guest book—it was love at first sight and they returned again and again to enjoy quiet getaways in this lovely part of Wales. When the hotel came up for sale they forsook their careers in shipping and teaching and became hoteliers. A measure of their success is that almost 80 percent of their guests are return customers. When I visited late on a Sunday morning I was unable to see rooms as every one was occupied, but photographs showed the bedrooms to be as delightful as the public rooms. The cozy bar doubles as reception and guests gather here or in the cottagey little lounge with its stone walls and wood-burning stove. If you are traveling with friends, ask to dine at the polished oak trestle table and enjoy the privacy of having your own dining room. The stone-walled dining room has little tables and chairs set with pale-green tablecloths. The surrounding area offers over 1,000 miles of walking paths and the roads are so quiet it's a delight to drive along them. Castles abound in the vicinity: Careg Cennen, Kidwelly, Llanstephan, and Laugharne. Guests often visit Dylan Thomas's boathouse at Laugharne. *Directions:* From Carmarthen take the A40 towards Llandeilo, then after 5 miles turn left at Nantgaredig on the B4310 for the 6-mile drive to Brechfa.

TY MAWR   **NEW**
Owners: Beryl & Richard Tudhope
Brechfa
Dyfed SA32 7RA, Wales
Tel: (01267) 202332 Fax: (01267) 202437
5 rooms
Double: from £76
Closed most of December and January
Credit cards: all major
Children over welcome

Tan-y-Foel, "the house under the hillside," sits high above the Conwy Valley overlooking a tapestry of green fields, little toy houses, and distant hills. Operating on the premise that smaller is better, Janet and Peter Pitman run their small country house single-handedly: Janet is the chef and Peter works the front of house. A sign on the door asks guests not to check in before 3:30 pm, which allows the Pitmans time for shopping and errands between guests departing in the morning and those arriving in the afternoon. Dinner is a three-course meal with choices of starter and main course and either cheese or dessert. Bedrooms have a more vibrant, colorful decor than the more traditionally decorated public rooms. Rooms 4, 5, and 6 enjoy spectacular countryside views—room 6 with its lime-green-and-lemon four-poster bed was a particular favorite. There are two very private rooms in the adjoining barn. The rugged grandeur of the mountain passes in nearby Snowdonia National Park is in complete contrast to the pretty countryside around Tan-y-Foel where the nearby Bodnant Gardens are the finest in Wales. A magnificent drive takes you over Llanberis Pass to Llanberis where you can ride the rack-and-pinion railway to the summit of Mount Snowdon. *Directions:* From Conwy take the A 470 towards Betws-y-Coed through Llanrwst. Turn left at the signpost for Capel Garmon and Nebo (do not take the single-track road) and Tan-y-Foel is on your left after 1½ miles.

TAN-Y-FOEL   **NEW**
Owners: Janet & Peter Pitman
Capel Garmon
Near Betws-y-Coed
Gwynedd LL26 0RE, Wales
Tel: (01690) 710507 Fax: (01690) 710681
7 rooms
Double: from £99
Open all year
Credit cards: all major
Children over 7

Ynyshir Hall shares its location on the Dover river estuary with a 1,000-acre bird reserve, home to herons, oyster catchers, curlews, and cormorants. Nestled in acres of gardens full of azaleas and rhododendrons, the hall was built in the 16th century, its most illustrious owner being Queen Victoria. Now it is home to professional artist Rob Reen and his wife Joan who have done the most wonderful job of decorating their country house hotel in rich colors, with each room accented by Rob's oils, acrylics, and watercolors. Relax round the fire in the elegant blue drawing room, enjoy a drink in the richly decorated bar, and dine on country-house fare in the turquoise-blue dining room. Bedrooms are named after famous artists. Monet, a ground-floor suite, has a conservatory sitting room. A frieze of wispy clouds adds whimsy to the bathroom in the Renoir suite which has particularly lovely views of the garden. Ynyshir Hall's central location makes it an ideal base for exploring the rugged Snowdonia National Park to the north and coastal paths to the south. Outstanding castles in the vicinity include Harlech, Powys, and Chirk. In nearby Machynlleth a traditional Welsh street market is held every Wednesday. *Directions:* From Aberystwyth take the A487 for 11 miles (towards Machynlleth) to Eglwysfach. Turn left in the village and Ynyshir Hall is on your right after half a mile.

YNYSHIR HALL   **NEW**
Owners: Joan & Rob Reen
Eglwysfach, Machynlleth
Powys SY20 8TA, Wales
Tel: (01654) 781209 Fax: (01654) 781366
4 rooms, 4 suites
Double: from £100 Suite: from £140
Open all year
Credit cards: all major
Children over 9

Tucked away in a fold of green hills, The West Arms nestles in one of the loveliest valleys in Wales. The low-ceilinged, heavily beamed reception/sitting room welcomes you with logs blazing in the inglenook fireplace and a settle and pink-and-green-chintz-covered chairs drawn round the fire. In the adjacent parlor the same warm fabric has been used for the chairs while the walls have been painted a dark apple-green. The dining room, too, has a large inglenook fireplace and ancient beams. Narrow, uneven stairs lead up to the most charming bedrooms with sloping ceilings and beamed walls. I preferred rooms facing the front of the inn to the large suite which does not have as high a standard of decor. (In addition there are several plainer, modern rooms.) While Chester and all the attractions of north Wales are easily accessible, there is delightful scenery close at hand. Little lanes take you up and around Lake Vyrnwy and down stunning valleys to Dinas Mawddy or Llanuwchllyn. When traveling to the attractive town of Llangollen, head cross country from Glyn Ceiriog, following signs for the mine museum, and then straight up and over the mountain. *Directions:* Turn off the A5 at Chirk (midway between Oswestry and Llangollen) and follow the B4500 for 10 miles to Llanarmon Dyffryn Ceiriog.

THE WEST ARMS
Owner: Mavis Price
Llanarmon Dyffryn Ceiriog
near Llangollen
Clwyd LL20 7LD, Wales
Tel: (01691) 600665 Fax: (01691) 600622
13 rooms
Double: from £100 Suite: from £110
Open all year
Credit cards: all major
Children welcome

From taking bed-and-breakfast guests to help get the farm on its feet, through expanding the traditional slate-hung farmhouse, to leasing the land and hiring a chef, Ty'n Rhos is Nigel and Lynda Kettle's Welsh success story. Over the years guests have become friends, returning year after year for a countryside holiday in this exceptionally beautiful part of Wales. I was particularly impressed by the very good-value-for-money prices and the genuine warmth of welcome that Lynda and Nigel extend to new and old friends. Dinner is a set four-course meal and if the main course is not to your liking, you are encouraged to select an alternative from the à-la-carte menu. All the bedrooms are beautifully appointed—request a room with a view of wonderful open countryside across the Menai Straits to the island of Anglesey. I particularly liked the ground-floor rooms whose patio doors open onto the garden. Ty'n Rhos is located between the sea and the wild mountains of Snowdonia National Park. Caernarfon Castle is close at hand as is the Snowdon mountain railway, the little steam train that ascends Mount Snowdon. *Directions:* From Chester take the A55 just before Bangor and turn left on the A5 (signposted Betws-y-Coed) and immediately right on the B4366 (signposted Llanberis). After 4 miles cross the roundabout and take the first right towards Seion. Ty'n Rhos is on your left after half a mile.

TY'N RHOS   **NEW**
Owners: Lynda & Nigel Kettle
Llanddeiniolen
Caernarfon
Gwynedd LL55 3AE, Wales
Tel: (01248) 670489 Fax: (01248) 670079
11 rooms
Double: from £56
Closed Christmas
Credit cards: all major
Children over 5

Peter and Bridget Kindred bought Tyddyn Llan as a run-down farmhouse and have turned it into an absolutely delightful hotel with three cozy, informal sitting rooms, a tiny bar, and two interconnecting dining rooms decked out in blue and yellow. A chef has replaced Bridget in the kitchen so both she and Peter are on hand to see that everything runs smoothly. Bedrooms are lovely, decked out in country-house style—rooms on the first floor (second in America) are more spacious than those tucked under the eaves. Private fishing is available on the Kindreds' own 4 miles of the nearby River Dee. You can hike the old drovers' roads and tramp into the nearby Berwyn mountains. (Llandrillo was an important point on the drovers' route which was used for hundreds of years for driving livestock from Welsh farms to the markets in England.) On nearby Lake Bala, the largest natural lake in Wales, you can sail, canoe, windsurf, or row. Steam trains run on a narrow track down one side of the lake. A more scenic train ride is from Blaenau Ffestiniog, a slate town where slate crags overhang the houses, to Porthmadog on the coast. On the way to the train visit Llechwedd slate caverns. Many visitors head into the walled city of Chester with its half-timbered shops. *Directions:* Tyddyn Llan is near Llandrillo, on the B4401 between Corwen (A5) and Bala.

TYDDYN LLAN
Owners: Bridget & Peter Kindred
Llandrillo
near Corwen
Clwyd LL21 0ST, Wales
Tel: (01490) 440264 Fax: (01490) 440414
10 rooms
Double: from £88
Open all year
Credit cards: all major
Children welcome

I always hope that a beautiful region and a beautiful hotel will coincide and such is the case here. Snowdonia provides the most beautiful of Welsh scenery and Bodysgallen Hall provides the most beautiful of Welsh hotels. Built around a 13th-century watchtower and overlooking Conwy Castle, this large, rambling hotel looks surprisingly uniform, considering six centuries of additions, alterations, and restorations. The mellow elegance and character of the house are preserved throughout. The spacious, dark-oak-paneled Jacobean entrance hall and the drawing room on the first floor have large fireplaces, mullioned windows, and comfortable furniture that create a warm, relaxed atmosphere. Twenty beautiful bedrooms are found in the main house: none of the rooms are large, neither are their bathrooms, but they are all decorated to the highest of standards—I particularly enjoyed my stay in room 8 which has a sitting nook and the loveliest of views of the gardens. Nine suites are located in adjoining little cottages. The grounds are an absolute delight, a series of gardens divided by stone walls into "rooms." If you wish to leave the grounds, you have plenty to do: the hotel has outlined three day trips into northern Wales. *Directions:* Take the A55 from Chester to the roundabout on the outskirts of Conwy where you turn right on the A470. The hotel entrance is on your right after 1 mile.

BODYSGALLEN HALL
Manager: Nigel Taylor
Llandudno
Gwynedd LL30 1RS, Wales
Tel: (01492) 584466 Fax: (01492) 582519
29 rooms
Double: from £120 Suite: from £145*
*Breakfast not included
Open all year
Credit cards: all major
Children over 8

Sitting high above the River Conwy, overlooking the ramparts of Conwy Castle across the broad river estuary, The Old Rectory offers guests hospitality, dinner with fellow guests or at a separate table, and the chance to learn a little about the Welsh and their culture: in summer a harpist often plays for guests before they go in to dinner. The long dining table is elegantly set with crystal and silver, the polished wood floors are covered with lovely patterned carpets, and fine watercolors hang on the walls. Dinner here is a highlight as Wendy is Wales's highest rated female chef. After dinner Michael and Wendy join their guests in the pine-paneled drawing room. Bedrooms, though not large, are well equipped with an iron and small ironing board, television, telephone, and mineral water. Walnut, Mahogany, and the coach house rooms (where smoking is allowed) have splendid garden views. Mahogany has a half-tester bed and a bathroom with a large, bright, peacock-blue tub in the corner. Glorious Bodnant Gardens, best know for its azaleas and rhododendrons, is just down the road while also nearby is the attractive, well preserved medieval town of Conwy with its dramatic castle. Beyond lie all the rugged delights of Snowdonia. *Directions:* The Old Rectory is half a mile south of Conwy on the A470, just a one-and-a-half-hour drive from Manchester airport.

THE OLD RECTORY
Owners: Wendy & Michael Vaughan
Llanrwst Road
Llansanffraid Glan Conwy
Gwynedd LL28 5LF, Wales
Tel: (01492) 580611 Fax: (01492) 584555
6 rooms
Double: from £74
Open February to 20th December
Credit cards: MC, VS
Children over 10

This hotel has a superb location high in the mid-Wales mountains at the head of Lake Vyrnwy overlooking miles and miles of pine-forested mountaintops. A decidedly old-fashioned feeling permeates the building, from the pine-paneled entrance hall to the drawing room with its ornate ceiling, grand piano, and large windows opening up to views of the lake stretching into the distance with pine-forested hills rising from its shore. The bar and dining room share the same stunning view: sunsets are dramatic. Bedrooms face either the lake or the driveway behind the hotel—it is well worth the extra pounds to secure a bedroom with a lake view (room 1 is quite the loveliest and rooms 1 to 38 have lake-view terraces). The tavern that lies adjacent to the hotel offers a cozy pub full of locals and a casual dining room serving traditional pub meals. Walking and relaxing are the most popular pastimes. The lake is stocked with 5,000 trout every year and over 10,000 pheasants are released during the shooting season. Tennis, biking, and sailing are available for guests. *Directions:* Lake Vyrnwy is a one-hour drive from Shrewsbury—take the A458 towards Welshpool and just after Ford take the B4393 to Lake Vyrnwy. The hotel's driveway is on the right 400 yards after the dam.

LAKE VYRNWY HOTEL
Manager: Jim Talbot
Lake Vyrnwy
Llanwddyn
Powys SY10 0LY, Wales
Tel: (01691) 870692 Fax: (01691) 870259
36 rooms
Double: from £75 Suite: from £125
Open all year
Credit cards: all major
Children welcome

This ivy-covered inn sitting at the center of a tiny Welsh village is an old and long-established sporting inn. The small, cozy bars have lots of charm, with exposed stonework, old beams, and open fireplaces where cheery fires burn on chilly winter evenings. In the sporting tradition of this pub, bedrooms are named after and marked by different fishing flies. All but two are above and behind the inn, in a quite modern addition which blocks noise from the bar. Rooms are very pleasantly though simply decorated. Guests can dine in the cozy little country-style dining room or at a table in the bar and fresh fish or game, according to the season, are always on the menu. Fishing and shooting are arranged by Richard and the inn's full-time ghillie and keeper. They are well versed in their mile-and-a-half stretch of the Wye and take pride in assisting their sporting visitors to make full use of their fishing and shooting facilities. (With advanced notice Richard can also arrange demonstrations of gun-dog training.) The upper Wye valley is unspoilt and serene and Di directs guests on countryside walks through its pretty scenery. Hay-on-Wye, the attractive market town famous for its many second-hand bookshops, is just 7 miles away. *Directions:* The Griffin Inn is located in the center of Llyswen, on the A470 Buith Wells road, 9 miles from Brecon.

THE GRIFFIN INN
Owners: Di & Richard Stockton
Llyswen
Brecon
Powys LD3 0YP, Wales
Tel: (01874) 754241 Fax: (01874) 754592
8 rooms
Double: from £50
Open all year
Credit cards: all major
Children welcome

This grand and dignified house was designed by Sir Clough Ellis (of fanciful Portmeirion) and rescued from ruin by Sir Bernard Ashley (of Laura Ashley). The lounging rooms are a delight: a great hall with an open fire, antiques, huge sofas, and interesting pictures, a flowery sitting room, and a book-filled library with leather chairs and a snooker table. Each bedroom or suite is individually planned and quite different from the next—some are very flowery, others very masculine. The suites are up two long flights of stairs under the eaves. The smaller rooms of the north wing are most attractive—several have small four-poster beds and Welsh mineral water, sherry, heart-shaped shortbread biscuits, and fluffy robes are provided. The kitchen brigade won the Welsh Restaurant of the Year award within six months of opening, and have not looked back since. The Wye river valley offers several places of interest and nearby are the ruins of Tintern Abbey, celebrated by Wordsworth. You can visit Hereford, a lovely, sleepy, medieval city astride the River Wye, its cathedral built in several styles from the 11th century, and Hay-on-Wye with its many bookstores. There is an abundance of pretty countryside, from the stark beauty of the Brecon Beacons to the soft prettiness of the Wye valley. *Directions:* Llangoed Hall is on the A470, midway between Buith Wells and Brecon.

LLANGOED HALL
Managers: Helen & Gareth Pugh
Llyswen
Brecon
Powys LD3 0YP, Wales
Tel: (01874) 754525 Fax: (01874) 754545
23 rooms
Double: from £140 Suite: from £195
Open all year
Credit cards: all major
Children over 8

A soft pink colorwash brightens the exterior of this spacious home in the village of Newport. Cnapan House is very much a family-run affair, with John and Eluned Lloyd, their daughter Judith, and her husband Michael Cooper extending a warm welcome. John and Michael are your genial hosts while Eluned and Judith work together in the kitchen. Lunchtime fare emphasizes whole-food cooking with old-fashioned, hearty soups and puddings (vegetarian dishes available). Tables are covered with lace cloths for dinner, adding a romantic touch to a special meal where the main course is always served with five or six vegetables. Guests can enjoy before-dinner drinks in either the sitting room or the bar, both snug rooms filled with country antiques and overflowing with charm. The bedrooms are superb, artfully decorated in a light, airy style and immaculately furnished, with every nook and cranny filled with old family treasures. One guestroom is a family room with a small adjoining bunk-bedroom for the children. (Nursery teas are served in the early evening so that parents can put the children in bed or in front of the TV before coming down to dinner.) You will love the welcoming, free-and-easy atmosphere that pervades this home. Just down the lane you find Newport's pretty beach and a particularly lovely section of the Welsh coastal path. *Directions:* Newport is on the A487 11 miles west of Cardigan and 7 miles east of Fishguard.

CNAPAN HOUSE
Owners: The Lloyd & Cooper families
East Street
Newport
Pembrokeshire SA42 0WF, Wales
Tel: (01239) 820575 Fax: (01239) 820878
5 rooms
Double: from £50
Closed February
Credit cards: MC, VS
Children welcome

Penmaenuchaf Hall is a lovely country house hotel with a quite unpronounceable name. According to owners Lorraine Fielding and Mark Watson, "pen mine ich av" is a somewhat accurate pronunciation. Lorraine, Mark, and daughter Lara moved here in 1989 and spent two years converting this beautiful old home into a hotel. Lorraine says the most enjoyable part was deciding upon the color schemes and choosing the fabrics— you'll be pleased with her choices: the decor throughout is absolutely delightful. From the log fire that warms the hallway sitting room through the comfortable lounge to the cozy dining room, the house exudes a welcoming ambiance. The principal bedroom, Leigh Taylor, is named after the wealthy Lancashire cotton magnate who built Penmaenuchaf as a grand holiday home. Today it can be your holiday home in northern Wales. Venture to explore Snowdonia National Park and the central Welsh coast and return in the evening to enjoy an excellent dinner. Of particular interest are the rugged scenery of Snowdonia, Portmeirion village with its Italianate houses, the narrow-gauge Ffestiniog railway, 13th-century Harlech Castle, Llechwedd Slate Caverns, and Bodnant, one of the world's finest gardens. *Directions:* From the Dollgellau bypass (A470) take the A493 towards Tywyn and Fairbourne. The entrance to Penmaenuchaf Hall is on the left after three-quarters of a mile.

PENMAENUCHAF HALL **NEW**
Owners: Lorraine Fielding & Mark Watson
Penmaenpool, Dolgellau
Gwynedd LL40 1YB, Wales
Tel: (01341) 422129 Fax: (01341) 422129
14 rooms
Double: from £95
Open all year
Credit cards: all major
Children welcome

Portmeirion is the dream of architect Sir Clough Ellis who bought this wooded hillside overlooking Tremadog Bay and built an Italianate fantasy village because he adored the Mediterranean fishing village of Portofino. It has ornate, color-washed houses and cottages, a campanile, sculptures, gardens of sub-tropical plants, and architectural oddments from all over Britain. Down by the sea, away from the visitors who come to Portmeirion every day, behind the façade of a seemingly unpretentious Victorian exterior, is the luxurious Portmeirion Hotel. The public rooms of the hotel are a decorator's extravaganza: a bright-turquoise sitting room, a glittering Indian bar, a maharajah-style dining room, and a wicker-and-marble, Chinese-motif dining room. There are 14 bedrooms in the main house and 20 more in cottages throughout the village. The most elaborate, and the most frequently requested, are the Indian Room with its four-poster bed constructed from the bases of Indian table lamps and the Peacock Suite. There is a delightful fantasy feel to the whole place as you stroll along the winding, cobbled streets in the quiet of an evening and gaze out across the vast, sandy estuary to distant hills. Remind yourself that you are in Wales by making excursions to nearby castles or ride the narrow-gauge railway from Porthmadog. *Directions:* Portmeirion is south of Minffordd on the A487, 2 miles from Porthmadog.

THE HOTEL PORTMEIRION
Manager: Menai Williams
Portmeirion
Gwynedd LL48 6ET, Wales
Tel: (01766) 770228 Fax: (01766) 771331
20 rooms village, 14 rooms hotel
Village Double: from £68
Hotel Double: from £92
Closed last 3 weeks of January
Credit cards: all major
Children welcome in village rooms

264

Key Map

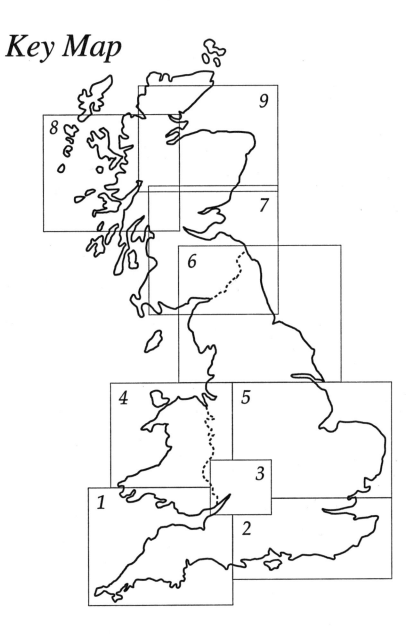

Map 1

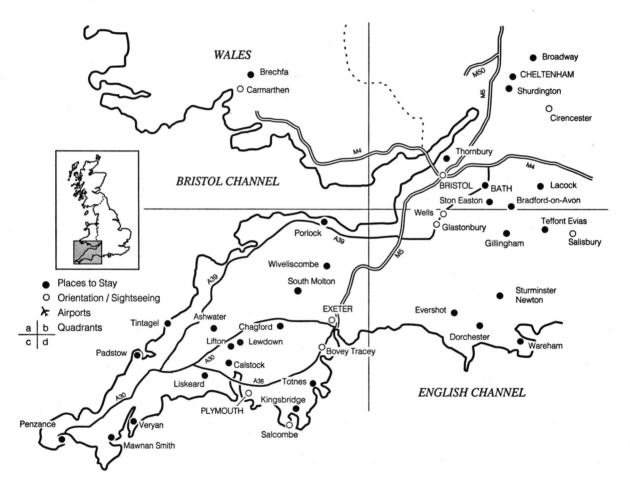

WALES

Brechfa

O Carmarthen

BRISTOL CHANNEL

M4

M50

M5

Broadway

CHELTENHAM

Shurdington

O Cirencester

Thornbury

BRISTOL · BATH

M4

Lacock

Ston Easton

Bradford-on-Avon

Wells

Glastonbury

Teffont Evias

O Salisbury

Porlock

A39

Gillingham

Wiveliscombe

South Molton

EXETER

Evers012

Dorchester

Sturminster Newton

Wareham

Places to Stay

O Orientation / Sightseeing

✈ Airports

a	b
c	d

Quadrants

Tintagel

Ashwater

Chagford

Lifton Lewdown

Bovey Tracey

Calstock

A30

Totnes

A38

Padstow

Liskeard

ENGLISH CHANNEL

Kingsbridge

A30

PLYMOUTH

Penzance

Veryan

Salcombe

Mawnan Smith

Map 2

Broadway

Buckland

Woodstock

Aylesbury

Burford

OXFORD

Ashton Clinton

Great Milton

Henley-on-Thames

A1

M1

M11

CAMBRIDGE

Bury St Edmunds

Lavenham

IPSWICH

Hintlesham

Dedham

Colchester

M40

M25

M4

LONDON

M3

M25

M25

M20

M2

Canterbury

Teffont Evias

Winchester

Horley

East Grinstead

Ashford

Gillingham

Salisbury

M23

Rushlake
Green

Rye

Sturminster
Newton

New Milton

SOUTHHAMPTON

M27

Cuckfield

Storrington

Battle

BRIGHTON

Wareham

PORTSMOUTH

ENGLISH
CHANNEL

● Places to Stay
○ Orientation
✈ Airports

a	b
c	d

Quadrants

267

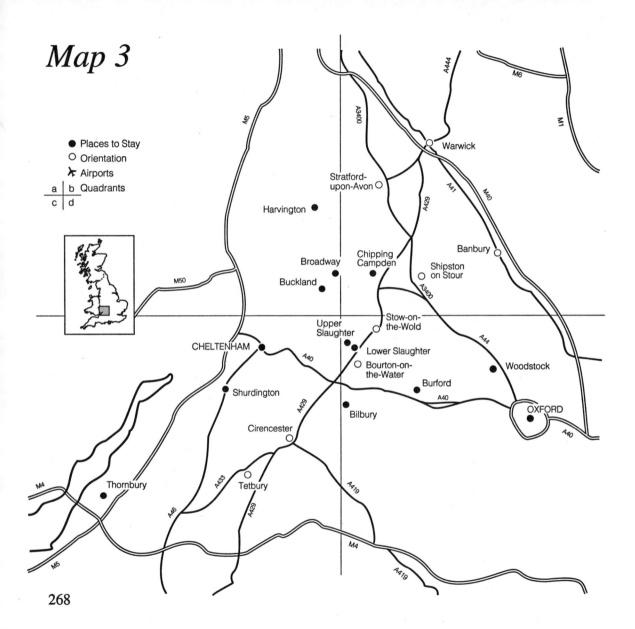

Map 3

- ● Places to Stay
- ○ Orientation
- ✈ Airports

a	b
c	d

Quadrants

M5

M50

A3400

A444

M6

M1

Warwick

A429

A41

M40

Stratford-upon-Avon ○

Harvington ●

Banbury ○

Broadway ●

Chipping Campden ●

Shipston on Stour ○

Buckland ●

A3400

Upper Slaughter ●

Stow-on-the-Wold ○

A44

CHELTENHAM ●

A40

Lower Slaughter ●

Bourton-on-the-Water ○

Woodstock ●

Shurdington ●

Burford ●

A40

A429

Bilbury ●

OXFORD ●

Cirencester ○

A40

Thornbury ●

A433

Tetbury ○

A46

A429

A419

M4

M4

M5

A419

268

Map 4

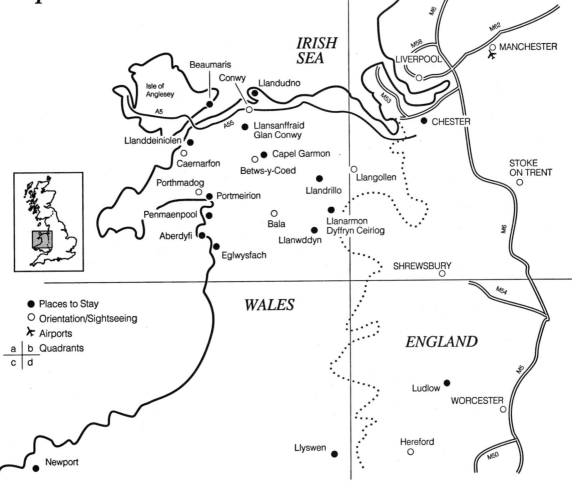

IRISH SEA

Isle of Anglesey

Beaumaris

Conwy

Llandudno

Llansanffraid Glan Conwy

Llanddeiniolen

Caernarfon

Capel Garmon

Betws-y-Coed

Llangollen

Porthmadog

Portmeirion

Llandrillo

Penmaenpool

Bala

Llanarmon Dyffryn Ceiriog

Aberdyfi

Llanwddyn

Eglwysfach

SHREWSBURY

WALES

ENGLAND

LIVERPOOL

MANCHESTER

CHESTER

STOKE ON TRENT

Ludlow

WORCESTER

Hereford

Llyswen

Newport

A5

A55

M6

M58

M62

M53

M6

M54

M5

M50

● Places to Stay
○ Orientation/Sightseeing
✈ Airports

a	b
c	d

Quadrants

269

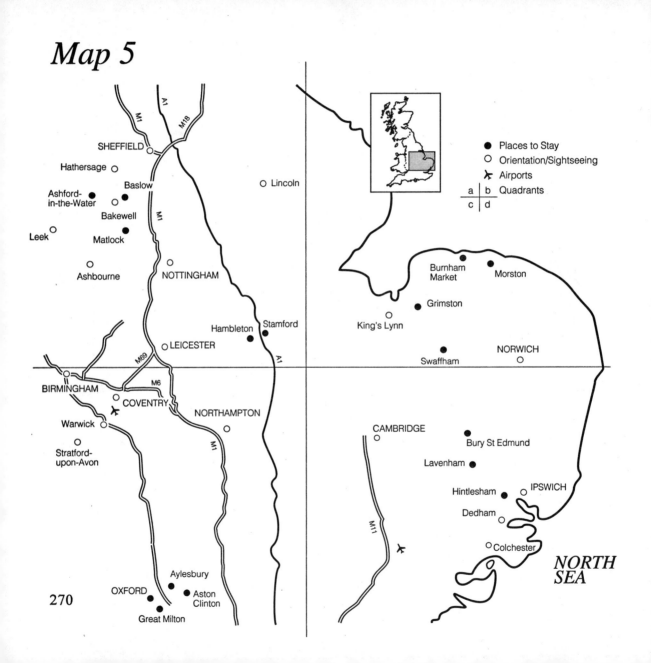

Map 5

SHEFFIELD

Hathersage

Baslow

Ashford-in-the-Water

Bakewell

Leek

Matlock

Ashbourne

NOTTINGHAM

Lincoln

Hambleton

Stamford

LEICESTER

Burnham Market

Morston

Grimston

King's Lynn

NORWICH

Swaffham

BIRMINGHAM

COVENTRY

NORTHAMPTON

Warwick

Stratford-upon-Avon

CAMBRIDGE

Bury St Edmund

Lavenham

Hintlesham

IPSWICH

Dedham

Colchester

Aylesbury

OXFORD

Aston Clinton

Great Milton

NORTH SEA

270

● Places to Stay
○ Orientation/Sightseeing
✈ Airports

a	b
c	d

Quadrants

Map 6

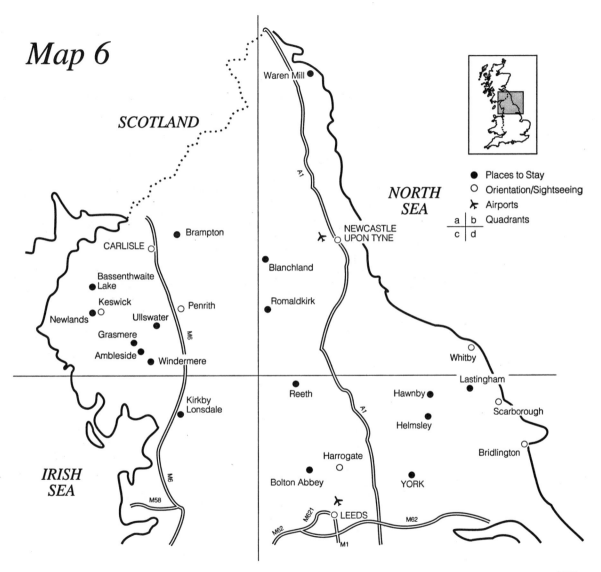

SCOTLAND

NORTH
SEA

IRISH
SEA

● Places to Stay
○ Orientation/Sightseeing
✈ Airports

| a | b | Quadrants |
| c | d | |

Waren Mill ●

CARLISLE ○

● Brampton

Bassenthwaite
● Lake

Keswick
○   Penrith ○

Newlands ○

Ullswater ●

Grasmere ●

Ambleside ●   ● Windermere

M6

Kirkby
Lonsdale

M6

M58

A1

✈   NEWCASTLE
○ UPON TYNE

● Blanchland

● Romaldkirk

Whitby ○

Lastingham ○

● Reeth

Hawnby ●

Scarborough ○

A1

Helmsley ●

Bridlington ○

Harrogate ○

● Bolton Abbey

● YORK

✈
○ LEEDS

M621

M62   M62

M1

271

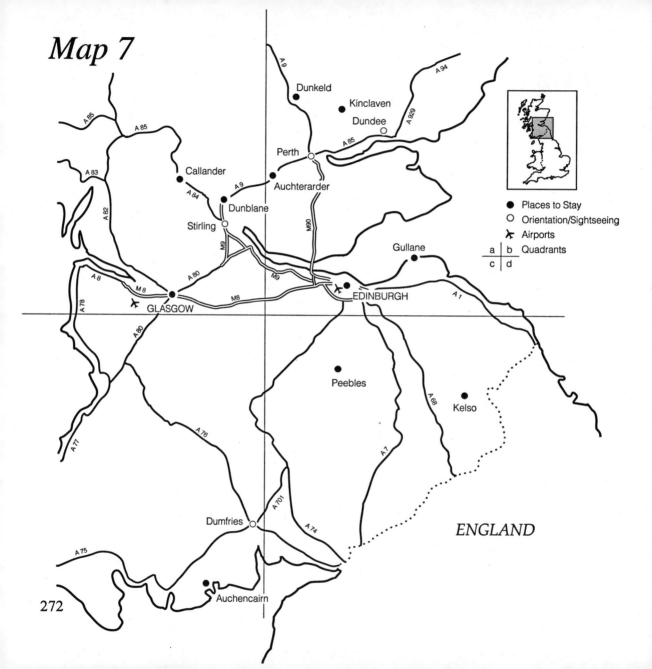

Map 7

272

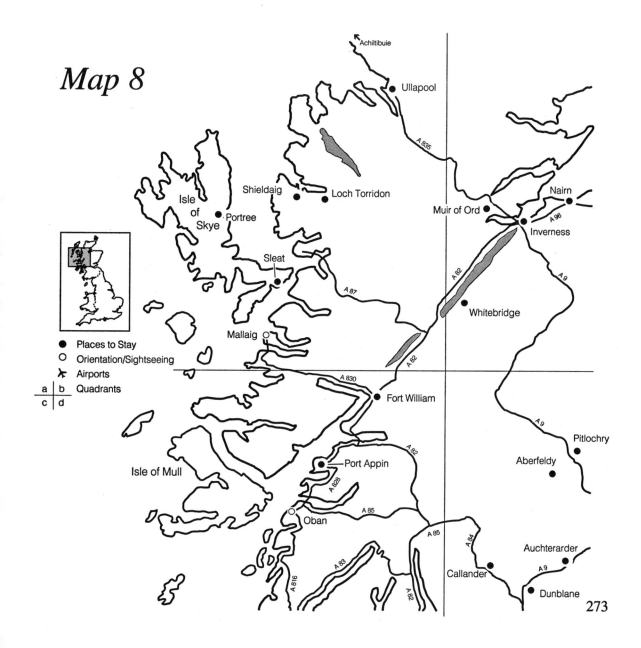

Map 8

Places to Stay
○ Orientation/Sightseeing
✈ Airports

a	b
c	d	Quadrants

Achiltibuie

Ullapool

A 835

Shieldaig • • Loch Torridon

Isle of Skye

• Portree

Muir of Ord • • Nairn

A 96

Inverness

Sleat

A 87

A 82

Whitebridge

Mallaig ○

A 830

A 9

Fort William

A 82

A 9

Isle of Mull

Port Appin

A 828

Pitlochry

Aberfeldy

A 82

A 85

○ Oban

A 85

A 84

Auchterarder

A 9

A 616

A 83

Callander

Dunblane

A 82

273

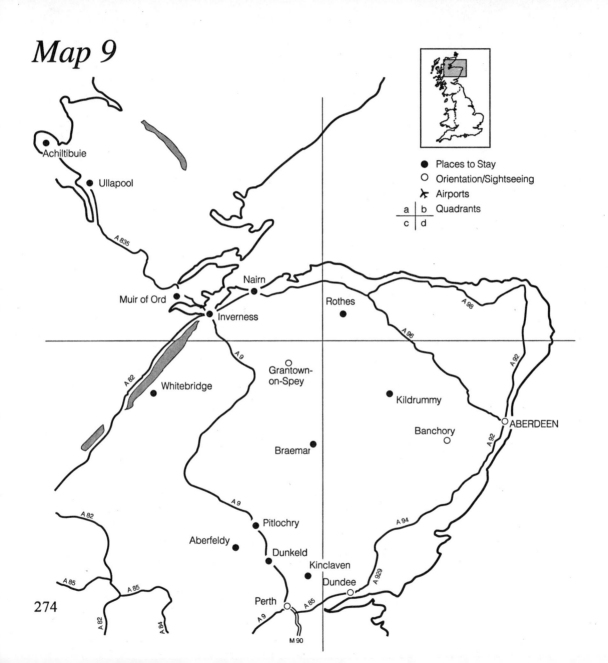

Map 9

Places to Stay
Orientation/Sightseeing
Airports

a	b
c	d

Quadrants

Achiltibuie

Ullapool

A 835

Nairn

Muir of Ord

Rothes

A 98

Inverness

A 96

A 9

A 82

Grantown-
on-Spey

Kildrummy

Whitebridge

A 92

Banchory

ABERDEEN

Braemar

A 92

A 9

A 94

A 82

Pitlochry

Aberfeldy

A 929

Dunkeld

A 85

Kinclaven

274

A 85

A 85

Perth

Dundee

A 9

A 85

A 82

A 84

M 90

USA Hotel Representatives

Forte Hotels 800-225-5843

Helmsley, The Black Swan
Lavenham, The Swan

Josephine Barr 800-323-5463

Josephine Barr often answers the phone. She is very familiar with all her hotels.
Ambleside, Rothay Manor
Auchterarder, Auchterarder House
Bath, The Queensberry Hotel
Bibury, The Swan Hotel
Bradford-on-Avon, Woolley Grange
Callander, Roman Camp Hotel
Edinburgh, Channings
Edinburgh, The Howard
Glasgow, One Devonshire Gardens
Kelso, Sunlaws
Kildrummy, Kildrummy Castle Hotel
Kinclaven, Ballathie House
Lifton, Arundell Arms
Llansanffraid Glan Conwy, The Old Rectory
London, Dorset Square Hotel
Whitebridge, Knockie Lodge
Winchester, Hotel du Vin
Wiveliscombe, Langley House
Woodstock, The Feathers
York, The Grange

Leading Hotels of the World 800-223-6800
Broadway, The Lygon Arms
New Milton, Chewton Glen

Pride of Britain Hotels 800-987-7433
Pride of Britain in a consortium of owner-managed hotels in Britain. Their USA booking agent is Josephine Barr. Josephine and her staff are very familiar with all the hotels.
Battle, Netherfield Place
Cuckfield, Ockenden Manor
Dunblane, Cromlix House
Eglwysfach, Ynyshir Hall
Goveton, Buckland Tout Saints
Grasmere, Michael's Nook
Grimston, Congham Hall
Gullane, Greywalls
Kelso, Sunlaws House Hotel
Lewdown, Lewtrenchard Manor
Shurdington, The Greenway
South Molton, Whitechapel Manor
Storrington, Little Thakeham
Sturminster Newton, Plumber Manor
Thornbury, Thornbury Castle
Whitebridge, Knockie Lodge

Utell International 800-448-8355
Bath, The Royal Crescent Hotel
London, The Stafford

Relais & Chateaux 212-856-0115

Aylesbury, Hartwell House
Brampton, Farlam Hall
Buckland, Buckland Manor
Chagford, Gidleigh Park
Dunkeld, Kinnaird
Evershot, Summer Lodge
Fort William, Inverlochy Castle
Gillingham, Stock Hill House
Great Milton, Le Manoir aux Quat' Saisons
Hambleton, Hambleton Hall
New Milton, Chewton Glen
Port Appin, The Airds Hotel
Ston Easton, Ston Easton Park
Ullswater, Sharrow Bay

Small Luxury Hotels 800-346-8480

Auchterarder, Auchterarder House
Chester, Chester Grosvenor Hotel
Hintlesham, Hintlesham Hall
Llandudno, Bodysgallen Hall
Llyswen, Llangoed Hall
London, 22 Jermyn Street
London, Dukes Hotel
London, The Stafford
Upper Slaughter, Lords of the Manor Hotel
Windermere, Holbeck Ghyll
York, Middlethorpe Hall

Index

—B—

—H—

—K—

Kelso
    Sunlaws House Hotel, 229
Kersey, 52
Keswick, 77
    Moot Hall, 78
Kettlewell, 71
Kiftsgate Court, 41
Kilburn, 69
Kildrummy
    Castle, 88
    Kildrummy Castle Hotel, 88, 230
Kildrummy Castle Hotel, Kildrummy, 88
Killin, 99
Kinclaven
    Ballathie House, 231
King's Lynn, 47
    Customs House, 47
    Guildhall, 47
    St. Margaret's Church, 47
King Harry Ferry, 32
Kingsbridge
    Buckland Tout Saints, 167
Kinnaird, Dunkeld, 221
Knightsbridge Green Hotel, London, 118
Knockie Lodge, Whitebridge, 245
Kyle of Lochalsh, 91, 97

—L—

L'Hotel, London, 119
Lacock, 26
    At The Sign of the Angel, 169
Lake Vyrnwy Hotel, Llanwddyn, 258
Lamb Inn, The, Burford, 39, 143
Land's End, 31
Langley House, Wiveliscombe, 209
Langshott Manor, Horley, 166
Lastingham
    Lastingham Grange, 170
Lastingham Grange, Lastingham, 170
Lavenham, 52
    Guildhall, 52
    The Great House, 171
    The Swan, 52, 172
Le Manoir Aux Quat' Saisons, Great Milton, 159
Levens Hall, 75
Lewdown
    Lewtrenchard Manor, 173
Lewtrenchard Manor, Lewdown, 173
Lifton
    Arundell Arms, 174
Liskeard, 33
Little Barrington, 39
Little Langdale, 76
    Three Shires, 76
Little Thakeham, Storrington, 194

We Love to Hear from Karen Brown's Readers

ACCOLADES: We'd love to hear which accommodations you have especially enjoyed—even the shortest of notes is greatly appreciated. It is reassuring to know that places we recommend meet with your approval.

COMPLAINTS: Please let us know when a place we recommend fails to live up to the standards you have come to expect from Karen Brown. Constructive criticism is greatly appreciated. We sometimes make a mistake, places change, or go downhill. Your letters influence us to re-evaluate a listing.

RECOMMENDATIONS: If you have a favorite hideaway that you would like to recommend, please write to us. Give us a feel for the place, if possible send us a brochure and photographs (which we regret we cannot return). Convince us that on our next research trip, your discovery deserves a visit. All accommodations included in our guides are ones we have seen and enjoyed. Many of our finest selections are those that readers have discovered—wonderful places we would never have found on our own.

Please send information to:

KAREN BROWN'S GUIDES
Post Office Box 70
San Mateo, California 94401, USA
Telephone (415) 342-9117   Fax (415) 342-9153

SEAL COVE INN—LOCATED IN THE SAN FRANCISCO AREA

Karen Brown Herbert (best known as author of the Karen Brown's Guides) and her husband, Rick, have put 19 years of experience into reality and opened their own superb hideaway, Seal Cove Inn. Spectacularly set amongst wild flowers and bordered by towering cypress trees, Seal Cove Inn looks out to the ocean over acres of county park: an oasis where you can enjoy secluded beaches, explore tidepools, watch frolicking seals, and follow the tree-lined path that traces the windswept ocean bluffs. Country antiques, original watercolors, flower-laden cradles, rich fabrics, and the gentle ticking of grandfather clocks create the perfect ambiance for a foggy day in front of the crackling log fire. Each bedroom is its own haven with a cozy sitting area before a wood-burning fireplace and doors opening onto a private balcony or patio with views to the distant ocean. Moss Beach is a 35-minute drive south of San Francisco, 6 miles north of the picturesque town of Half Moon Bay, and a few minutes from Princeton harbor with its colorful fishing boats and restaurants. Seal Cove Inn makes a perfect base for whale-watching, salmon-fishing excursions, day trips to San Francisco, exploring the coast, or, best of all, just a romantic interlude by the sea, time to relax and be pampered. Karen and Rick look forward to the pleasure of welcoming you to their hideaway by the sea.

Seal Cove Inn, 221 Cypress Avenue, Moss Beach, California 94038, USA
Telephone: (415) 728-7325   Fax: (415) 728-4116

Be a Karen Brown's Preferred Reader

If you would like to be the first to know when new editions of Karen Brown's Guides go to press, and also to be included in any special promotions, simply send us your name and address. We encourage you to buy new editions and throw away the old ones so that you don't miss a wealth of wonderful new discoveries or run the risk of staying in places that no longer meet our standards—you'll be glad you did. We cover the miles searching for special places so that you don't have to spend your valuable vacation time doing so.

Name _____

Street _____

Town _____ State _____ Zip _____

Telephone: _____ Fax: _____

Please send information to:

KAREN BROWN'S GUIDES
Post Office Box 70
San Mateo, California 94401, USA
Telephone (415) 342-9117   Fax (415) 342-9153

JUNE BROWN, who hails from Sheffield, England, has an extensive background in travel, dating back to her school girl days when she "youth hosteled" throughout Europe. June lives in San Mateo, California, with her husband, Tony, and their children, Simon and Clare.

KAREN BROWN wrote her first travel guide in 1976. Her personalized travel series has grown to 12 titles and Karen and her small staff work diligently to keep all the guides updated. Karen, her husband, Rick, and their children, Alexandra and Richard, live on the coast south of San Francisco at their own country inn, Seal Cove Inn, in Moss Beach.

BARBARA TAPP, the talented artist who produces all of the hotel sketches and delightful illustrations in this guide, was raised in Australia where she studied in Sydney at the School of Interior Design. Although Barbara continues with freelance projects, she devotes much of her time to illustrating the Karen Brown guides. Barbara lives in Kensington, California, with her husband, Richard, their two sons, Jonothan and Alexander, and daughter, Georgia.

JANN POLLARD, the artist responsible for the beautiful painting on the cover of this guide, has studied art since childhood, and is well-known for her outstanding impressionistic-style watercolors which she has exhibited in numerous juried shows, winning many awards. Jann travels frequently to Europe (using Karen Brown's guides) where she loves to paint historical buildings. Jann lives in Burlingame, California, with her husband, Gene.

USA Order Form

Please ask in your local bookstore for KAREN BROWN'S GUIDES.
If the books you want are unavailable, you may order directly from the publisher.

Austria: Charming Inns & Itineraries $16.95

California: Charming Inns & Itineraries $16.95

England: Charming Bed & Breakfasts $15.95

England, Wales & Scotland: Charming Hotels & Itineraries $16.95

French Country Bed & Breakfasts $15.95

France: Charming Inns & Itineraries $16.95

Germany: Charming Inns & Itineraries $16.95

Ireland: Charming Inns & Itineraries $16.95

Italy: Charming Bed & Breakfasts $15.95

Italy: Charming Inns & Itineraries $16.95

Spain: Charming Inns & Itineraries $16.95

Swiss Country Inns & Itineraries $16.95

Name _____ Street _____

Town _____ State _____ Zip _____ tel. _____

Credit Card [MasterCard or Visa] _____ Exp: _____

Add $4 for the first book and 50 cents for each additional book for postage & packing.
California residents add 8.25% sales tax. Order form **only** for shipments within the USA.
Indicate number of copies of each title; send form with check or credit card information to:

KAREN BROWN'S GUIDES
Post Office Box 70, San Mateo, California, 94401
Telephone: (415) 342-9117   Fax: (415) 342-9153